MW01283690

Peach Recipes 365

(Peach Recipes - Volume 1)

Enjoy 365 Days with Amazing Peach Recipes in Your Own Peach Cookbook!

Emily Chan

Copyright: Published in the United States by Emily Chan/ © EMILY CHAN

Published on November 18, 2018

All rights reserved. No part of this publication may be reproduced, stored in retrieval system, copied in any form or by any means, electronic, mechanical, photocopying, recording or otherwise transmitted without written permission from the publisher. Please do not participate in or encourage piracy of this material in any way. You must not circulate this book in any format. EMILY CHAN does not control or direct users' actions and is not responsible for the information or content shared, harm and/or actions of the book readers.

In accordance with the U.S. Copyright Act of 1976, the scanning, uploading and electronic sharing of any part of this book without the permission of the publisher constitute unlawful piracy and theft of the author's intellectual property. If you would like to use material from the book (other than just simply for reviewing the book), prior permission must be obtained by contacting the author at *chefemilychan@gmail.com*

Thank you for your support of the author's rights.

Contents

Introduction

***

Did you know that people need to eat at least five vegetables and fruits daily? However, many of us don't even eat half of this. Everyone knows that eating more fruits and veggies is good for the health, as it helps prevent flu, fight colds, reduce the risk of cancer, and provide your much-needed energy for the day ahead. Considering these facts, why aren't we eating more healthy food? Convenience is definitely to blame for this.

I've lost count of the times I've been walking around London on an empty stomach, craving food that I know will nourish my body. However, the available choices are the exact opposites of what our body needs. There's your buttery croissants, overly sweet soda, muffins loaded with sugar, chocolate bars, coffees with lots of milk, pre-packed sandwiches, and more. How frequently do you encounter baskets of veggies or mounds of fresh fruits? Maybe, I'd be the only one in the world who'd rejoice upon seeing a vending machine along a train platform that churns out fruits and vegetables (I might even do cartwheels out of sheer joy!). Well, just a wishful thinking that might come true someday... For now, I'll wait for my train in Balham with a basket full of cherry tomatoes. Or you may spot me heartily eating a bag of peas, my favorite healthy on-the-go snack. I simply put some peas in my bag before I leave the house. Just by munching on peas, I can easily get two servings of vegetables that provide a sustained dose of energy better than that post-carb crash.

If you're living a sedentary or inactive lifestyle, our series about Fruit & Vegetable and the book "Peach Recipes 365 Volume 1" as well might inspire you to eat more fruits and vegetables. I've begun with breakfast and explained dessert in detail, with very simple yet tasty recipes. Almost every single recipe includes at least one portion of vegetable and fruit. A number of recipes even have five portions in just one serving.

Although this isn't a vegetarian book, the recipes are angled in such a way that encourages people to eat less meat and more fruit & vegetable, and it presents a variety of vegan choices. There's also an attempt to meet certain dietary requirements. Midway through writing this cookbook series, I had to begin a strict detox program after suffering from parasite infestation. I consulted a nutritionist who provided me with a list of foods to avoid such as dairy, sugar, and wheat. I was also given a list of foods I MUST EAT. Loads of vegetables and fruits were at the top of the nutritionist's list. And they worked! Most of the recipes in this book came from my detox program. I strongly believe in a healthy balance. Sometimes, everyone needs a slice of the cake.

You also see more different types of fruit and vegetable recipes such as:

- ✓ *Banana Recipes*
- ✓ *Broccoli Recipes*
- ✓ *Mushroom Recipes*
- ✓ *Potato Recipes*
- ✓ *Squash Recipes*
- ✓ *...*

Thank you for choosing "Peach Recipes 365 Volume 1". I really hope that each book in the series will be always your best friend in your little kitchen.

Let's live happily and eat more fruits and vegetables every day!

Enjoy the book,

365 Amazing Peach Recipes

***

1. 120 Calorie Peach Pies

"An easy, great-tasting recipe when you're watching calories and need to tame your sweet tooth."

Serving: 8 | Prep: 15 m | Cook: 10 m | Ready in: 25 m

Ingredients

- 1 recipe pastry for a single 9-inch pie crust
- 1 large fresh peach, sliced into 8 pieces
- 1 teaspoon white sugar
- 1 teaspoon ground cinnamon

Direction

- Preheat oven to 450 degrees F (230 degrees C).
- Roll pie pastry onto a cutting board. Cut crust into eight 4-inch circles using a cookie cutter. Place 1 peach slice in the center of each circle. Fold circle in half to enclose each peach slice; seal edges together. Place mini pies on a baking sheet.
- Mix cinnamon and sugar together in a small bowl; sprinkle over mini pies.
- Bake in the preheated oven until crust is lightly browned, 10 to 13 minutes.

Nutrition Information

- Calories: 121 calories
- Total Fat: 7.5 g
- Cholesterol: 0 mg
- Sodium: 118 mg
- Total Carbohydrate: 12 g
- Protein: 1.4 g

2. 3Ingredient Cake Mix Cobbler

"Yummy peach cobbler made with cake mix. It makes you feel as though you are in the South on a warm sunny day. This recipe is inexpensive, easy, and surprisingly delicious!"

Serving: 8 | Prep: 5 m | Cook: 50 m | Ready in: 55 m

Ingredients

- 2 (15.25 ounce) cans peaches in light syrup
- 1 (18.25 ounce) box yellow cake mix
- 1 stick butter, melted

Direction

- Preheat the oven to 350 degrees F (175 degrees C).
- Pour peaches into a baking dish. Sprinkle cake mix on top and pour melted butter all over.
- Bake in the preheated oven until golden brown, about 50 minutes.

Nutrition Information

- Calories: 439 calories
- Total Fat: 19 g
- Cholesterol: 32 mg
- Sodium: 512 mg
- Total Carbohydrate: 66.2 g
- Protein: 3.5 g

3. A Very Intense Fruit Smoothie

"Gorgeous colour and absolutely refreshing. Use your favorite canned fruit - I prefer peaches or pears."

Serving: 2 | Prep: 3 m | Ready in: 3 m

Ingredients

- 1 (10 ounce) package frozen mixed berries
- 1 (15 ounce) can sliced peaches, drained
- 2 tablespoons honey

Direction

- In a blender, combine frozen fruit, canned fruit and honey. Blend until smooth.

Nutrition Information

- Calories: 293 calories
- Total Fat: 0.3 g
- Cholesterol: 0 mg
- Sodium: 13 mg
- Total Carbohydrate: 75.5 g
- Protein: 3.4 g

4. Absolute Stress

"One is enough to relieve most stress levels!"

Serving: 1 | Prep: 5 m | Ready in: 5 m

Ingredients

- 1 fluid ounce vodka
- 1 fluid ounce dark rum
- 1 fluid ounce peach schnapps
- 1 fluid ounce orange juice
- 1 fluid ounce cranberry juice

Direction

- In a cocktail shaker, combine vodka, rum, peach liqueur, orange juice and cranberry juice. Shake well.
- Pour over ice in a tall glass and garnish with a slice of orange and a cherry.

5. Alyssas Mango Peach Salsa

"An amazing recipe thought up by yours truly. Also good on ice cream, plain or pureed."

Serving: 16 | Prep: 10 m | Ready in: 10 m

Ingredients

- 1 cup diced mango
- 1 cup diced peaches
- 1 tablespoon vegetable oil
- 1/8 teaspoon salt

Direction

- Stir mango, peaches, vegetable oil, and salt together in a bowl.

Nutrition Information

- Calories: 16 calories
- Total Fat: 0.9 g
- Cholesterol: 0 mg
- Sodium: 19 mg
- Total Carbohydrate: 2.2 g
- Protein: 0.1 g

---

6. American Girls Peach Cobbler

"The first person I served this for didn't like peach cobbler (unknown to me). He really enjoyed it. I just made it because it sounded yummy and I was dieting. No one will ever guess it's 'lighter' than any other cobbler. I hope you like it. Oh! and it's quick and easy."

Serving: 12 | Prep: 10 m | Cook: 35 m | Ready in: 45 m

Ingredients

- 1/2 cup reduced-calorie margarine, melted
- 1 1/2 cups all-purpose flour
- 2 teaspoons baking powder
- 1 1/2 cups white sugar
- 1/2 cup skim milk
- 4 (15 ounce) cans sliced peaches packed in juice, drained and juice reserved

Direction

- Preheat the oven to 375 degrees F (190 degrees C).
- Pour the melted margarine into the bottom of a 9x13 inch baking dish; set aside. In a medium bowl, combine the flour, baking powder and white sugar. Stir in 1 cup of the reserved liquid from the peaches and the milk until smooth. Pour the batter evenly into the bottom of the dish over the margarine. Do not stir. Spoon peaches over the batter.

- Bake for 35 to 40 minutes in the preheated oven, or until the top is golden.

Nutrition Information

- Calories: 252 calories
- Total Fat: 3.5 g
- Cholesterol: < 1 mg
- Sodium: 157 mg
- Total Carbohydrate: 53.8 g
- Protein: 2.8 g

---

7. Amish Peach Dumplings

"Flour dumplings are added to a peach syrupy mixture to create a wonderful dessert. This is an Amish recipe. Using cream or canned milk instead of the milk gives this a creamier texture but also more calories. You can use fresh, frozen, or canned peaches."

Serving: 8 | Prep: 15 m | Cook: 25 m | Ready in: 40 m

Ingredients

- 2 cups hot water
- 1 cup sugar
- 1 tablespoon butter
- 2 cups sliced peeled peaches
- 1 cup flour
- 2 teaspoons baking powder
- 1/2 teaspoon salt
- 1 cup milk

Direction

- Stir water, sugar, and butter together in a pot over medium-high heat until sugar dissolves and mixture has a syrupy texture, 5 to 10 minutes. Add peaches to syrup; bring to a boil.
- Whisk flour, baking powder, and salt together in a bowl. Stir milk into flour mixture until a stiff batter forms.
- Drop batter by large spoonfuls into boiling peach syrup; cover the pot with a lid, reduce heat to medium, and cook until dumplings are set, about 20 minutes.

Nutrition Information

- Calories: 190 calories
- Total Fat: 2.2 g
- Cholesterol: 6 mg
- Sodium: 293 mg
- Total Carbohydrate: 40.6 g
- Protein: 2.6 g

8. AnnieBells Peach Cobbler

"This is my mom's recipe that's been handed down to all of her daughters."

Serving: 6 | Prep: 10 m | Cook: 45 m | Ready in: 55 m

Ingredients

- 2 prepared pie pastries (such as Pillsbury®)
- 2 cups brown sugar
- 1 cup white sugar
- 1 tablespoon ground cinnamon
- 1/2 teaspoon ginger
- 1 pinch ground nutmeg, or to taste
- 2 (15 ounce) cans peach slices, drained, liquid reserved
- 1/3 cup water
- 1/4 cup salted butter, melted
- 1/4 cup salted butter, cut into small pieces
- 1 teaspoon white sugar
- 1 teaspoon ground cinnamon

Direction

- Preheat oven to 375 degrees F (190 degrees C). Line a pie plate with 1 of the prepared pie pastries.
- Whisk brown sugar, 1 cup white sugar, 1 tablespoon cinnamon, ginger, and nutmeg together in a bowl. Stir reserved peach liquid, water, and melted butter into sugar mixture until sugar dissolves into liquid. Stir in peaches.
- Spoon peach mixture into prepared pie plate and place remaining pie pastry over the top; pinch and crimp edges together. Dot with butter pieces, remaining sugar, and remaining cinnamon.
- Bake in the preheated oven until crust is light brown, about 45 minutes.

Nutrition Information

- Calories: 821 calories
- Total Fat: 35.4 g
- Cholesterol: 41 mg
- Sodium: 440 mg
- Total Carbohydrate: 126.4 g
- Protein: 4.9 g

9. Apricot and Peach Fried Pies

"Apricot and peach fried pies have the best flavor of any fried pie I've ever eaten. My family loves these great pies. My grandmother made this up years ago. I have made this delicious fried pie for over 40 years. Enjoy!"

Serving: 18 | Cook: 30 m | Ready in: 30 m

Ingredients

- Dough:
- 4 cups all-purpose flour
- 2 teaspoons salt
- 1 cup shortening
- 1 cup milk
- Filling:
- 8 ounces dried apricots
- 1 (6 ounce) package dried peaches
- 3/4 cup white sugar
- water to cover
- 2 cups vegetable oil for frying

Direction

- To Make Crust: In a large bowl, mix together flour and salt. Cut in shortening until mixture is crumbly. Mix in milk and stir until dough forms a ball. Roll out dough and cut into 18 6-inch circles. Set aside.
- To Make Filling: In a large saucepan, combine apricots, peaches, and sugar. Add enough water to cover fruit. Cover pan and cook over low heat until fruit is falling apart. Remove lid

and continue to cook until water is evaporated.

- Place oil or shortening in small high-sided skillet. Place over medium heat. Spoon equal amounts of filling into each pastry circle and fold in half. Seal pastry with a fork dipped in cold water.
- Fry a few pies at a time in hot oil, browning on both sides. Drain pies on paper towels.

Nutrition Information

- Calories: 280 calories
- Total Fat: 14.4 g
- Cholesterol: 1 mg
- Sodium: 266 mg
- Total Carbohydrate: 34.8 g
- Protein: 3.6 g

10. Arctic Peach

"Very similar to a popular drink and a particular chain restaurant."

Serving: 1 | Prep: 10 m | Ready in: 10 m

Ingredients

- 1 cup frozen peach slices
- 4 fluid ounces peach nectar (such as Kern's®)
- 2 fluid ounces champagne
- 1 fluid ounce peach schnapps
- 1 fluid ounce vodka
- 2 cubes ice, or more if desired

Direction

- Blend peaches, peach nectar, champagne, peach schnapps, vodka, and ice in a blender on high until smooth, about 30 seconds.

Nutrition Information

- Calories: 319 calories
- Total Fat: 0.1 g
- Cholesterol: 0 mg
- Sodium: 20 mg
- Total Carbohydrate: 40 g
- Protein: 0.4 g

11. Aunt Patsis Easy Peach Jam

"I got this recipe from my great-aunt and tried it the first time on some fresh summer peaches. It was super easy and super yummy. It also works with frozen fruit. Store in a cool, dark place."

Serving: 60 | Prep: 20 m | Cook: 32 m | Ready in: 12 h 52 m

Ingredients

- 2 1/2 pounds fresh peaches
- 5 cups white sugar
- 3 (3 ounce) packages peach gelatin
- 2 teaspoons lemon juice
- 1/2 teaspoon almond extract

Direction

- Heat five 12-ounce jars in simmering water until ready for use. Wash lids and rings in warm soapy water.
- Fill a large pot with water; bring to a boil. Add peaches; cook until skin loosens, about 20 seconds. Drain and cool until easily handled. Peel, pit, and cut the peaches into chunks.
- Measure out 5 cups of peach chunks into the pot. Mash with a potato masher. Add sugar, peach gelatin, lemon juice, and almond extract; mix well. Bring to a rolling boil and cook jam for 1 minute. Remove from heat.
- Pack jam into hot jars, filling to within 1/4 inch of the top. Wipe rims with a clean, damp cloth. Top with lids and screw on rings.
- Place a rack in the bottom of a large stockpot and fill halfway with water. Bring to a boil and lower in jars using a holder, placing them 2 inches apart. Pour in more boiling water to cover the jars by at least 1 inch. Bring the water to a rolling boil, cover the pot, and process for 10 minutes.
- Remove the jars from the stockpot and place onto a cloth-covered or wood surface, several inches apart, until cool, about 12 hours. Press

the top of each lid with a finger, ensuring that lid does not move up or down and seal is tight.

Nutrition Information

- Calories: 84 calories
- Total Fat: 0 g
- Cholesterol: 0 mg
- Sodium: 16 mg
- Total Carbohydrate: 21.3 g
- Protein: 0.4 g

manufacturer's instructions. Ladle the jam into the jars, leaving 1/4 inch of headspace. Wipe the rims with a clean damp cloth or paper towel, and seal with lids and rings. Process according to guidelines suggested by your local extension.

Nutrition Information

- Calories: 103 calories
- Total Fat: 0 g
- Cholesterol: 0 mg
- Sodium: < 1 mg
- Total Carbohydrate: 26.7 g
- Protein: 0.1 g

12. Auntie Doriss Peach Jam

"My great Auntie Doris passed down this old farmhouse recipe, made with very simple ingredients, for a fresh and delicious peach jam. It is wonderful on toast, oatmeal or ice-cream."

Serving: 48 | Prep: 30 m | Cook: 3 h | Ready in: 11 h 30 m

Ingredients

- 12 fresh peaches - peeled, pitted and chopped
- 4 oranges
- 6 cups white sugar

Direction

- Place the peaches into a large bowl. Scrub the oranges then chop into pieces - including the peel. This is easiest done in a food processor so you don't lose as much juice. Transfer to the bowl with the peaches. Stir in sugar, cover, and refrigerate overnight.
- The next day, pour the entire contents of the bowl into a large pot. Bring to a simmer over low heat and cook for 2 to 3 hours, stirring occasionally. Make sure the heat is low enough, or the jam will burn and stick to the bottom of the pot. This does not need to come to a rolling boil.
- While the jam simmers, sterilize your jars in boiling water for at least 5 minutes, and keep hot. Prepare new lids according to the

13. Avons End of Summer Sunday Morning Peach Coffee Cake

"Picking peaches with my daughter and watching her create a peach/blueberry muffin inspired me to make this really nice and flavorful coffee cake with a tender crumb. Peaches and bananas are great together. The aroma while baking is heavenly. Not really restricted to Sunday mornings!"

Serving: 9 | Prep: 25 m | Cook: 40 m | Ready in: 2 h 15 m

Ingredients

- 1/2 cup brown sugar
- 1/4 cup maple syrup
- 3/4 cup peach yogurt
- 1 very ripe banana, mashed
- 1/4 cup butter, melted
- 1 egg, beaten
- 1/2 cup steel cut oats
- 1 cup all-purpose flour
- 3/4 cup whole wheat flour
- 2 teaspoons baking powder
- 1/2 teaspoon baking soda
- 2 teaspoons ground cinnamon
- 1/4 teaspoon salt
- 1 cup chopped ripe peach
- 1/2 cup chopped pecans

- 1/2 cup whole wheat flour
- 1/4 cup brown sugar
- 1/4 cup butter, melted
- 1 pinch ground cinnamon

Direction

- Preheat an oven to 375 degrees F (190 degrees C). Grease a 9x9-inch baking pan.
- Mix together 1/2 cup brown sugar, maple syrup, peach yogurt, banana, 1/4 cup melted butter, egg, and oats in a large bowl until well blended. Allow mixture to rest until the oats have softened, 10 to 20 minutes. Combine all-purpose flour, 3/4 cup whole wheat flour, baking powder, baking soda, 2 teaspoons cinnamon, and salt in a bowl. Stir the flour mixture and peaches into the banana mixture until just combined. Pour the mixture into the prepared baking pan.
- Mix the pecans, 1/2 cup whole wheat flour, 1/4 cup brown sugar, 1/4 cup melted butter, and a pinch of cinnamon in a bowl. Spread pecan mixture over the cake batter.
- Bake in the preheated oven until a toothpick inserted into the center comes out clean, 40 to 50 minutes. Cool in the pan for 10 minutes before removing to cool completely on a wire rack.

Nutrition Information

- Calories: 416 calories
- Total Fat: 16.6 g
- Cholesterol: 49 mg
- Sodium: 345 mg
- Total Carbohydrate: 62.4 g
- Protein: 7.6 g

14. Baby Blintz Stacks

"Blintz stacks with peach filling."

Serving: 10 | Prep: 35 m | Cook: 40 m | Ready in: 1 h 15 m

Ingredients

- 1 (24 ounce) carton cottage cheese
- 2 fresh peaches - peeled, pitted and chopped
- 3 tablespoons white sugar
- 1/2 teaspoon ground nutmeg
- 1/4 teaspoon salt
- 1/4 teaspoon almond extract
- 1/2 cup sour cream
- 2 tablespoons brown sugar
- 1 1/2 cups all-purpose flour
- 1 tablespoon white sugar
- 1/2 teaspoon baking powder
- 1/2 teaspoon salt
- 1/2 teaspoon ground nutmeg
- 2 cups milk
- 2 eggs
- 2 tablespoons melted butter
- 1/2 teaspoon vanilla extract
- 2 fresh peaches, pitted and sliced

Direction

- Stir together the cottage cheese, chopped peaches, 3 tablespoons white sugar, 1/4 teaspoon salt, and the almond extract in a bowl until evenly combined. Stir together the sour cream and brown sugar in a separate bowl. Refrigerate both fillings until ready to use.
- Whisk together the flour, 1 tablespoon of white sugar, the baking powder, 1/2 teaspoon salt, and the nutmeg in a bowl. Beat the eggs, milk, butter, and vanilla extract in a separate bowl until smooth. Stir in the flour mixture until no lumps remain.
- Heat a lightly oiled griddle over medium-high heat. Drop batter by large spoonfuls onto the griddle to form silver dollar-sized blintzes. Cook until bubbles form and the edges are dry, about 2 minutes. Flip, and cook until

browned on the other side. Repeat with remaining batter.

- To assemble, spread 1 tablespoon of peach filling on top of each blintz. Stack together 5 blintzes to make a serving portion, and spoon the sweetened sour cream overtop. Garnish with peach slices.

Nutrition Information

- Calories: 264 calories
- Total Fat: 10 g
- Cholesterol: 62 mg
- Sodium: 534 mg
- Total Carbohydrate: 29.3 g
- Protein: 13.7 g

15. Baked Chicken with Peaches

"Rushed? Need an elegant main dish to serve for an important occasion, that doesn't take a lot of preparation or time? This is it. This dish is not only easy and quick, it serves up beautifully as well. My family loves it. Tip: For a delicious sauce to serve over the chicken and peaches, mix 1/2 tablespoon cornstarch with 1/2 cup cold water and pour mixture into cooking juices. This mixture will thicken and become a sauce to pour over the chicken and peaches."

Serving: 8 | Prep: 15 m | Cook: 30 m | Ready in: 45 m

Ingredients

- 8 skinless, boneless chicken breast halves
- 1 cup brown sugar
- 4 fresh peaches - peeled, pitted, and sliced
- 1/8 teaspoon ground ginger
- 1/8 teaspoon ground cloves
- 2 tablespoons fresh lemon juice

Direction

- Preheat oven to 350 degrees F (175 degrees C). Lightly grease a 9x13 inch baking dish.
- Place chicken in the prepared baking dish, and sprinkle with 1/2 cup of brown sugar. Place peach slices over chicken, then sprinkle with

remaining 1/2 cup brown sugar, ginger, cloves, and lemon juice.

- Bake for about 30 minutes in the preheated oven, basting often with juices, until chicken is cooked through and juices run clear.

Nutrition Information

- Calories: 248 calories
- Total Fat: 2.8 g
- Cholesterol: 67 mg
- Sodium: 68 mg
- Total Carbohydrate: 30.3 g
- Protein: 24.6 g

16. Baked Pancake with Peaches

"A delicious way to add fruit into breakfast! Okay, it should probably serve 4 but if you have big eaters, don't be surprised if it is divided! Fortunately, you can put this together fast. Serve with vanilla yogurt."

Serving: 4 | Prep: 10 m | Cook: 20 m | Ready in: 30 m

Ingredients

- 1 tablespoon butter
- 2 large peaches, peeled and cut into 1/4-inch slices
- 1 tablespoon brown sugar
- 1 teaspoon ground cinnamon
- 3 eggs
- 1/2 cup milk
- 1/2 cup all-purpose flour
- 1 drop vanilla extract
- 1 pinch salt
- 1 pinch ground nutmeg

Direction

- Preheat oven to 425 degrees F (220 degrees C).
- Melt butter in a cast-iron skillet in the preheating oven.
- Combine peach slices, brown sugar, and cinnamon in a bowl; gently toss to coat the peaches well.

- Beat eggs, milk, flour, vanilla extract, salt, and nutmeg together in a bowl until batter well-combined but a little lumpy; pour into skillet. Top batter with the peach mixture.
- Bake in preheated oven until set in the middle, about 20 minutes.

Nutrition Information

- Calories: 178 calories
- Total Fat: 7 g
- Cholesterol: 133 mg
- Sodium: 83 mg
- Total Carbohydrate: 21.6 g
- Protein: 6.9 g

17. Baked Peaches

"Easy to keep ingredients on hand for this quick dessert."

Serving: 6 | Prep: 10 m | Cook: 20 m | Ready in: 30 m

Ingredients

- 1 (16 ounce) package frozen peach slices
- 1/3 cup brown sugar substitute
- 1/4 cup pecans
- 1 tablespoon all-purpose flour
- 1 teaspoon vanilla extract

Direction

- Preheat oven to 350 degrees F (175 degrees C).
- Spread peach slices into a baking dish in a single layer. Stir brown sugar substitute, pecans, flour, and vanilla extract together; spread over the peach slices.
- Bake in preheated oven until the peaches are heated through, 20 to 30 minutes.

Nutrition Information

- Calories: 113 calories
- Total Fat: 3.4 g
- Cholesterol: 0 mg
- Sodium: 11 mg
- Total Carbohydrate: 20.8 g

- Protein: 1 g

18. Baked Peaches n Cream

"These baked peaches taste like pie, minus the guilt of eating one! Of course all pie is even better with ice cream. Perfect way to make those summer peaches disappear."

Serving: 4 | Prep: 10 m | Cook: 15 m | Ready in: 25 m

Ingredients

- 8 teaspoons brown sugar
- 2 tablespoons butter, cut into 8 pieces
- 1 pinch ground cinnamon, or more to taste
- 4 ripe peaches, halved and pitted
- 4 scoops vanilla ice cream

Direction

- Preheat oven to 400 degrees F (200 degrees C).
- Arrange brown sugar, 1 teaspoon per peach, in a 9x13-inch baking dish. Top each brown sugar mound with a piece of butter and a sprinkle of cinnamon. Place a peach half, cut-side down, on top of brown sugar-butter.
- Bake in the preheated oven until peaches are soft, 15 to 20 minutes.
- Plate 2 warm peaches per serving and top with 1 scoop vanilla ice cream.

Nutrition Information

- Calories: 141 calories
- Total Fat: 8.1 g
- Cholesterol: 25 mg
- Sodium: 63 mg
- Total Carbohydrate: 17 g
- Protein: 0.8 g

19. Banana Coconut Smoothie Bowl

"This banana and peach smoothie is topped with coconut, almonds, and raisins creating a paleo-friendly smoothie bowl for a quick breakfast."

Serving: 1 | Prep: 15 m | Ready in: 15 m

Ingredients

- Smoothie:
- 1 banana, divided
- 1/2 cup frozen peach slices
- 2 tablespoons unsweetened applesauce
- 2 tablespoons water
- 2 teaspoons coconut oil
- Toppings:
- 1 tablespoon shredded unsweetened coconut
- 1 tablespoon sliced almonds
- 1 tablespoon raisins

Direction

- Blend 1/2 banana, peaches, applesauce, water, and coconut oil together in a blender until smooth; pour into a serving bowl.
- Slice remaining half banana and arrange on top of smoothie. Add shredded coconut, almonds, and raisins.

Nutrition Information

- Calories: 317 calories
- Total Fat: 16.3 g
- Cholesterol: 0 mg
- Sodium: 9 mg
- Total Carbohydrate: 45 g
- Protein: 3.3 g

20. Banana Peach Bread

"I was looking for a new banana bread and started trying some things. When I came up with this one, the kids and wife just loved it and my mother in-law wants me to make it for her."

Serving: 16 | Prep: 20 m | Cook: 50 m | Ready in: 2 h 10 m

Ingredients

- 3/4 cup white sugar
- 1/2 cup butter, softened
- 1 tablespoon brown sugar
- 1 tablespoon instant hot chocolate mix
- 3 bananas, peeled
- 1 large fresh peach - peeled, pitted, and diced
- 1/4 cup milk
- 2 eggs
- 1 tablespoon vanilla extract
- 2 cups all-purpose flour
- 1/2 cup chopped walnuts (optional)
- 1 teaspoon baking soda
- 1 teaspoon salt

Direction

- Preheat oven to 350 degrees F (175 degrees C). Grease the bottom of a 5x9-inch loaf pan.
- Beat white sugar and butter together in a large bowl with an electric mixer until light and fluffy. Add brown sugar and hot chocolate mix; stir well.
- Place bananas, peach, milk, eggs, and vanilla extract in a blender; blend until smooth. Stir into butter mixture until well incorporated.
- Mix flour, walnuts, baking soda, and salt together in a separate bowl; stir into banana-butter mixture until flour mixture is just moistened. Pour batter into the prepared loaf pan.
- Bake in the preheated oven until a toothpick inserted in the center of bread comes out clean, 50 to 60 minutes. Cool in pan for 5 minutes before transferring bread to a wire rack to cool completely.

Nutrition Information

- Calories: 208 calories
- Total Fat: 9.1 g
- Cholesterol: 39 mg
- Sodium: 279 mg
- Total Carbohydrate: 28.9 g
- Protein: 3.4 g

21. Barbequed Peaches

"Take some ripe, juicy peaches, slather them in barbecue sauce, and grill them until just heated through. Your favorite brand or recipe for barbeque sauce should work, especially ones that have a little spicy kick to them."

Serving: 4 | Prep: 5 m | Cook: 7 m | Ready in: 12 m

Ingredients

- 2 firm, ripe freestone peaches, halved and pitted
- 4 tablespoons barbeque sauce

Direction

- Preheat grill for medium heat and lightly oil the grate.
- Slice flesh-side of peach halves diagonally about 1/4-inch deep, twice in each direction.
- Drizzle flesh-side of each peach half with barbeque sauce; brush sauce for an even coat.
- Place peaches, flesh-side up, on the grill. Cook until barbeque sauce bubbles slightly and peaches are a little softer than when you put them on the grill, 7 to 10 minutes.

Nutrition Information

- Calories: 36 calories
- Total Fat: 0 g
- Cholesterol: 0 mg
- Sodium: 177 mg
- Total Carbohydrate: 8.7 g
- Protein: 0 g

22. Basic Fruit Smoothie

"This is a great smoothie consisting of fruit, fruit juice and ice. I like to use whatever fresh fruits I crave that day. Any kind of berry, mangos, papayas, kiwi fruit, et cetera make a great smoothie. Experiment with your favorites!"

Serving: 4 | Prep: 10 m | Cook: 5 m | Ready in: 15 m

Ingredients

- 1 quart strawberries, hulled
- 1 banana, broken into chunks
- 2 peaches
- 1 cup orange-peach-mango juice
- 2 cups ice

Direction

- In a blender, combine strawberries, banana and peaches. Blend until fruit is pureed. Blend in the juice. Add ice and blend to desired consistency. Pour into glasses and serve.

Nutrition Information

- Calories: 118 calories
- Total Fat: 0.6 g
- Cholesterol: 0 mg
- Sodium: 16 mg
- Total Carbohydrate: 28.5 g
- Protein: 1.6 g

23. Basil Peach Pepper Parmesan Cobbler

"I know it sounds completely wacky, but it is unbelievably delicious. If you've ever enjoyed a fruit-and-cheese Danish, you know that mixing cheese with fruit really isn't that crazy. It works so well together. These are time-tested flavor combinations."

Serving: 2 | Prep: 15 m | Cook: 35 m | Ready in: 1 h 20 m

Ingredients

- Batter:
- 4 teaspoons butter, melted
- 2/3 cup self-rising flour
- 1/2 cup white sugar
- 2/3 cup cold milk
- 1 tablespoon finely shredded Parmigiano-Reggiano cheese
- 1 pinch freshly ground black pepper
- Peaches:
- 1 large fresh peach - peeled, pitted, and sliced
- 2 tablespoons white sugar
- 2 leaves fresh basil, torn
- 1/2 teaspoon balsamic vinegar
- 1 teaspoon water

Direction

- Preheat oven to 375 degrees F (190 degrees C). Pour 2 teaspoons melted butter into the bottoms of two 6-ounce glass or ceramic ramekins.
- Combine self-rising flour with 1/2 cup sugar in a bowl; whisk in milk to make a smooth batter. Whisk Parmigiano-Reggiano cheese and black pepper into the batter; divide equally between the prepared ramekins.
- Place peach slices into a bowl and top with 2 tablespoons sugar and basil. Drizzle with balsamic vinegar and water; mix. Allow peaches to rest and let sugar draw out the moisture, about 10 minutes. Divide sliced peaches and their juice over the batter.
- Bake in the preheated oven until the cobbler batter rises up over the peaches and cobblers are browned and bubbling, about 35 minutes.

Let cool for about 20 minutes before serving for cobblers set up. Serve warm.

Nutrition Information

- Calories: 531 calories
- Total Fat: 10.8 g
- Cholesterol: 30 mg
- Sodium: 666 mg
- Total Carbohydrate: 101.9 g
- Protein: 7.9 g

24. Beach Goers Wraps

"Grill up some sweet ripe pineapple, peach, and mango slices, toss with raspberry vinegar and fresh salad mix for a perfect, summer wrap."

Serving: 4 | Prep: 20 m | Cook: 10 m | Ready in: 30 m

Ingredients

- 2 peaches
- 1/2 mango
- 6 slices fresh or canned DOLE® Pineapple
- Olive oil for brushing
- 2 teaspoons raspberry vinegar
- 1/4 teaspoon salt
- Ground black pepper, to taste
- 1 (13 ounce) package DOLE All Natural Endless Summer™ Kit
- 4 (10 inch) wraps or tortillas

Direction

- Cut peaches in half, remove seed. Cut into 1/4-inch slices. Cut mango half into 1/2-inch slices. Brush peaches, mango and pineapple slices with oil and grill on each side until tender. Cool slightly, cut into chunks. Toss fruit with raspberry vinegar, salt and pepper, to taste.
- Combine all ingredients in salad kit except Summer Vinaigrette, in large bowl. Add fruit chunks, toss well. Toss with dressing.

- Heat wraps in microwave for 30 seconds. Lay out wraps and divide salad filling equally. Fold over one end and wrap sides over filling.

Nutrition Information

- Calories: 485 calories
- Total Fat: 27.1 g
- Cholesterol: 5 mg
- Sodium: 880 mg
- Total Carbohydrate: 61 g
- Protein: 10.1 g

25. Beef Peach Pie

"A meatloaf with a twist. The peaches add a sweet touch and go well with the ground beef."

Serving: 8 | Prep: 10 m | Cook: 50 m | Ready in: 1 h

Ingredients

- 1 pound ground beef
- 1 egg
- 1/2 cup milk
- 1/4 cup chopped onion
- 1 cup soft bread crumbs
- 1 teaspoon salt
- 1 pinch pepper
- 1 (15 ounce) can sliced peaches, drained
- 1 tablespoon vinegar
- 1 tablespoon ketchup
- 1/4 cup brown sugar

Direction

- Preheat the oven to 350 degrees F (175 degrees C).
- In a medium bowl, mix together the ground beef, egg, milk, onion, bread crumbs, salt and pepper. Press into a 9 inch pie pan like a crust. Prick meat all over using a fork.
- Bake for 25 to 30 minutes in the preheated oven. Remove from the oven, and pour off any excess fat. Arrange the sliced peaches over the beef. Mix together the vinegar, ketchup and

brown sugar, and spoon over the top of the peaches.
- Bake for an additional 20 minutes. Let stand for at least 10 minutes before serving.

Nutrition Information

- Calories: 261 calories
- Total Fat: 16.2 g
- Cholesterol: 73 mg
- Sodium: 408 mg
- Total Carbohydrate: 17.4 g
- Protein: 11.6 g

26. Bellini Meanie Martini

"Peach schnapps and vodka are shaken, then topped off with a splash of champagne, and a few fresh raspberries. Yuuuuuummmmmm!"

Serving: 1 | Prep: 5 m | Ready in: 5 m

Ingredients

- 1/4 cup good quality vodka
- 2 fluid ounces peach schnapps
- 1 cup ice cubes
- 2 fluid ounces champagne
- 3 fresh raspberries for garnish

Direction

- Pour the vodka and peach schnapps into a shaker with the ice. Shake until frothy. Strain into a martini glass, and top off with champagne. Garnish with fresh raspberries.

27. Berry Good Smoothie II

"A delicious way to get your '5-a-day.' It's a quick and easy breakfast, but great any time of day! Nectarines, strawberries, and blueberries blended with nonfat milk and ice!"

Serving: 2 | Prep: 10 m | Ready in: 10 m

Ingredients

- 1 nectarine, pitted
- 3/4 cup strawberries, hulled
- 3/4 cup blueberries, rinsed and drained
- 1/3 cup nonfat dry milk powder
- 1 cup crushed ice

Direction

- In a blender combine nectarine, strawberries, blueberries, milk powder and crushed ice. Blend until smooth. Pour into glasses and serve.

Nutrition Information

- Calories: 151 calories
- Total Fat: 0.7 g
- Cholesterol: 4 mg
- Sodium: 110 mg
- Total Carbohydrate: 29.6 g
- Protein: 8.7 g

28. Best Peach Cobbler Ever

"This is a very moist cobbler - easy to make and delicious to eat!"

Serving: 18 | Prep: 30 m | Cook: 1 h | Ready in: 1 h 30 m

Ingredients

- 1 (29 ounce) can sliced peaches
- 2 tablespoons butter, melted
- 1 pinch ground cinnamon
- 1 pinch ground nutmeg
- 1 tablespoon cornstarch
- 1/2 cup water
- 1 cup milk

- 1 cup white sugar
- 1 cup all-purpose flour
- 2 teaspoons baking powder
- 1 pinch salt
- 1/2 cup butter
- 1 teaspoon ground cinnamon
- 1/4 teaspoon ground nutmeg

Direction

- Preheat oven to 350 degrees F (175 degrees C.) In a large bowl, combine sliced peaches with juice, 2 tablespoons melted butter, a pinch of cinnamon and a pinch of nutmeg. Dissolve cornstarch in water, then stir into peach mixture; set aside.
- In another bowl, combine milk, sugar, flour, baking powder and salt. Beat until smooth - mixture will be thin.
- Melt 1/2 cup butter in a 9x13 inch pan. Pour batter over melted butter. Spoon peaches over batter. Sprinkle top with additional cinnamon and nutmeg.
- Bake in preheated oven for 1 hour, or until knife inserted comes out clean.

Nutrition Information

- Calories: 263 calories
- Total Fat: 6.8 g
- Cholesterol: 18 mg
- Sodium: 138 mg
- Total Carbohydrate: 48.4 g
- Protein: 1.2 g

29. Beths PeachNectarine Muffins

"These are simple, delicious muffins ... a must try. Enjoy right out of the oven or let cool."

Serving: 8 | Prep: 10 m | Cook: 20 m | Ready in: 30 m

Ingredients

- 1 1/2 cups all-purpose flour
- 3/4 cup white sugar
- 1/2 teaspoon salt

- 2 teaspoons baking powder
- 1/3 cup vegetable oil
- 1 egg
- 1/3 cup milk
- 1 large ripe peach - peeled, pitted and diced
- 1 very ripe nectarine, pitted and diced
- 1 tablespoon brown sugar

Direction

- Preheat oven to 400 degrees F (200 degrees C). Grease 8 muffin cups or line with paper muffin liners.
- In a large bowl, combine flour, sugar, salt and baking powder. Add vegetable oil, egg and milk; mix well. Fold in diced peach and nectarine. Fill each muffin tin to the top with muffin mix. Sprinkle a little brown sugar onto the top of each uncooked muffin.
- Bake in preheated oven for 18 to 20 minutes. Check muffins regularly after 15 minutes of baking. Serve warm or cool.

Nutrition Information

- Calories: 271 calories
- Total Fat: 10.2 g
- Cholesterol: 24 mg
- Sodium: 250 mg
- Total Carbohydrate: 41.9 g
- Protein: 3.7 g

30. Biscuit Wedges with Fruit in Vanilla Syrup

"Fresh fruit in vanilla syrup joins homemade biscuits and Reddi-wip in a luscious dessert."

Serving: 6 | Ready in: 40 m

Ingredients

- 1 cup all-purpose baking mix
- 2 teaspoons vanilla extract
- 1 teaspoon cinnamon sugar
- 1/2 cup water

- 3 tablespoons granulated sugar
- 2 teaspoons vanilla extract
- 3 cups cut-up mixed fresh fruit (sliced strawberries, bananas, peaches and/or blueberries)
- Reddi-wip Original Whipped Light Cream

Direction

- Preheat oven and prepare the baking mix according to package directions for rolled biscuits, adding 2 teaspoons vanilla with the measure of water listed in the package directions. Roll out or pat dough into 6-inch circle on lightly floured surface; cut into 6 wedges. Place, 2 inches apart, on ungreased baking sheet. Brush tops lightly with additional water; sprinkle with cinnamon sugar.
- Bake according to package directions.
- Mix 1/2 cup water and granulated sugar in small saucepan. Bring to a boil over medium-high heat. Reduce heat to low; simmer 5 minutes, or until slightly thickened, to a syrup-like consistency. Remove from heat; cool slightly. Stir in remaining 2 teaspoons vanilla. Pour over the fruit in large bowl; toss gently to coat.
- Split biscuits horizontally in half. Place bottom halves of biscuits on 6 dessert plates; cover evenly with half of the fruit mixture. Top each with a serving of Reddi-wip and top half of biscuit. Spoon remaining fruit mixture evenly over biscuits; top with additional serving of Reddi-wip.

Nutrition Information

- Calories: 243 calories
- Total Fat: 10.1 g
- Cholesterol: 34 mg
- Sodium: 254 mg
- Total Carbohydrate: 32.2 g
- Protein: 1.9 g

31. Blackberry Peach Pie

"You can't go wrong with blackberries, peaches, and some spices."

Serving: 8 | Prep: 15 m | Cook: 50 m | Ready in: 1 h 5 m

Ingredients

- 3 cups fresh blackberries
- 3 fresh peaches - peeled, pitted, and sliced
- 3 tablespoons cornstarch
- 3/4 cup white sugar
- 1 double crust ready-to-use pie crust
- 2 tablespoons butter, melted
- 1 tablespoon ground cinnamon
- 1/2 teaspoon ground nutmeg

Direction

- Preheat oven to 450 degrees F (230 degrees C).
- Mix the blackberries, peaches, cornstarch, and sugar in a large bowl.
- Press one of the pie crusts into the bottom of a 9-inch pie pan. Pour the blackberry mixture into the pie crust. Cover with the remaining pie crust. Crimp the edges of the two crusts together to seal. Cut slits in the top of the pie to vent. Brush the top with the melted butter. Sprinkle the cinnamon and nutmeg over the top.
- Bake in preheated oven for 15 minutes. Reduce the oven temperature to 350 degrees F (175 degrees C) and continue to cook until top crust is golden brown, 35 to 40 minutes.

Nutrition Information

- Calories: 363 calories
- Total Fat: 18.2 g
- Cholesterol: 8 mg
- Sodium: 255 mg
- Total Carbohydrate: 48 g
- Protein: 3.6 g

32. Blueberry Peach Muffins

"My whole family requests these muffins as soon as peaches are in season! If you like blueberry muffins, you will love these!"

Serving: 16 | Prep: 15 m | Cook: 20 m | Ready in: 35 m

Ingredients

- 3 cups all-purpose flour
- 1/2 cup white sugar
- 1/2 cup brown sugar
- 1 tablespoon baking powder
- 1 pinch salt
- 3 eggs
- 1 cup milk
- 1/2 cup melted butter
- 1 cup blueberries
- 1 cup peeled and diced fresh peaches
- 2 teaspoons white sugar
- 1 teaspoon ground cinnamon
- 1/2 teaspoon ground nutmeg
- 2 tablespoons melted butter

Direction

- Preheat the oven to 400 degrees F (200 degrees C). Grease muffin tins, or line with paper liners.
- In a large bowl, stir together the flour, 1/2 cup white sugar, brown sugar, baking powder and salt. In a separate bowl, mix together the eggs, milk and 1/2 cup of melted butter until well blended. Pour the wet ingredients into the dry, and mix until just blended. Fold in the blueberries and peaches. Fill muffin cups with batter.
- Bake for 18 to 20 minutes in the preheated oven, or until the tops spring back when lightly touched. In a small bowl, stir together the remaining sugar, cinnamon and nutmeg. Brush muffins with remaining melted butter, and sprinkle with the cinnamon mixture. Cool in the pan over a wire rack.

Nutrition Information

- Calories: 231 calories
- Total Fat: 8.7 g

- Cholesterol: 55 mg
- Sodium: 136 mg
- Total Carbohydrate: 34.3 g
- Protein: 4.3 g

33. Boars Head Bold BourbonRidge Uncured Smoked Ham Summer Salad

"Inspired by the rich traditions born in the rolling hills and hidden waterways of Kentucky, Bold BourbonRidge™ Uncured Smoked Ham embodies the American epicurean spirit and captures the sophistication of the majestic thoroughbreds this region is known for. Masterfully crafted with a refined bourbon and patiently smoked with reclaimed charred oak bourbon barrels, each slice celebrates the heritage and pride of the bluegrass state."

Serving: 4 | Prep: 20 m | Ready in: 20 m

Ingredients

- For the Dressing:
- 1/2 cup champagne vinegar
- 3 tablespoons Boar's Head Real Mayonnaise
- 1 green onion, white and green parts, minced
- 1 1/2 teaspoons honey
- 2 teaspoons Dijon mustard
- 1 small garlic clove, minced
- 1 tablespoon fresh lemon juice
- 1 teaspoon chopped fresh dill
- 1 teaspoon chopped fresh parsley leaves
- 1 teaspoon kosher salt
- 1/2 teaspoon freshly ground black pepper
- 1 cup canola oil
- 2 1/2 cups mixed salad greens
- 8 ounces Boar's Head Bold® BourbonRidge™ Uncured Smoked Ham, sliced thin
- 1 cup peaches, sliced thin
- 1/2 cup blueberries
- 1/2 cup raspberries
- 1/2 cup blackberries

Direction

- To make the dressing, combine the vinegar, mayonnaise, green onion, honey, Dijon mustard, garlic, lemon juice, dill, parsley, salt, and pepper in a blender or food processor with a metal blade. With the machine running, gradually add the oil in a thin, steady stream to form an emulsion. Set aside when complete.
- Place mixed greens into a large salad bowl, top with dressing and remaining ingredients, and serve.

Nutrition Information

- Calories: 713 calories
- Total Fat: 67.1 g
- Cholesterol: 38 mg
- Sodium: 1021 mg
- Total Carbohydrate: 18 g
- Protein: 11.4 g

34. BourbonSoaked Grilled Peaches with Burrata and Prosciutto

"I hope I had you at bourbon-soaked peaches. Sometimes ingredients come together so perfectly all you need to do is assemble and enjoy.
These juicy, ripe peaches soaked in bourbon, combined with rich, salty prosciutto, creamy Burrata, and peppery arugula hit all the right flavor notes making this the most amazing harmonious dish I've had in a long time. Plus grilling fruit deepens its flavor which enhances everything. I'm not kidding about this one. Time to hit the patio and put this dish on heavy summer rotation."

Serving: 4 | Prep: 20 m | Cook: 6 m | Ready in: 56 m

Ingredients

- 3 fresh peaches, sliced
- 1/4 cup bourbon
- 1 (1 pound) loaf crusty bread, sliced
- 8 ounces Burrata cheese
- 3 cups arugula
- 2 tablespoons olive oil, or to taste

- salt and ground black pepper to taste
- 2 tablespoons balsamic vinegar glaze (such as Trader Joe's®)
- 8 slices prosciutto, chopped

Direction

- Combine peaches and bourbon in a bowl. Let soak for 30 minutes.
- Preheat grill for medium heat and lightly oil the grate. Grill bread slices until grill marks appear, about 2 minutes per side. Transfer to a plate.
- Grill peaches until dark grill marks form, 2 to 3 minutes. Transfer to a bowl.
- Place Burrata cheese and arugula on a platter. Drizzle olive on top; season with salt and pepper. Add grilled peaches to the platter. Drizzle balsamic glaze over Burrata cheese, arugula, and peaches. Scatter prosciutto on top. Serve with grilled bread.

Nutrition Information

- Calories: 719 calories
- Total Fat: 30 g
- Cholesterol: 65 mg
- Sodium: 1471 mg
- Total Carbohydrate: 70.3 g
- Protein: 27.1 g

35. Brandy Baked Peaches

"Peaches are cut into halves, topped with a brandy-cinnamon sauce, and baked for 30 minutes. Place peaches on individual serving dishes, top with ice cream, and drizzle with sauce for a light summer dessert."

Serving: 6 | Prep: 10 m | Cook: 35 m | Ready in: 45 m

Ingredients

- cooking spray
- 3 fresh peaches, halved and pitted
- 1/4 cup butter
- 1 tablespoon sliced almonds
- 1/4 cup honey

- 1/4 cup brown sugar
- 1 1/2 teaspoons ground cinnamon
- 2 tablespoons brandy
- 1 pinch salt
- 1 teaspoon vanilla extract

Direction

- Preheat oven to 350 degrees F (175 degrees C). Prepare a baking dish with cooking spray.
- Arrange peaches cut-side up in the prepared baking dish.
- Put butter in a saucepan over medium-low heat, add almonds, and heat together until butter melts, about 2 minutes. Stir honey, brown sugar, and cinnamon into the melted butter; bring to a simmer and add brandy and salt. Stir to dissolve the salt, remove saucepan from heat, and add vanilla extract; pour the mixture over the peaches.
- Bake peaches in preheated oven until the peaches are cooked through, about 30 minutes.

Nutrition Information

- Calories: 182 calories
- Total Fat: 8.2 g
- Cholesterol: 20 mg
- Sodium: 86 mg
- Total Carbohydrate: 24.4 g
- Protein: 0.4 g

36. Bread Pudding with Whiskey Sauce and Fruit

"A great dessert for a Sunday dinner."

Serving: 14 | Prep: 20 m | Cook: 1 h | Ready in: 1 h 20 m

Ingredients

- 3 eggs, beaten
- 1 cup white sugar
- 2 1/2 cups whole milk
- 1 1/2 teaspoons ground cinnamon
- 1/2 teaspoon ground nutmeg

- 4 fresh peaches - peeled, pitted, and sliced
- 4 apples - peeled, cored and sliced
- 6 cups day-old bread cubes
- 6 tablespoons butter, cut into pieces
- 1 cup whiskey
- 1 pound butter
- 2 cups white sugar

Direction

- Coat a 9x13 baking dish with cooking spray. Preheat oven to 350 degrees F (175 degrees C).
- In a large bowl, combine eggs, 1 cup sugar, milk, cinnamon and nutmeg and stir until smooth. Fold in peaches, apples and bread cubes, until bread is well coated. Pour into prepared baking dish. Dot with 6 tablespoons butter.
- Bake in preheated oven for 1 hour, until set. Serve warm with whiskey sauce.
- To make whiskey sauce: In a medium saucepan over medium heat, combine whiskey, 1 pound butter and 2 cups sugar. Cook and stir until sugar dissolves and sauce is smooth. Remove from heat and serve hot.

Nutrition Information

- Calories: 593 calories
- Total Fat: 34.3 g
- Cholesterol: 127 mg
- Sodium: 358 mg
- Total Carbohydrate: 59.9 g
- Protein: 4.4 g

37. Busy Mom Peach Cobbler

"This yummy cobbler recipe has been in my family (and probably most southern families) for ages. I have added and taken away a few things over the years, but I love it any way I make it."

Serving: 6 | Prep: 10 m | Cook: 1 h 10 m | Ready in: 1 h 20 m

Ingredients

- 1/2 cup butter
- 1 (16 ounce) can sliced peaches in heavy syrup
- 2 tablespoons white sugar
- 1 cup self-rising flour
- 1 cup white sugar
- 1/4 teaspoon ground cinnamon, or to taste
- 1/8 teaspoon ground nutmeg, or to taste
- 1 cup 2% milk
- 2 tablespoons white sugar

Direction

- Preheat an oven to 325 degrees F (165 degrees C). Put the butter in an 8x8 inch baking dish and place in the oven to melt while you prepare the remaining ingredients.
- Bring the peaches with syrup and 2 tablespoons of sugar to a boil in a saucepan. Reduce heat to medium-low and simmer 10 minutes; set aside. Whisk together the flour, 1 cup sugar, cinnamon, and nutmeg in a bowl. Stir in the milk until the mixture is just moistened. Pour into the hot baking dish over the butter. Spoon the peach slices and most of the syrup over the batter.
- Bake in the preheated oven for 30 minutes. Sprinkle with the remaining 2 tablespoons of sugar. Return to the oven and bake until the top is golden brown, 30 to 45 minutes longer.

Nutrition Information

- Calories: 450 calories
- Total Fat: 16.4 g
- Cholesterol: 44 mg
- Sodium: 396 mg
- Total Carbohydrate: 73.1 g
- Protein: 4.2 g

38. Byrdhouse Spicy Chicken and Peaches

"This was a recipe of my mom's that I manipulated in true Byrdhouse form. Everyone loves this one, even the kids if you take it easy with the red pepper. I always serve this on broad, flat noodles."

Serving: 4 | Prep: 20 m | Cook: 30 m | Ready in: 50 m

Ingredients

- 1 (15 ounce) can peaches, drained and chopped
- 4 cloves garlic, pressed
- 1 1/2 cups orange juice
- 2 tablespoons distilled white vinegar
- 2 tablespoons brown sugar
- 1 1/2 teaspoons nutmeg
- 1/2 teaspoon red pepper flakes
- 2 teaspoons dried basil
- salt and pepper to taste
- 4 (6 ounce) skinless, boneless chicken breast halves - cut into bite-size pieces
- 2 tablespoons flour
- 3 tablespoons butter

Direction

- Bring peaches, garlic, orange juice, vinegar, sugar, nutmeg, red pepper flakes, and basil to a boil in a saucepan over high heat. Reduce heat to medium-low, and simmer for 15 minutes, stirring occasionally.
- Meanwhile, season the chicken to taste with salt and pepper, then dust with flour and shake off the excess. Melt the butter in a large skillet over medium-high heat. Add the chicken, and cook until lightly brown on both sides, but still pink in the center.
- Season peach sauce with salt and pepper, and pour over browned chicken. Return the chicken to a simmer, then reduce heat to medium-low, cover, and simmer 15 minutes more until the chicken is no longer pink in the center.

Nutrition Information

- Calories: 390 calories
- Total Fat: 12.9 g
- Cholesterol: 111 mg
- Sodium: 141 mg
- Total Carbohydrate: 33.4 g
- Protein: 35.3 g

39. Cabbage Peach and Carrot Smoothie

"The cabbage spices this up a little."

Serving: 4 | Prep: 10 m | Ready in: 10 m

Ingredients

- 1 cup grapes
- 1 cup sliced frozen peaches
- 3/4 cup chopped cabbage
- 1 large carrot
- 1/4 cup ice cubes, or as desired
- 1/4 cup water, or as desired

Direction

- Blend grapes, peaches, cabbage, carrot, ice cubes, and water in a high-powered blender (such as a Vitamix(R)) until desired consistency is reached.

Nutrition Information

- Calories: 52 calories
- Total Fat: 0.3 g
- Cholesterol: 0 mg
- Sodium: 17 mg
- Total Carbohydrate: 13.3 g
- Protein: 0.9 g

40. California Fusion Peach Salsa

"This is a fusion Peach salsa that combines hot and sweet with Asian spices. Great as a dip with tortilla chips or served as a garnish to meat dishes."

Serving: 4 | Prep: 5 m | Ready in: 5 m

Ingredients

- 2 (15 ounce) cans peaches, drained and chopped
- 2 green onions with tops, thinly sliced
- 2 teaspoons chopped fresh cilantro
- 2 tablespoons lime juice
- 1/4 teaspoon Asian five-spice powder
- 2 teaspoons garlic chile paste
- 1/8 teaspoon white pepper

Direction

- In a medium bowl, combine peaches, green onion, cilantro, and lime juice. Mix in five-spice powder, garlic chile paste, and white pepper. Cover, and refrigerate until ready to serve.

Nutrition Information

- Calories: 103 calories
- Total Fat: 0.4 g
- Cholesterol: 0 mg
- Sodium: 32 mg
- Total Carbohydrate: 27.1 g
- Protein: 1.5 g

41. California Peach Cobbler

"This has been in my family ever since I can remember. It was always a favorite during holidays."

Serving: 8 | Prep: 15 m | Cook: 55 m | Ready in: 1 h 10 m

Ingredients

- 8 large fresh yellow peaches - peeled, pitted, and sliced
- 1 1/2 cups white sugar, divided
- 1/2 cup water
- 1/2 cup butter
- 1 1/2 cups all-purpose flour
- 1 1/2 cups 2% milk
- 1/2 cup brown sugar
- 1 pinch ground cinnamon, or more to taste

Direction

- Preheat oven to 350 degrees F (175 degrees C).
- Combine peaches, 1 cup white sugar, and water in a saucepan; bring to a boil. Reduce heat and simmer, stirring carefully, until peaches are tender and syrup is thickened, about 10 minutes.
- Put butter in a 3-quart baking dish and place in oven until butter melts, 2 to 3 minutes.
- Mix flour, milk, brown sugar, and remaining 1/2 cup white sugar together in a bowl until batter is smooth; pour over melted butter without stirring. Spoon peach mixture over batter, allowing the syrup to drip over peaches into the batter. Sprinkle cinnamon over the top.
- Bake in the preheated oven until cobbler is cooked through and bubbling, about 45 minutes.

Nutrition Information

- Calories: 441 calories
- Total Fat: 12.6 g
- Cholesterol: 34 mg
- Sodium: 111 mg
- Total Carbohydrate: 79.2 g
- Protein: 4.1 g

42. Captain Jacks Peach Pie

"Rum and butter...mmm. A smooth and softly sweet peach pie with lots of layers of distinctive flavor. An original recipe of mine which is the favorite fruit pie in our house."

Serving: 8 | Prep: 30 m | Cook: 45 m | Ready in: 2 h 15 m

Ingredients

- 1 (15 ounce) package double crust ready-to-use pie crust
- 1 cup white sugar
- 1/3 cup all-purpose flour
- 1 tablespoon cornstarch
- 1/4 teaspoon ground cinnamon
- 1/4 teaspoon ground cardamom
- 1/4 teaspoon ground allspice
- 1/4 cup butter, melted
- 8 fresh peaches - peeled, pitted, and sliced
- 2 tablespoons rum
- 2 tablespoons milk

Direction

- Preheat oven to 400 degrees F (200 degrees C). Lightly grease a 9-inch pie dish with butter.
- Press one pie crust into the prepared pie dish.
- Mix sugar, flour, cornstarch, cinnamon, cardamom, and allspice together in a bowl. Slowly stir butter into the sugar mixture until fully incorporated.
- Toss peaches and rum together in a separate bowl; add sugar mixture to peaches. Gently toss to coat peaches. Pour peach mixture into pie crust. Top with remaining pie crust; seal the two crust edges together. Cut 4 to 5 slits in the top crust for ventilation. Brush with milk.
- Bake in the preheated oven for 15 minutes. Lower heat to 350 degrees F (175 degrees C); bake until top is golden brown, about 30 more minutes. Turn off the oven and let the pie rest in the oven as it cools, at least 1 hour.

Nutrition Information

- Calories: 452 calories
- Total Fat: 22.1 g
- Cholesterol: 16 mg
- Sodium: 300 mg
- Total Carbohydrate: 58.5 g
- Protein: 3.8 g

43. Caribbean Sangria

"This is a wonderful refreshment and so easy to make. When we have barbeques, I usually have to make a couple of gallons because it goes quick!"

Serving: 8 | Prep: 25 m | Ready in: 2 h 25 m

Ingredients

- 1 small orange, sliced
- 1 peach, sliced (optional)
- 1 lemon, sliced
- 1 lime, sliced
- 3 cups dry red wine
- 1 (12 fluid ounce) can or bottle lemon-lime soda
- 1 1/2 cups rum
- 3/4 cup white sugar
- 3 strawberries, sliced, or more to taste

Direction

- Place orange slices, peach slices, lemon slices, and lime slices in the bottom of a pitcher. Pour in red wine, lemon-lime soda, rum, and sugar; stir until sugar is dissolved.
- Cover and refrigerate sangria until flavors combine, at least 2 hours.
- Garnish each serving with a strawberry slice.

Nutrition Information

- Calories: 276 calories
- Total Fat: 0.1 g
- Cholesterol: 0 mg
- Sodium: 10 mg
- Total Carbohydrate: 30 g
- Protein: 0.4 g

44. Chef Jimmie Joness Drunken Peaches

"These grilled peaches with extra spirit are the perfect accompaniment for ice cream. Recipe by Food City's corporate chef, Jimmie Jones."

Serving: 4 | Prep: 10 m | Cook: 4 m | Ready in: 1 h 14 m

Ingredients

- 3 peaches, or more to taste
- 1/2 cup Chardonnay
- 1/4 cup Full Circle™ 100% Pure Honey
- 1/4 cup Food Club® Light Brown Sugar
- 1 tablespoon Food Club® Pure Vanilla Extract
- 1/2 teaspoon Food Club® Cinnamon
- 1/4 cup Food Club® Pecan Halves
- Salt to taste
- 1 pint Kay's® Classic Vanilla Bean Ice Cream
- 4 leaves fresh mint

Direction

- Halve peaches and remove pits.
- In a large bowl, stir Chardonnay, honey, brown sugar, vanilla, and cinnamon together.
- Add peaches, ensuring they are liberally coated by marinade. Allow to marinate for 1 to 2 hours.
- Preheat grill to hot.
- Lay peaches face-down over the grill for 4 to 6 minutes, or until exterior is seared and fruit is tender, basting with the wine-honey marinade. Remove peaches from heat.
- Coarsely chop pecans and lightly salt.
- Scoop vanilla bean ice cream into bowls. Immediately top with warm grilled peaches, a drizzling of the wine-honey marinade, chopped pecans, a dusting of cinnamon, and mint garnish.

Nutrition Information

- Calories: 350 calories
- Total Fat: 12.1 g
- Cholesterol: 29 mg
- Sodium: 101 mg
- Total Carbohydrate: 53.4 g
- Protein: 3.1 g

45. Chef Johns Nectarine Salsa

"I've always loved the marvelous contrast between a hot, smoky piece of meat, and a cold, fruity salsa; and this version featuring nectarines did not disappoint. In fact, the only thing that pairs better with this fresh fruit salsa is a basket of crispy tortilla chips."

Serving: 6 | Prep: 20 m | Ready in: 50 m

Ingredients

- 1 cup finely diced nectarine
- 1/2 cup finely diced red bell pepper
- 1/3 cup finely diced onions
- 2 tablespoons finely diced jalapeno pepper
- 1 tablespoon chopped fresh cilantro
- 1 tablespoon fresh lime juice
- 2 teaspoons olive oil
- 1/2 teaspoon salt, plus more to taste
- 1 pinch cayenne pepper
- 1 pinch freshly ground black pepper

Direction

- Combine nectarines, bell pepper, onions, jalapeno pepper, and cilantro in a bowl. Stir in lime juice, olive oil, salt, and cayenne pepper.
- Cover bowl with plastic wrap. Refrigerate to let flavors develop, 30 minutes to 1 hour.
- Before serving, stir in black pepper. Add a pinch more salt, if needed.

Nutrition Information

- Calories: 33 calories
- Total Fat: 1.7 g
- Cholesterol: 0 mg
- Sodium: 195 mg
- Total Carbohydrate: 4.5 g
- Protein: 0.5 g

46. Chef Johns Peach Blackberry Flognarde

"I was looking around for a name for this unusual clafoutis-like combination of peaches, blackberries, thyme, and black pepper. I saw an article that said in France a clafoutis that uses fruit other than cherries is called a flognarde. I enjoy saying flognarde so much that I think even if this recipe hadn't come out as well as it did I would still make it regularly, just to say 'flognarde'."

Serving: 8 | Prep: 15 m | Cook: 45 m | Ready in: 1 h 30 m

Ingredients

- 1 1/4 cups milk
- 2/3 cup white sugar
- 1/2 cup whole wheat flour
- 3 eggs
- 1/2 teaspoon vanilla extract
- 1/2 teaspoon fresh thyme leaves
- 1/4 teaspoon ground black pepper
- 1 pinch salt
- 1 pint fresh blackberries
- 1 fresh peach, sliced

Direction

- Preheat oven to 350 degrees F (175 degrees C). Butter a casserole dish.
- Whisk milk, sugar, and flour together in a large bowl. Add eggs, vanilla extract, thyme leaves, black pepper, and salt; whisk until batter is smooth.
- Spread blackberries and peach slices out in the prepared casserole dish. Pour batter over the top.
- Bake in the preheated oven until fruit is hot and batter is set, about 45 minutes. Cool completely.

Nutrition Information

- Calories: 155 calories
- Total Fat: 2.9 g
- Cholesterol: 73 mg
- Sodium: 63 mg
- Total Carbohydrate: 28.3 g
- Protein: 5.2 g

47. Chef Johns Peach Cobbler

"There was a time when being called a shoemaker was the ultimate kitchen insult. It meant that your cooking skills were so weak, the cobbler down the street could have come into the kitchen and done just as well. This beautiful peach cobbler recipe is so easy, any shoemaker could master it."

Serving: 6 | Prep: 15 m | Cook: 55 m | Ready in: 1 h 10 m

Ingredients

- 5 cups fresh peaches - peeled, pitted, and sliced
- 1/8 teaspoon Chinese five-spice powder
- 1 teaspoon grated lemon zest
- 1 cup white sugar
- 1 cup water
- 1/2 cup butter, melted
- 1 cup white sugar
- 1 1/2 cups self-rising flour
- 1 1/2 cups milk

Direction

- Preheat oven to 350 degrees F (175 degrees C).
- Combine peaches, Chinese five-spice powder, and lemon zest in a bowl.
- Stir sugar and water together in saucepan pan over medium heat until simmering, 2 to 3 minutes. Stir in peach mixture; cook and stir for 2 minutes. Remove from heat and set aside.
- Combine sugar and self-rising flour in a large bowl. Pour in milk; whisk to form a smooth batter.
- Pour melted butter into a Dutch oven. Pour batter over the melted butter.
- Gently place peaches and syrup on top of batter. As the cobbler bakes, they will sink down into the batter.
- Bake until syrup is bubbling and crust has risen and is golden brown, about 50 minutes.

Nutrition Information

- Calories: 562 calories

- Total Fat: 16.9 g
- Cholesterol: 46 mg
- Sodium: 536 mg
- Total Carbohydrate: 99.3 g
- Protein: 5.3 g

48. Chef Johns Peach Melba

"Peach Melba was created for Victorian era opera star Nellie Melba by the greatest chef of the time, Auguste Escoffier, who also named some thin, crispy toasts in her honor years later."

Serving: 6 | Prep: 15 m | Cook: 15 m | Ready in: 4 h 30 m

Ingredients

- 3 cups fresh or frozen raspberries
- 1/3 cup white sugar
- 1 tablespoon lemon juice
- 1 tablespoon water
- 1/8 teaspoon balsamic vinegar
- 2 cups white sugar
- 2 cups water
- 2 tablespoons lemon juice
- 1 vanilla bean, split lengthwise
- 3 peaches, halved and pitted
- 6 scoops vanilla ice cream
- 1/4 cup sliced almonds

Direction

- Combine raspberries, 1/3 cup sugar, 1 tablespoon lemon juice, water, and balsamic vinegar in a saucepan over medium heat. Bring to a simmer and cook until sugar dissolves and berries collapse, 2 to 3 minutes. Remove from heat and strain into a bowl. Cool to room temperature, cover and refrigerate until thoroughly chilled.
- Combine 2 cups sugar, 2 cups water, 2 tablespoons lemon juice, and split vanilla bean in a large saucepan and bring to a simmer over medium heat.

- Place peach halves with cut sides up in the syrup and simmer until tender, 5 to 8 minutes per side, basting with the syrup occasionally. Remove from heat and allow to cool in the syrup. Transfer to a bowl, cover, and refrigerate until thoroughly chilled, about 4 hours.
- Remove peach skins and serve each peach half on top of a scoop of ice cream in a bowl. Spoon the raspberry sauce over the top. Garnish with toasted, slivered almonds.

Nutrition Information

- Calories: 420 calories
- Total Fat: 4.6 g
- Cholesterol: 9 mg
- Sodium: 21 mg
- Total Carbohydrate: 96.5 g
- Protein: 2.2 g

49. Cherry Berry Peach Pie

"This recipe was given to me by a friend who is the best pie maker I know. When Bing cherries aren't in season I use raspberries."

Serving: 8 | Prep: 30 m | Cook: 55 m | Ready in: 1 h 25 m

Ingredients

- 1 (15 ounce) package pastry for a double crust 9-inch pie
- 3 cups peeled, sliced peaches
- 1 cup Bing cherries, pitted and halved
- 1 cup blueberries
- 1 tablespoon lemon juice
- 1/2 cup white sugar
- 1/4 cup brown sugar
- 3 tablespoons all-purpose flour
- 1/4 teaspoon ground cinnamon
- 1/8 teaspoon salt
- 1 tablespoon milk, or as needed
- 1 teaspoon white sugar, or as needed

Direction

- Preheat oven to 450 degrees F (230 degrees C). Press one pie crust pastry into a 9-inch pie plate. Cut the remaining pie crust pastry into 3/4-inch strips to be used for the lattice top.
- Mix peaches, cherries, blueberries, and lemon juice together in a large bowl. Add 1/2 cup white sugar, brown sugar, flour, cinnamon, and salt; stir to coat. Pour fruit mixture into the prepared pie crust. Weave a lattice top over the fruit filling using the pie crust strips. Brush top crust with milk; sprinkle with about 1 teaspoon white sugar.
- Bake in the preheated oven for 10 minutes. Reduce heat to 350 degrees F (175 degrees C); bake until fruit filling is bubbling and lattice top is lightly browned, 45 to 50 minutes.

Nutrition Information

- Calories: 370 calories
- Total Fat: 16.5 g
- Cholesterol: < 1 mg
- Sodium: 294 mg
- Total Carbohydrate: 53.1 g
- Protein: 3.7 g

50. Chicken Salad with Peaches and Walnuts

"For this salad use whatever fruit is fresh and ripe. If peaches are not in season, try using melons or oranges. Nectarines are also delicious in this recipe."

Serving: 4 | Prep: 15 m | Ready in: 15 m

Ingredients

- 2 large fresh peaches
- 2 cups chopped, cooked chicken meat
- 1/2 cup thinly sliced red onion
- 1/2 cup poppyseed salad dressing
- 6 cups mixed salad greens
- 1/2 cup toasted walnuts, chopped

Direction

- Chop 1 peach into 1/2 inch pieces; place in large bowl. Add chicken and onion; toss with enough dressing to coat.
- Add greens and walnuts to bowl and toss to coat. Mound salad on large plate. Cut remaining peach in thin wedges and place on top to garnish.

Nutrition Information

- Calories: 398 calories
- Total Fat: 25.4 g
- Cholesterol: 63 mg
- Sodium: 273 mg
- Total Carbohydrate: 18.3 g
- Protein: 22.7 g

51. Chilled Peach Soup

"So tasty that people were actually scraping their bowls!"

Serving: 10 | Prep: 10 m | Cook: 15 m | Ready in: 55 m

Ingredients

- 1 cup dry white wine
- 1 cup peach schnapps
- 1/2 cup sugar
- 1 teaspoon chopped fresh mint leaves
- 1/2 teaspoon ground cinnamon
- 1/4 teaspoon ground nutmeg
- 2 cups half-and-half cream
- 10 fresh peaches, sliced

Direction

- Place white wine, peach schnapps, sugar, mint leaves, cinnamon, nutmeg, and half-and-half together in a bowl, and stir until well blended and sugar is dissolved. Add sliced peaches, and transfer to a saucepan.
- Cook over medium heat for 15 minutes, stirring frequently and reducing heat if necessary to prevent scorching cream. Remove from heat when peaches are tender. Cool to a

safe temperature for blending. Process in a blender or food processor until completely smooth. Cover, and refrigerate until ready to serve. Serve chilled.

Nutrition Information

- Calories: 232 calories
- Total Fat: 5.7 g
- Cholesterol: 18 mg
- Sodium: 27 mg
- Total Carbohydrate: 29.4 g
- Protein: 1.5 g

52. Chipotle Peach Salsa with Cilantro

"*I came up with this fresh-tasting, spicy recipe one night as we fired up steaks smothered in a smoky hickory BBQ sauce on our new grill. The combination was a hit and this has definitely become a new favorite. We like our food spicy, so adjust the amount of chipotle and onion to suit your taste.*"

Serving: 4 | Prep: 10 m | Ready in: 10 m

Ingredients

- 1 cup sliced canned peaches, drained and chopped
- 1/3 cup chopped red onion
- 2 cloves garlic, minced
- 1 1/2 teaspoons minced fresh ginger root
- 2 teaspoons minced chipotle peppers in adobo sauce
- 1/3 cup chopped fresh cilantro
- 1/2 lime, juiced
- salt and pepper to taste

Direction

- In a bowl, mix the peaches, onion, garlic, ginger, chipotle peppers in adobo sauce, cilantro, and lime. Season with salt and pepper. Chill until serving.

Nutrition Information

- Calories: 41 calories
- Total Fat: 0.1 g
- Cholesterol: 0 mg
- Sodium: 17 mg
- Total Carbohydrate: 10.3 g
- Protein: 0.8 g

53. Christas Peach Pecan Scones

"*Sweet peaches and crunchy pecans add a twist to this flaky tea time favorite.*"

Serving: 8 | Prep: 15 m | Cook: 20 m | Ready in: 35 m

Ingredients

- 2 cups all-purpose flour
- 1/3 cup white sugar
- 1 tablespoon baking powder
- 1 teaspoon salt
- 1/2 teaspoon ground cinnamon
- 1/2 cup cold unsalted butter
- 1/2 cup heavy whipping cream
- 2 eggs
- 1/2 cup diced canned peaches
- 1/4 cup chopped pecans
- Topping:
- 1 egg
- 2 tablespoons water
- 1 teaspoon raw sugar, or to taste

Direction

- Preheat oven to 400 degrees F (200 degrees C). Line a baking sheet with parchment paper.
- Mix flour, white sugar, baking powder, salt, and cinnamon together in a bowl. Cut in butter until it forms pea-sized pieces.
- Whisk heavy cream and 2 eggs together in a small bowl. Add to the flour-butter mixture. Mix in peaches and pecans until just combined.
- Turn dough out onto a floured surface. Pat into a round disc about 1/2-inch thick. Cut

into 8 wedges. Transfer wedges to the baking sheet.
- Whisk 1 egg and water together in a small bowl. Brush over wedges. Sprinkle raw sugar on top.
- Bake in the preheated oven until golden brown, 20 to 25 minutes.

Nutrition Information

- Calories: 356 calories
- Total Fat: 21.4 g
- Cholesterol: 112 mg
- Sodium: 505 mg
- Total Carbohydrate: 36.1 g
- Protein: 6.1 g

54. Cinnamon Peach Crunch Yogurt Cup

"Combine the flavor of fresh peaches and blueberries and the crunch of cinnamon cereal in this easy yogurt cup."

Serving: 1 | Prep: 5 m | Ready in: 5 m

Ingredients

- 1 (6 ounce) container Yoplait® Original Harvest Peach yogurt
- 4 teaspoons diced fresh peaches, divided
- 4 teaspoons fresh blueberries, divided
- 1 tablespoon Cinnamon Toast Crunch ™ cereal

Direction

- Remove 1 tablespoon yogurt from yogurt container.
- Stir in 3 teaspoons of the diced peaches and 3 teaspoons of the blueberries.
- Top yogurt cup with remaining peaches, blueberries and the cereal.

Nutrition Information

- Calories: 165 calories
- Total Fat: 1.4 g

- Cholesterol: < 1 mg
- Sodium: 180 mg
- Total Carbohydrate: 30.9 g
- Protein: 5.9 g

55. CinnamonPeach Cottage Cheese Pancakes

"A cottage cheese-based pancake with fruit for extra flavor."

Serving: 4 | Prep: 10 m | Cook: 30 m | Ready in: 40 m

Ingredients

- 4 eggs
- 1 cup cottage cheese
- 1/2 cup milk
- 1 teaspoon vanilla extract
- 2 tablespoons butter, melted
- 1 peach, shredded
- 1 cup all-purpose flour
- 2 tablespoons white sugar
- 1 pinch salt
- 3/4 teaspoon baking soda
- 1 teaspoon ground cinnamon

Direction

- Mix eggs, cottage cheese, milk, vanilla, butter, and peach in a large bowl. Combine flour, sugar, salt, baking soda, and cinnamon in a small bowl. Stir flour mixture into the cottage cheese mixture until just combined.
- Heat a lightly oiled griddle over medium-high heat. Drop batter by large spoonfuls onto the griddle, and cook until bubbles form and the edges are dry. Flip, and cook until browned on the other side. Repeat with remaining batter.

Nutrition Information

- Calories: 344 calories
- Total Fat: 14.2 g
- Cholesterol: 212 mg
- Sodium: 589 mg

- Total Carbohydrate: 35.5 g
- Protein: 17.6 g

56. Citrus Marinated Beef Fruit Kabobs

"Cubes of Top Sirloin are marinated for flavor in a mixture of orange peel, cilantro and smoked paprika. They are then grilled alongside skewers of watermelon, peaches, and mango."

Serving: 4 | Ready in: 40 m

Ingredients

- 1 pound beef top sirloin steak boneless, cut 1 inch thick
- 1 medium orange
- 1/4 cup chopped fresh cilantro leaves
- 1 tablespoon smoked paprika
- 1/4 teaspoon ground red pepper (optional)
- 4 cups cubed mango, watermelon, peaches and/or plums
- Salt

Direction

- Grate peel and squeeze 2 tablespoons juice from orange; reserve juice. Combine orange peel, cilantro, paprika, and ground red pepper, if desired, in small bowl. Cut beef Steak into 1-1/4-inch pieces. Place beef and 2-1/2 tablespoons cilantro mixture in food-safe plastic bag; turn to coat. Place remaining cilantro mixture and fruit in separate food-safe plastic bag; turn to coat. Close bags securely. Marinate beef and fruit in refrigerator 15 minutes to 2 hours.
- Soak eight 9-inch bamboo skewers in water 10 minutes; drain. Thread beef evenly onto four skewers leaving small space between pieces. Thread fruit onto remaining four separate skewers.
- Place kabobs on grid over medium, ash-covered coals. Grill beef kabobs, covered, 8 to 10 minutes (over medium heat on preheated gas grill, 9 to 11 minutes) for medium rare (145 degrees F) to medium (160 degrees F) doneness, turning occasionally. Grill fruit kabobs 5 to 7 minutes or until softened and beginning to brown, turning once.
- Season beef with salt, as desired. Drizzle reserved orange juice over fruit kabobs.

Nutrition Information

- Calories: 256 calories
- Total Fat: 4.6 g
- Cholesterol: 39 mg
- Sodium: 87 mg
- Total Carbohydrate: 34.1 g
- Protein: 22 g

57. Classic Bisquick Peach Cobbler

"Whether you use canned, fresh or frozen peaches will probably depend on the time of year. Whatever the season, this homey dessert will bring you praises. Try this favorite from the Betty Crocker Kitchens tonight."

Serving: 6 | Prep: 10 m | Cook: 1 h | Ready in: 1 h 10 m

Ingredients

- 1 cup Original Bisquick® mix
- 1 cup milk
- 1/2 teaspoon ground nutmeg
- 1/2 cup butter or margarine, melted
- 1 cup sugar
- 1 (29 ounce) can sliced peaches, drained

Direction

- Heat oven to 375 degrees F.
- Stir together Bisquick mix, milk and nutmeg in ungreased square baking dish, 8x8x2 inches. Stir in butter until blended. Stir together sugar and peaches; spoon over batter.
- Bake 50 to 60 minutes or until golden.

Nutrition Information

- Calories: 427 calories
- Total Fat: 19.3 g
- Cholesterol: 44 mg
- Sodium: 383 mg
- Total Carbohydrate: 63.3 g
- Protein: 3.8 g

58. Conchis Sangria

"This is the sangria that my friends taught me to make in Spain. It's quick and easy and makes a great drink to mix up for a summer party."

Serving: 48 | Prep: 10 m | Ready in: 10 m

Ingredients

- 4 (750 milliliter) bottles red wine
- 1 1/4 cups white sugar
- 2 Granny Smith apples - peeled, cored and sliced
- 4 sliced fresh peaches
- 2 bananas, peeled and sliced
- 2 cinnamon sticks, crushed
- 3 liters lemon-lime flavored carbonated beverage

Direction

- In a large pitcher, combine red wine, sugar, apples, peaches, bananas and cinnamon sticks. Refrigerate for 6 hours or overnight.
- When you're ready to serve, stir in the lemon-lime soda.

59. CookieCrusted Peach Cobbler

"This recipe makes a very rich peach cobbler. The crust is very sweet and cookie-like. Serve warm with vanilla ice cream. Definitely not for those watching their weight!"

Serving: 12 | Prep: 20 m | Cook: 45 m | Ready in: 1 h 5 m

Ingredients

- 8 fresh peaches - peeled, pitted, and sliced
- 1/2 cup butter, cut into pieces
- 1/2 cup brown sugar
- 2 cups all-purpose flour
- 2 cups white sugar
- 2 teaspoons baking powder
- 1 teaspoon salt
- 2 eggs, lightly beaten
- 1 cup vegetable oil
- 1 teaspoon ground cinnamon

Direction

- Preheat an oven to 350 degrees F (175 degrees C). Spray a 9x13-inch baking pan with cooking spray.
- Arrange the peaches in the prepared pan. Scatter the butter over the peaches, then sprinkle the brown sugar evenly on top. Set aside. Mix flour, white sugar, baking powder, and salt in a bowl. Stir the oil into the beaten eggs, then stir the egg mixture into the dry ingredients. Spoon the batter over the peaches, then sprinkle cinnamon on top.
- Bake in the preheated oven until the crust is lightly browned, about 45 minutes.

Nutrition Information

- Calories: 497 calories
- Total Fat: 26.9 g
- Cholesterol: 51 mg
- Sodium: 325 mg
- Total Carbohydrate: 62.6 g
- Protein: 3.3 g

60. CoolDown Grapefruit Smoothie

"Great grapefruit smoothie for the Summer. All you need are some simple fruits."

Serving: 1 | Prep: 10 m | Ready in: 10 m

Ingredients

- 1 1/2 cups grapefruit juice
- 1 fresh peach - peeled, pitted, and diced
- 1 tablespoon milk
- 4 pitted cherries
- 4 ice cubes

Direction

- Place grapefruit juice, peach, milk, cherries, and ice cubes in a blender. Blend until smooth.

Nutrition Information

- Calories: 196 calories
- Total Fat: 0.9 g
- Cholesterol: 1 mg
- Sodium: 16 mg
- Total Carbohydrate: 45.3 g
- Protein: 2.7 g

61. Cop Cobbler

"A twist on a old favorite, great for dessert or even breakfast! Yummy with a scoop of vanilla ice cream and a cup of hot coffee!
"

Serving: 24 | Prep: 15 m | Cook: 1 h | Ready in: 1 h 15 m

Ingredients

- 24 glazed doughnuts
- 1 (14 ounce) can sweetened condensed milk
- 2 eggs, beaten
- 1 (29 ounce) can sliced peaches, not drained
- 1 teaspoon ground cinnamon
- 1 pinch salt
- 1/2 cup butter, melted
- 1 (16 ounce) package confectioners' sugar
- 2 teaspoons vanilla extract

Direction

- Preheat an oven to 350 degrees F (175 degrees C). Grease a 9x13 inch baking dish, and set aside.
- Tear the doughnuts into bite-size pieces, and place them in a large bowl. Pour in the sweetened condensed milk, eggs, peaches with juice, cinnamon, and salt, and mix. Spoon the mixture into the greased baking dish.
- Bake in the preheated oven for 1 hour, until a knife inserted in the center comes out clean.
- While the cobbler is baking, make a glaze by combining the melted butter, confectioners' sugar, and vanilla extract in a bowl. Stir until smooth. Drizzle the glaze over the baked cobbler.

Nutrition Information

- Calories: 423 calories
- Total Fat: 19.4 g
- Cholesterol: 35 mg
- Sodium: 261 mg
- Total Carbohydrate: 58.1 g
- Protein: 5.9 g

62. Creamy Chicken Salad with Peaches

"A perfect summer lunch! Serve on toast or fresh lettuce. Can be eaten immediately or chilled before serving."

Serving: 2 | Prep: 10 m | Ready in: 10 m

Ingredients

- 2 ounces cream cheese, softened
- 1 tablespoon poppy seed salad dressing
- 3/4 cup diced cooked chicken
- 1/2 fresh peach, diced
- 1/4 cup chopped walnuts (optional)
- 1 tablespoon chopped green onions

Direction

- Mix cream cheese and poppy seed dressing together in a bowl; fold in chicken, peach, walnuts, and green onions until well coated.

Nutrition Information

- Calories: 336 calories
- Total Fat: 26.3 g
- Cholesterol: 73 mg
- Sodium: 168 mg
- Total Carbohydrate: 6.5 g
- Protein: 18.8 g

63. Creamy Peach Pie

"An easy single-crust pie. Apples also work well in this pie."

Serving: 8

Ingredients

- 1 recipe pastry for a 9 inch single crust pie
- 4 cups fresh peaches - peeled, pitted, and sliced
- 3/4 cup white sugar
- 1/4 cup all-purpose flour
- 1/4 teaspoon salt
- 1/4 teaspoon freshly grated nutmeg
- 1 cup heavy whipping cream

Direction

- Peel and slice peaches.
- Combine sugar, flour, salt and nutmeg. Add to the peaches and toss lightly. Turn out into pie shell. Pour whipping cream evenly over top.
- Bake in a preheated 400 degree F (205 degrees C) oven for 35-45 minutes or until firm and golden brown on top. Chill for several hours before serving.

Nutrition Information

- Calories: 320 calories
- Total Fat: 18.5 g

- Cholesterol: 41 mg
- Sodium: 204 mg
- Total Carbohydrate: 36.8 g
- Protein: 2.4 g

64. Creamy White Tea and Peach Smoothie

"Blend up this creamy, refreshing smoothie to start your morning right or as the perfect reward for a busy active day."

Serving: 4 | Prep: 5 m | Ready in: 5 m

Ingredients

- 1 1/2 cups chilled, brewed white tea
- 2 cups frozen sliced peaches or mango
- 1 cup Nordica 1% or Fat Free Cottage Cheese
- 2 tablespoons honey
- 1 tablespoon lime or lemon juice

Direction

- Combine tea, peaches, cottage cheese, honey and lime juice in a blender. Blend on high speed for 2 minutes or until very smooth. (Adjust sweetness to taste.) Serve immediately.

Nutrition Information

- Calories: 109 calories
- Total Fat: 0.8 g
- Cholesterol: 5 mg
- Sodium: 148 mg
- Total Carbohydrate: 19.7 g
- Protein: 8 g

65. Crisp Peach Cobbler

"This recipe was inspired by one from Renee Erickson's in cookbook, 'A Boat, a Whale, and a Walrus.' It's a lot crispier than a regular cobbler, and you can use the technique for other fruit cobblers. Serve warm with vanilla ice cream."

Serving: 8 | Prep: 20 m | Cook: 45 m | Ready in: 1 h 35 m

Ingredients

- 6 large fresh peaches, pitted and cut into eighths
- 1 lemon, zested and juiced
- Batter:
- 1/2 cup unsalted butter, at room temperature
- 1 1/4 cups white sugar
- 1 1/3 cups self-rising flour
- 1/3 cup rolled oats
- 2/3 cup whole milk
- Glaze:
- 1/4 cup white sugar
- 2 tablespoons cold water, or as needed to wet topping sugar

Direction

- Preheat oven to 375 degrees F (190 degrees C). Place a baking sheet on the rack under the middle rack to catch drips. Generously butter a 2-inch deep (2-quart) baking dish.
- Place peach sections into prepared baking dish. Sprinkle with lemon juice and zest.
- Stir butter and sugar together in a mixing bowl. Mix until creamed and resembles a sugary, buttery paste, 4 to 5 minutes. Add oats and flour; stir until flour and oats are incorporated into the butter-sugar mixture and mixture resembles coarse crumbs, 4 to 5 minutes. Pour in milk; stir until mixture is wet and creamy, like a thick spreadable batter, 3 to 4 minutes.
- Drop batter by spoonful on top of the peaches. Spread batter evenly over the surface of the peaches. Sprinkle 1/4 cup sugar on the batter. Spritz with water until sugar is wet and surface glistens.
- Bake in preheated oven on middle rack until browned and crispy, about 45 minutes. Let cool at least 30 minutes before serving.

Nutrition Information

- Calories: 371 calories
- Total Fat: 12.6 g
- Cholesterol: 33 mg
- Sodium: 279 mg
- Total Carbohydrate: 62.3 g
- Protein: 3.3 g

66. Danes Frozen Peach Margaritas

"Peach season equals margarita season! Garnish with peach slice and lime slice. Enjoy."

Serving: 3 | Prep: 10 m | Ready in: 10 m

Ingredients

- 2 cups ice cubes, or as desired
- 1 fresh peach, pitted and sliced
- 2 1/2 (1.5 fluid ounce) jiggers tequila
- 1 (1.5 fluid ounce) jigger triple sec
- 1 (1.5 fluid ounce) jigger peach schnapps
- 1 lime, juiced
- 1 tablespoon agave nectar

Direction

- Blend ice cubes, peach, tequila, triple sec, peach schnapps, lime juice, and agave nectar together in a blender until smooth, about 30 seconds.

Nutrition Information

- Calories: 218 calories
- Total Fat: 0.1 g
- Cholesterol: 0 mg
- Sodium: 9 mg
- Total Carbohydrate: 21.7 g
- Protein: 0.1 g

67. Double Dare Peaches

"I double dare ya to try this insane concoction that will give your mouth a bad case of schizophrenia. Take a bite and enjoy the sweet peaches, feel the heat sneak up on you, and put out the fire with ice cream. Peach ice cream is good as well."

Serving: 8 | Prep: 20 m | Cook: 10 m | Ready in: 30 m

Ingredients

- 1/4 cup butter
- 2 habanero peppers, seeded and halved
- 8 fresh peaches - peeled, pitted and sliced
- 1/4 cup brown sugar
- 1 teaspoon ground cinnamon
- 1/2 gallon vanilla ice cream
- 1/4 cup crushed jalapeno and habanero peanut brittle (such as Klondike Candies®) (optional)

Direction

- Melt the butter in a large skillet over medium-low heat. Add the habanero peppers, and cook 5 to 8 minutes, stirring frequently. Remove and discard the peppers, then stir the peaches into the flavored butter. Increase the heat to medium-high. Cook and stir until the peaches begin to sizzle in the butter, then stir in the brown sugar and cinnamon. Continue stirring until the peaches are tender and the sugar has turned into a golden brown glaze, 3 to 5 minutes more.
- Spoon the peaches into individual bowls. Scoop the ice cream over the peaches, and sprinkle with peanut brittle to serve.

Nutrition Information

- Calories: 403 calories
- Total Fat: 21.6 g
- Cholesterol: 74 mg
- Sodium: 184 mg
- Total Carbohydrate: 49.2 g
- Protein: 5.3 g

68. Down Home Summer Peaches

"A chewier version of a no-bake peach cobbler or peach crisp. I make this for my husband in our 'down home' farming community where Calhoun County peaches are extra-sweet! The peaches must be in their peak season to be sweet enough; canned peaches will not be as good!"

Serving: 2 | Prep: 5 m | Cook: 2 m | Ready in: 17 m

Ingredients

- 3 tablespoons butter
- 4 cups quick-cooking oats
- 1 tablespoon maple syrup, or to taste
- 1 tablespoon corn syrup, or to taste
- 1/4 cup brown sugar
- 1/3 cup miniature semisweet chocolate chips
- 1/2 teaspoon almond extract
- 1/2 teaspoon vanilla extract
- 2 fresh peaches, pitted and sliced

Direction

- Melt butter in a large skillet over medium heat. Pour quick oats over butter; cook and stir until oats are warmed, about 30 seconds. Drizzle maple syrup and corn syrup over the oats and stir to coat. Sprinkle brown sugar over the oats and immediately remove skillet from heat; stir mixture until the sugar melts and the oats are coated, 1 to 2 minutes.
- Pour the oats mixture into a bowl; add chocolate chips, almond extract, and vanilla extract. Gently stir the mixture to distribute chocolate chips throughout the oats mixture; spread onto a flat, shallow pan to cool completely.
- Divide peach slices between 2 bowls. Sprinkle oats mixture over the peaches.

Nutrition Information

- Calories: 1095 calories
- Total Fat: 36.5 g
- Cholesterol: 46 mg
- Sodium: 155 mg

- Total Carbohydrate: 175.6 g
- Protein: 22.8 g

69. Drumsticks with Peach and Honey

"My neighbor used to have a restaurant in Indonesia. He was kind enough to share one of his most popular item on the menu with me. My kids who are big fans of peaches, canned or fresh, and drumsticks love this recipe, especially on a hot,summer day. These are good when served hot over rice, or bring to the park for a picnic."

Serving: 10 | Prep: 25 m | Cook: 45 m | Ready in: 1 h 10 m

Ingredients

- 2 teaspoons butter
- 1 teaspoon minced garlic
- 10 chicken drumsticks
- 1/2 teaspoon salt
- 1/4 teaspoon ground black pepper
- 1 teaspoon butter
- 1/2 onion, sliced
- 5 teaspoons honey
- 2 teaspoons soy sauce
- 1/2 teaspoon ground ginger
- 1 cup water
- 1 lemon, thinly sliced
- 1 teaspoon cornstarch
- 2 teaspoons water
- 1 peach, peeled and sliced

Direction

- Heat 2 teaspoons of butter in a large skillet over medium-low heat. Stir in the garlic, and cook for a minute or two until the garlic softens and mellows. Season the chicken with salt and pepper, and add to the skillet. Cook until the chicken has browned on all sides, about 15 minutes.
- When the drumsticks have browned, remove, and set aside. Melt the remaining 1 teaspoon butter in the skillet, and stir in the sliced onion. Cook and stir until the onion begins to soften, about 5 minutes, then stir in the honey, soy sauce, ginger, and 1 cup of water. Return the drumsticks to the skillet, and bring to a boil over high heat. Reduce heat to medium-low, spread the lemon slices overtop, cover with a lid, and simmer until the drumsticks are tender and no longer pink at the bone, about 15 minutes.
- Once the drumsticks have cooked, remove them to a serving platter and keep warm. Dissolve the cornstarch in 2 teaspoons of water, and stir into the simmering sauce. Add the peach, and cook until the sauce thickens and returns to a simmer. Pour sauce over the drumsticks to serve.

Nutrition Information

- Calories: 246 calories
- Total Fat: 12.4 g
- Cholesterol: 90 mg
- Sodium: 266 mg
- Total Carbohydrate: 5.9 g
- Protein: 26.9 g

70. Dutch Oven Peach Pecan Cobbler

"Great scout or family camping recipe shared by a veteran scout leader. Use parchment Dutch oven liners to speed up cleanup."

Serving: 12 | Prep: 20 m | Cook: 30 m | Ready in: 50 m

Ingredients

- 2 (21 ounce) cans peach pie filling
- 1 (15.25 ounce) package yellow cake mix
- 1 cup chopped pecans, divided
- 1/2 cup butter, cubed
- 2 cups toffee baking bits

Direction

- Build a campfire and allow the fire to burn until it has accumulated a bed of coals. Rake the coals into a flat bed on one side of the fire.
- Line a 12-inch Dutch oven with parchment paper. Pour in peach filling; spread evenly. Sprinkle cake mix on top, followed by 1/2 cup pecans. Stir peach mixture briefly.
- Sprinkle butter cubes, the remaining 1/2 cup pecans, and toffee chips evenly over the peach mixture. Cover with lid.
- Carefully place medium-hot coals over and under the Dutch oven; cook until golden brown, 30 to 35 minutes.

Nutrition Information

- Calories: 603 calories
- Total Fat: 33.1 g
- Cholesterol: 54 mg
- Sodium: 504 mg
- Total Carbohydrate: 73.1 g
- Protein: 3.6 g

71. Easiest Ever Fruit Cobbler

"This is the quickest, easiest and best ever cobbler versatile enough for any canned fruit. We like it best with peaches. Serve warm. Best topped with vanilla ice cream!"

Serving: 6 | Prep: 10 m | Cook: 35 m | Ready in: 45 m

Ingredients

- 1/2 cup butter, melted
- 1 (29 ounce) can sliced peaches with juice
- 1 cup self-rising flour
- 1 cup white sugar
- 1 pinch salt
- 1 cup milk

Direction

- Preheat oven to 400 degrees F (200 degrees C). Grease a 2-quart baking dish.
- Stir together peaches and juice with melted butter. Pour into prepared pan. In a small

bowl mix flour, sugar and salt. Stir in milk. Pour mixture over peaches.
- Bake on bottom rack of preheated oven 15 minutes, or until lightly browned, then move to top rack for 20 minutes more. Serve warm.

Nutrition Information

- Calories: 418 calories
- Total Fat: 16.4 g
- Cholesterol: 44 mg
- Sodium: 396 mg
- Total Carbohydrate: 66.4 g
- Protein: 4.4 g

72. Easy French Peach Pie

"This very rich and easy-to-make pie is a modified family recipe. It can be made with either peaches or apples."

Serving: 8 | Prep: 10 m | Cook: 55 m | Ready in: 1 h 5 m

Ingredients

- 1 recipe pastry for a single 9-inch pie crust
- 1 (28 ounce) can sliced peaches, drained
- 1 cup white sugar
- 1 egg
- 1 tablespoon all-purpose flour
- 1 teaspoon butter
- 1/4 teaspoon ground cinnamon, or to taste

Direction

- Preheat an oven to 450 degrees F (230 degrees C). Press pie pastry into a 9-inch pie pan.
- Fill prepared pie crust with peaches. Mix sugar, egg, flour, butter, and cinnamon together in a bowl; pour over peaches.
- Bake in the preheated oven for 15 minutes. Reduce heat to 350 degrees F (175 degrees C); bake until peach filling is bubbling and crust is lightly browned, 40 to 45 minutes.

Nutrition Information

- Calories: 271 calories

- Total Fat: 8.6 g
- Cholesterol: 25 mg
- Sodium: 133 mg
- Total Carbohydrate: 47.6 g
- Protein: 2.9 g

73. Easy Fruit Cobbler

"This cobbler can be made with peaches, apples, cherries, or berries."

Serving: 8 | Prep: 15 m | Cook: 1 h | Ready in: 1 h 15 m

Ingredients

- 1 cup all-purpose flour
- 2 teaspoons baking powder
- 3/4 cup white sugar
- 3/4 cup milk
- 1/4 cup butter
- 2 cups sliced fresh peaches

Direction

- Preheat oven to 325 degrees F (165 degrees C). Melt butter in a 9 x 9 inch baking dish.
- Blend together flour, baking powder, sugar, and milk.
- Pour batter in baking dish over the butter. Sprinkle fruit on top of the batter, do not stir. Bake for 1 hour or until golden brown.

Nutrition Information

- Calories: 200 calories
- Total Fat: 6.4 g
- Cholesterol: 17 mg
- Sodium: 174 mg
- Total Carbohydrate: 34 g
- Protein: 2.4 g

74. Easy Peach Cobbler

"This is a great peach cobbler--so easy a child can make it! It is great right out of the oven served with vanilla ice cream."

Serving: 6 | Prep: 10 m | Cook: 30 m | Ready in: 40 m

Ingredients

- 1 cup white sugar
- 1/2 cup butter, room temperature
- 1 cup self-rising flour
- 1 cup milk
- 1 (15 ounce) can peaches

Direction

- Preheat oven to 350 degrees F (175 degrees C).
- Watch Now
- In a one-quart baking dish or 9 inch square pan, cream together sugar and butter. Mix in flour and milk until smooth. Pour peaches and their juice over the top.
- Watch Now
- Bake 25 to 30 minutes in the preheated oven, until golden brown.
- Watch Now

Nutrition Information

- Calories: 390 calories
- Total Fat: 16.4 g
- Cholesterol: 44 mg
- Sodium: 393 mg
- Total Carbohydrate: 58.8 g
- Protein: 4 g

75. Easy Peach Crisp II

"My family actually calls this peach cobbler but the crispy shortbread-type crust makes it a crisp. Very good with ice cream or sprinkled with pecans before baking."

Serving: 24 | Prep: 10 m | Cook: 35 m | Ready in: 45 m

Ingredients

- 1 (29 ounce) can sliced peaches, drained

- 2 cups all-purpose flour
- 1 1/2 cups white sugar
- 1 pinch salt
- 1 1/2 teaspoons ground cinnamon
- 1 cup butter, chilled

Direction

- Preheat oven to 350 degrees F (175 degrees C).
- Layer the peaches in a 9x13 inch baking pan. In a large bowl, mix the flour, sugar, salt and cinnamon. Slice the butter into chunks and mix it into the dry ingredients until it looks like pea size crumbs. Sprinkle crumbs over peaches.
- Bake for 30 to 40 minutes in the preheated oven, until lightly golden.

Nutrition Information

- Calories: 169 calories
- Total Fat: 7.8 g
- Cholesterol: 20 mg
- Sodium: 56 mg
- Total Carbohydrate: 24.5 g
- Protein: 1.4 g

76. Easy Peach Pie

"It is everything you want. Can be frozen and thawed to eat later."

Serving: 10 | Prep: 30 m | Ready in: 30 m

Ingredients

- 1 (9 inch) deep dish graham cracker pie crust
- 5 fresh peaches - peeled, pitted, and sliced
- 1 (18 ounce) jar peach glaze
- 1/4 cup white sugar
- 1 (12 ounce) container frozen whipped topping, thawed
- 2 (8 ounce) packages cream cheese

Direction

- Combine peaches and glaze in a mixing bowl. Let stand for a couple of minutes.
- Combine sugar and cream cheese. Mix with an electric mixer on high speed for one minute. Gradually add in the nondairy whipped topping, and mix on medium speed until you have a smooth consistency. Pour mixture into pie shell. Pour peach mixture on top. Cover, and chill for 1 hour.

Nutrition Information

- Calories: 496 calories
- Total Fat: 31.4 g
- Cholesterol: 66 mg
- Sodium: 373 mg
- Total Carbohydrate: 49.5 g
- Protein: 5 g

77. Easy Peachy Cobbler Bake

"Canned peaches in light syrup are baked in a sweetened baking mix topping for an easy, comforting cobbler."

Serving: 18 | Prep: 5 m | Cook: 50 m | Ready in: 1 h 5 m

Ingredients

- 1 (29 ounce) can peaches in light syrup
- 2/3 cup white sugar
- 3 tablespoons butter
- 2/3 cup brown sugar
- 1 1/2 cups all-purpose baking mix
- 1 1/3 cups buttermilk

Direction

- Preheat oven to 350 degrees F (175 degrees C).
- In a medium bowl, combine peaches in syrup with sugar. Pour into a 9x13 inch baking dish. Dot with butter. In a separate bowl, combine brown sugar and baking mix. Stir in buttermilk until smooth. Pour over peaches.
- Bake in preheated oven 50 minutes, or until lightly browned and bubbly. Let rest 10 minutes before serving.

Nutrition Information

- Calories: 148 calories
- Total Fat: 3.6 g
- Cholesterol: 6 mg
- Sodium: 163 mg
- Total Carbohydrate: 28.8 g
- Protein: 1.5 g

78. Elnoras Peach Cobbler

"This is my grandmother's simple recipe. Only peaches and cobbler in Pennsylvania, no hiding the peach flavor with too many spices."

Serving: 8 | Prep: 20 m | Cook: 40 m | Ready in: 1 h

Ingredients

- 1 cup milk
- 1 cup self-rising flour
- 1 cup white sugar
- 1/2 cup butter, melted
- 4 cups sliced peaches
- 1 tablespoon white sugar, or to taste (optional)

Direction

- Preheat oven to 375 degrees F (190 degrees C). Grease an 11x17-inch baking dish.
- Whisk milk, flour, and 1 cup sugar together in a bowl until blended; add butter. Stir to combine.
- Arrange peaches in prepared baking dish; sprinkle with 1 tablespoon sugar. Cover peaches with batter, without stirring.
- Bake in the preheated oven until browned and bubbling, about 40 minutes.

Nutrition Information

- Calories: 291 calories
- Total Fat: 12.3 g
- Cholesterol: 33 mg
- Sodium: 295 mg
- Total Carbohydrate: 43.5 g
- Protein: 2.7 g

79. English Trifle

"I got this recipe from my English cousin. It's very easy to make and this is her recipe for the cake."

Serving: 12 | Prep: 30 m | Cook: 30 m | Ready in: 1 h 30 m

Ingredients

- 1/2 cup margarine
- 1/2 cup white sugar
- 2 eggs
- 1 3/4 cups all-purpose flour
- 1/2 teaspoon baking powder
- 1/2 teaspoon salt
- 1 pint heavy cream
- 1/4 cup white sugar
- 1 teaspoon vanilla extract
- 1 (4.6 ounce) package non-instant vanilla pudding mix
- 1 (8 ounce) jar seedless raspberry jam
- 1/2 cup sherry
- 4 fresh peaches - peeled, pitted, and sliced
- 1 pint fresh strawberries, rinsed and sliced
- 1 pint blueberries

Direction

- Preheat oven to 350 degrees F (175 degrees C). Grease and flour an 8x8 inch cake pan.
- In large bowl, cream together margarine and 1/2 cup sugar. Beat in eggs, one at a time. Combine flour, baking powder and salt. Fold dry ingredients into butter mixture. Pour into prepared pan.
- Bake 25 minutes, or until cake springs back when lightly touched in center. Cool in pan for five minutes, then remove from pan and cool completely on wire rack. Cut into narrow pieces about 1 1/2 inches by 4 inches. Set aside.
- In large bowl, beat cream with electric mixer until soft peaks form. Beat in 1/4 cup sugar and vanilla and continue to beat until stiff peaks form. Set aside.

- Prepare vanilla pudding according to package directions. Set aside.
- To Assemble Trifle: Brush each piece of cake with raspberry jam. Use half the cake pieces to line the bottom of a trifle bowl or other glass serving dish. Sprinkle half of the sherry over cake. Layer half the peaches, strawberries and blueberries on top. Cover with half the pudding and a third of the whipped cream. Repeat layers with remaining cake, sherry, fruit and pudding. Top with remaining whipped cream. Chill in refrigerator at least 30 minutes before serving.

Nutrition Information

- Calories: 432 calories
- Total Fat: 23.5 g
- Cholesterol: 86 mg
- Sodium: 305 mg
- Total Carbohydrate: 51.7 g
- Protein: 4.6 g

80. Erics Grilled Pork on Pork Rollatini

"Pork cutlets are stuffed with peaches, jalapeno, and sausage and rolled into rollatini and grilled for a quick and easy weeknight dinner that looks gourmet. This recipe was made in a Panasonic CIO and appears on an episode of the Dinner Spinner TV Show on The CW!"

Serving: 4 | Prep: 20 m | Cook: 40 m | Ready in: 1 h

Ingredients

- 1/2 cup balsamic vinegar
- 1 pound pork cutlets, thinly sliced
- 3 fully cooked andouille sausages, diced
- 1/4 cup diced onion
- 1/4 cup chopped jalapeno
- 2 peaches, pitted and chopped into 1/4-inch pieces
- 1/2 cup diced apple
- kitchen twine

Direction

- Preheat oven to 400 degrees F (200 degrees C) and place a grill pan in the oven. (Or preheat countertop induction oven on medium heat with grill pan inside.)
- Bring balsamic vinegar to a boil in a saucepan; reduce heat and simmer until balsamic is reduced and thickened into a glaze, 10 to 15 minutes.
- Pound pork cutlets with a mallet to about 1/2-inch thickness.
- Cook and stir sausage, onion, and jalapeno in a skillet over medium heat until onion slightly translucent and sausage is cooked through, about 5 minutes. Add peaches and apple; cook and stir filling until fruit is softened, about 5 more minutes. Add about 1 tablespoon balsamic glaze to the top and stir.
- Spoon filling into the center of each pork cutlet, reserving leftover filling in the skillet. Roll up culet and tie with roasting twine. Place rolled pork onto heated grill pan and return to oven.
- Bake in the preheated oven, turning pork halfway through, until pork is cooked through and browned on the outside, 20 to 25 minutes. (Or grill on medium heat in the countertop induction oven for 15 minutes (7 1/2 minutes each side.)
- Pour balsamic glaze over leftover filling in the skillet; cook and stir over low heat just until warm. Spoon filling onto cooked stuffed pork.

Nutrition Information

- Calories: 173 calories
- Total Fat: 5.3 g
- Cholesterol: 55 mg
- Sodium: 137 mg
- Total Carbohydrate: 11.3 g
- Protein: 19.1 g

81. Freezer Peach Pie Filling

"Peach filling is prepared ahead of time and frozen inside a pie plate. When ready to bake, simply place it in a crust-filled pie plate of the same size, and bake."

Serving: 8 | Prep: 15 m | Cook: 55 m | Ready in: 3 h 10 m

Ingredients

- 2 1/2 cups sliced peaches
- 3/4 cup white sugar
- 1 tablespoon cornstarch
- 1 tablespoon MINUTE Tapioca
- 1 dash Dash of nutmeg

Direction

- Place sliced peaches in a bowl with sugar, cornstarch, tapioca, and nutmeg. Toss until evenly coated and sugar is mostly dissolved.
- Transfer peaches to a 9 inch foil-lined pie plate. Cover with another piece of foil and freeze immediately to prevent peaches from discoloring. Once frozen solid, remove peaches from pie plate, with foil, and transfer to a zipper locked plastic bag for later use. When ready to use, line a pie plate with prepared crust and place frozen peaches on top.
- Preheat oven to 450 degrees F (230 degrees C).
- Bake in the preheated oven on the bottom rack for 20 minutes. Lower heat to 350 degrees F (175 degrees C) and continue baking for another 30 to 35 minutes, or until completely warmed through.

Nutrition Information

- Calories: 118 calories
- Total Fat: 0.2 g
- Cholesterol: 0 mg
- Sodium: 1 mg
- Total Carbohydrate: 30.2 g
- Protein: 0.6 g

82. French Peach Pie

"This is an easy impressive pie. It is also very good with fresh fruit."

Serving: 8 | Prep: 15 m | Cook: 5 m | Ready in: 1 h 30 m

Ingredients

- 1 (9 inch) pie shell, baked
- 1 (15 ounce) can sliced peaches, juice reserved
- 1 (3.5 ounce) package instant vanilla pudding mix
- 1 cup milk
- 1 cup sour cream
- 1/4 teaspoon almond extract
- 1 tablespoon cornstarch
- 1 teaspoon lemon juice

Direction

- Drain peaches, reserving 2/3 cup of syrup. Stir together pudding mix, milk, sour cream, and almond extract for 2 minutes, until very smooth. Pour filling into pie shell. Chill for 10 minutes.
- Arrange peach slices in a nice pattern over custard in pie shell.
- In a small saucepan, mix together reserved peach syrup and corn starch. Bring to a boil, and cook for 2 minutes. Remove from heat, and stir in lemon juice. Pour glaze over peaches. Chill until set. Serve.

Nutrition Information

- Calories: 268 calories
- Total Fat: 14.5 g
- Cholesterol: 15 mg
- Sodium: 328 mg
- Total Carbohydrate: 31.7 g
- Protein: 3.7 g

83. Fresh Fruit Basket Cobbler

"Summer stone fruits combined with a sweet-tart sauce nestled under a flaky biscuit crust...yummy!"

Serving: 8 | Prep: 20 m | Cook: 20 m | Ready in: 1 h

Ingredients

- 2 cups sliced fresh peaches
- 2 cups sliced fresh nectarines
- 2 cups pitted and quartered plums
- 1 teaspoon cornstarch
- 1 cup currant jelly
- 1/2 teaspoon apple pie spice
- 1/8 teaspoon white pepper
- 1 (16.3 ounce) can refrigerated flaky biscuits (such as Pillsbury Grands!®)
- 1/4 cup white sugar
- 1/4 teaspoon ground cinnamon

Direction

- Preheat oven to 350 degrees F (175 degrees C). Spray an 8x13-inch baking dish with cooking spray.
- In a large bowl, lightly mix together the peach, nectarine, and plum slices until well mixed, and toss with the cornstarch to dust the fruit. Pour in the currant jelly, apple pie spice, and white pepper, and lightly mix again with your hands to coat the fruit with the jelly and seasonings. Spread the fruit into the prepared baking dish.
- Pop open the can of biscuits, and cut them in half. Arrange the biscuit dough halves on top of the fruit. Mix the sugar and cinnamon in a small bowl, and sprinkle the mixture evenly on the biscuit dough.
- Bake in the preheated oven until the biscuits are golden brown, 20 to 25 minutes. Allow to cool on a rack for at least 20 minutes to let the dish set up.

Nutrition Information

- Calories: 358 calories
- Total Fat: 8 g
- Cholesterol: < 1 mg
- Sodium: 571 mg

- Total Carbohydrate: 69.3 g
- Protein: 4.5 g

84. Fresh Fruit Cobbler

"Never use more than 1 quart of fruit. Only use fresh fruit for this recipe. Any variation will work! I usually do use sweetened peaches and lightly sugared berries, but this is optional. Serve warm with cream, ice cream, or whipped cream."

Serving: 6 | Prep: 30 m | Cook: 30 m | Ready in: 1 h

Ingredients

- 1 cup sliced fresh peaches
- 3/4 cup peeled, cored and sliced apple
- 3/4 cup peeled, cored and sliced pear
- 1/2 cup blueberries
- 1/2 cup pitted and sliced cherries
- 1/2 cup pitted and sliced plums
- 1 egg
- 3/4 cup white sugar
- 1/4 cup milk
- 1 cup all-purpose flour
- 1 teaspoon baking powder
- 1/2 teaspoon salt
- 1/2 teaspoon vanilla extract
- 2 tablespoons butter, melted

Direction

- Preheat oven to 350 degrees F (175 degrees C). Grease a 2 quart baking dish.
- Arrange the peaches, apple, pear, blueberries, cherries, and plums in the prepared baking dish. In a medium bowl, beat egg, sugar, and milk. In a separate bowl, sift together flour, baking powder, and salt; stir into the egg mixture. Stir in vanilla and melted butter. Cover the fruit with the batter mixture.
- Bake 30 minutes in the preheated oven. Cobbler should be bubbly and lightly browned. Serve warm.

Nutrition Information

- Calories: 272 calories
- Total Fat: 5.3 g

- Cholesterol: 42 mg
- Sodium: 320 mg
- Total Carbohydrate: 53.7 g
- Protein: 4 g

85. Fresh Peach Cobbler

"Nothing brings out the flavor of fresh peaches better than a fruit cobbler, and this one bakes up in 30 minutes."

Serving: 8

Ingredients

- 1/2 cup butter
- 2 cups biscuit baking mix
- 2 cups sugar, divided
- 3 tablespoons cinnamon, divided
- 3/4 cup Kikkoman Pearl® Organic Original Soymilk
- 5 cups fresh peaches, peeled and sliced
- 1 cup corn syrup

Direction

- Heat oven to 375 degrees F.
- Put butter in an 8 x 12-inch baking dish; place dish in oven until butter melts. In mixing bowl, mix biscuit mix with 1/2 cup sugar and 1 tablespoon cinnamon. Mix in soymilk. Place peaches in baking dish with butter. Add corn syrup, 1 1/2 cups sugar and 2 tablespoons cinnamon; toss to combine.
- Drop spoonfuls of biscuit mixture over peaches, spreading with the back of the spoon to cover all the peaches. Bake about 30 minutes or until crust has risen and is golden brown.

Nutrition Information

- Calories: 570 calories
- Total Fat: 16.4 g
- Cholesterol: 31 mg
- Sodium: 488 mg
- Total Carbohydrate: 108 g
- Protein: 3 g

86. Fresh Peach Cobbler I

"Serve warm with whipped cream, whipped topping, or vanilla ice cream!"

Serving: 6 | Prep: 30 m | Cook: 25 m | Ready in: 55 m

Ingredients

- Peach Filling:
- 1/2 cup white sugar
- 1 tablespoon cornstarch
- 1/4 teaspoon ground cinnamon
- 4 cups sliced fresh peaches
- 1 teaspoon lemon juice
- Cobbler Topping:
- 1 cup all-purpose flour
- 1 tablespoon white sugar
- 1 1/2 teaspoons baking powder
- 1/2 teaspoon salt
- 3 tablespoons shortening
- 1/2 cup milk

Direction

- Preheat oven to 400 degrees F (200 degrees C).
- Combine 1/2 cup sugar, cornstarch, and cinnamon in a saucepan and whisk to mix. Stir in sliced peaches (see Editor's Note) and lemon juice, tossing until peaches are evenly coated.
- Cook filling over medium heat, stirring constantly, until mixture thickens and boils. Boil 1 minute. Pour mixture into an ungreased 2-quart casserole dish. Keep mixture hot in oven while you make the topping.
- In a medium bowl combine flour, 1 tablespoon sugar, baking powder, and salt. Mix thoroughly, then cut in shortening until mixture looks like fine crumbs. Add milk and stir until mixture is evenly moistened.
- Remove peach filling from oven and drop dough onto peaches in 6 equal-size spoonfuls.
- Return cobbler to oven and bake until topping is golden brown, 25 to 30 minutes.

Nutrition Information

- Calories: 243 calories
- Total Fat: 7 g
- Cholesterol: 2 mg
- Sodium: 328 mg
- Total Carbohydrate: 42.5 g
- Protein: 2.9 g

---

87. Fresh Peach Cobbler II

"Simple old-fashioned peach cobbler; just like Grandma used to make. Tastes great."

Serving: 8 | Prep: 30 m | Cook: 40 m | Ready in: 1 h 10 m

Ingredients

- 3 cups sliced fresh peaches
- 1 cup white sugar
- 1 tablespoon lemon juice
- 1 teaspoon grated lemon zest
- 1/4 teaspoon almond extract
- 1 1/2 cups all-purpose flour
- 1 tablespoon white sugar
- 1 tablespoon baking powder
- 1/2 teaspoon salt
- 1/3 cup shortening
- 1/2 cup milk
- 1 egg, beaten
- 2 tablespoons white sugar

Direction

- Preheat oven to 400 degrees F (200 degrees C). Lightly grease an 8x8 inch square baking dish.
- Place sliced peaches in prepared baking dish. Mix together 1 cup sugar, lemon juice, lemon zest, and almond extract. Place in oven while preparing shortcake (heating peaches first helps prevent dough from getting soggy).
- In a large bowl, combine flour, 1 tablespoon sugar, baking powder, and salt. Cut in shortening until mixture resembles coarse crumbs. Add milk and egg; stir just until flour

is moistened. Spread over hot peaches. Sprinkle top with remaining sugar.
- Bake in preheated oven for 35 to 40 minutes, or until top is golden brown.

Nutrition Information

- Calories: 306 calories
- Total Fat: 9.7 g
- Cholesterol: 24 mg
- Sodium: 289 mg
- Total Carbohydrate: 51.8 g
- Protein: 3.7 g

---

88. Fresh Peach Dessert

"We look forward to peach season every year just so we can have this dessert. Make sure to use sweet, ripe peaches. You could also substitute other fruits such as raspberries or strawberries, but I think fresh peaches are the best."

Serving: 15 | Prep: 30 m | Cook: 10 m | Ready in: 40 m

Ingredients

- 16 whole graham crackers, crushed
- 3/4 cup butter, melted
- 1/2 cup white sugar
- 4 1/2 cups miniature marshmallows
- 1/4 cup milk
- 1 pint heavy cream
- 1/3 cup white sugar
- 6 large fresh peaches - peeled, pitted and sliced

Direction

- Combine the graham cracker crumbs, melted butter, and 1/2 cup sugar in a mixing bowl. Mix until evenly moistened, reserve 1/4 cup of the mixture for the topping. Press the remaining mixture into the bottom of a 9x13-inch baking dish.
- Heat marshmallows and milk in a large saucepan over low heat and stir until the marshmallows are completely melted. Remove from heat and cool.

- Whip cream in a large bowl until soft peaks form. Beat in 1/3 cup sugar until the cream forms stiff peaks. Fold the whipped cream into the cooled marshmallow mixture.
- Spread 1/2 the cream mixture over the crust, arrange the peaches on top of the cream, then spread the remaining cream mixture over the peaches. Sprinkle the reserved crumb mixture over the cream. Refrigerate until serving.

Nutrition Information

- Calories: 366 calories
- Total Fat: 22.5 g
- Cholesterol: 68 mg
- Sodium: 190 mg
- Total Carbohydrate: 39.2 g
- Protein: 1.9 g

89. Fresh Peach Dumplings Served with Hard Sauce

"This is fresh peaches wrapped in a rich flakey dough, and topped with a teaspoon of hard sauce after baked. No sugar is used on the peaches, just the sauce. Sugar free ice cream could be used instead of hard sauce."

Serving: 6 | Prep: 30 m | Cook: 30 m | Ready in: 1 h

Ingredients

- 2 cups all-purpose flour
- 1 teaspoon salt
- 3/4 cup butter flavored shortening
- 5 tablespoons ice water
- 6 fresh peaches - peeled, pitted and halved
- 1/4 cup butter, softened
- 1 egg
- 1/4 teaspoon ground nutmeg
- 1 teaspoon vanilla extract
- 1 pinch salt
- 2 cups confectioners' sugar

Direction

- In a medium bowl, stir together the flour and salt. Cut in the butter flavored shortening using your hands or a pastry blender until the mixture resembles coarse crumbs. Sprinkle the ice water over the dough, and stir until the mixture comes together. Knead the dough briefly, then divide into 6 pieces.
- Preheat the oven to 375 degrees F (190 degrees C).
- On a lightly floured surface roll out each piece of dough into a thin circle. Place two peach halves together, and wrap in each circle of dough, sealing at the top. Place the dumplings onto an ungreased baking sheet.
- Bake dumplings for 30 minutes in the preheated oven, or until golden brown. While the dumplings are baking, make the sauce. In a medium bowl, mix together the butter, egg, nutmeg, vanilla and salt using an electric mixer on low speed. Gradually mix in the confectioners' sugar. Spoon over warm dumplings.

Nutrition Information

- Calories: 658 calories
- Total Fat: 35.8 g
- Cholesterol: 51 mg
- Sodium: 459 mg
- Total Carbohydrate: 79.6 g
- Protein: 5.5 g

90. Fresh Peach Empanadas

"Super delicious empanadas! The pastry is so light, buttery, and flaky. It's just beautifully delicious!"

Serving: 15 | Prep: 30 m | Cook: 15 m | Ready in: 2 h 20 m

Ingredients

- 2 cups all-purpose flour
- 1 tablespoon white sugar
- 1/2 teaspoon salt

- 1 cup cold butter, cut into 1/2-inch pieces
- 1/4 cup cream cheese
- 1/4 cup sour cream
- Filling:
- 2 ripe peaches, peeled and cut into 1-inch pieces
- 3 1/2 tablespoons white sugar, divided, or more to taste
- 1 teaspoon ground cinnamon
- 1/2 teaspoon vanilla extract
- 1 pinch salt
- 1/2 egg, beaten, or as needed

Direction

- Place flour in a medium bowl. Whisk in sugar and salt. Cut in butter using 2 knives or a pastry cutter. Gently work in cream cheese and sour cream until dough is combined.
- Turn dough out onto your working surface. Quickly gather crumbs together into a square; fold square in half. Flatten dough out into a larger square using a rolling pin; fold in half again. Roll out one more time and fold into thirds, like a letter. Wrap dough in plastic wrap. Chill until firm, about 1 hour.
- Mix peaches, 3 tablespoons sugar, and cinnamon in a small bowl. Let sit for about 15 minutes. Transfer filling mixture into a strainer over a bowl to drain the excess juices for 15 minutes, stirring occasionally.
- Preheat the oven to 400 degrees F (200 degrees C). Line a baking sheet with parchment paper.
- Roll pastry dough onto a floured surface to about 3/8-inch thickness. Cut out 15 to 20 circles about 4- to 6-inches in diameter. Place 2 teaspoons of filling into the middle of each circle. Fold dough in half over the filling and seal edges together with your fingers. Press edges together with the tines of a fork to make a decorative seal, if desired.
- Place empanadas on the prepared baking sheet; brush with egg and sprinkle with remaining sugar.
- Bake in the preheated oven until golden brown, 12 to 15 minutes. Remove from oven and let cool for 5 minutes before serving.

Nutrition Information

- Calories: 212 calories
- Total Fat: 14.7 g
- Cholesterol: 44 mg
- Sodium: 191 mg
- Total Carbohydrate: 17.7 g
- Protein: 2.5 g

91. Fresh Peach Pie I

"This is one of the few unbaked peach pie recipes that I have been able to find."

Serving: 8

Ingredients

- 1 (9 inch) pie shell, baked
- 1 cup white sugar
- 1/2 cup water
- 3 tablespoons cornstarch
- 1 tablespoon butter
- 2 cups fresh peaches, pitted and mashed
- 1/4 teaspoon ground nutmeg
- 1 teaspoon vanilla extract
- 4 cups fresh peaches - pitted, skinned, and sliced

Direction

- Combine sugar, water, cornstarch, butter or margarine, mashed peaches, and nutmeg in a saucepan. Cook over medium heat until clear and thick. Stir in vanilla.
- Fill pie shell with sliced fresh peaches, alternating with the glaze. Refrigerate.

Nutrition Information

- Calories: 266 calories
- Total Fat: 9.3 g
- Cholesterol: 4 mg
- Sodium: 136 mg
- Total Carbohydrate: 44.4 g
- Protein: 1.5 g

92. Fresh Peach Pie II

"If you like fresh peaches, this is the pie for you. It's the only way my family wants it. It's delicious topped with whipped topping."

Serving: 16 | Prep: 20 m | Cook: 15 m | Ready in: 45 m

Ingredients

- 1 1/2 cups white sugar
- 1/4 cup cornstarch
- 2 cups water
- 1 (3 ounce) package peach flavored Jell-O® mix
- 4 cups fresh peaches - peeled, pitted, and sliced
- 2 (9 inch) pie shells, baked

Direction

- In a saucepan over medium heat, combine sugar and cornstarch. Add water and bring to a boil. Continue to boil or 3 minutes, stirring constantly. Stir in the peach gelatin mix. Remove from heat and allow to cool.
- In a large bowl, combine the sliced peaches with the gelatin mixture. Gently stir until peach slices are coated with gelatin. Pour into baked pie shells. Refrigerate until set.

Nutrition Information

- Calories: 226 calories
- Total Fat: 7.8 g
- Cholesterol: 0 mg
- Sodium: 143 mg
- Total Carbohydrate: 37.8 g
- Protein: 1.9 g

93. Fresh Peach Salsa

"This cool, refreshing salsa is a wonderful summertime treat. Peaches and orange marmalade blend perfectly with green onions and cider vinegar. The salsa may be served warm."

Serving: 16 | Prep: 15 m | Ready in: 15 m

Ingredients

- 6 large fresh peaches - peeled, pitted and chopped
- 2/3 cup orange marmalade
- 1/4 cup sliced green onions
- 3 tablespoons cider vinegar
- 1 ounce crystallized ginger
- 2 teaspoons white sugar

Direction

- In a medium bowl, mix together peaches, orange marmalade, green onions, cider vinegar, crystallized ginger and sugar. Cover and refrigerate until serving.

Nutrition Information

- Calories: 54 calories
- Total Fat: 0 g
- Cholesterol: 0 mg
- Sodium: 11 mg
- Total Carbohydrate: 14 g
- Protein: 0.1 g

94. Fresh Peach Trifle

"This dessert is one of my favorites. Although you have to put a little work into it, the results can be described with one word: Yummy!"

Serving: 8 | Prep: 35 m | Ready in: 35 m

Ingredients

- 6 large ripe peaches - peeled, pitted and sliced
- 1 tablespoon fresh lemon juice
- 2 (8 ounce) containers vanilla yogurt
- 1 teaspoon lemon zest

- 1 (10 inch) prepared angel food cake

Direction

- Place peaches in a large bowl, and gently toss with lemon juice. Place 1 cup of peaches in a blender, set aside remaining slices, and blend until smooth. Place yogurt into a bowl; stir in the peach puree and lemon zest until well blended.
- Cut the angel food cake into squares and place half in the bottom of a glass dish. Spoon half of the peach slices over the cake. Cover with half of the yogurt mixture. Place remaining cake squares over the yogurt. Top with peaches, reserving 5 or 6 slices for garnish. Cover with remaining yogurt mixture. Garnish with peach slices. Refrigerate until ready to serve.

Nutrition Information

- Calories: 182 calories
- Total Fat: 1 g
- Cholesterol: 3 mg
- Sodium: 356 mg
- Total Carbohydrate: 38.3 g
- Protein: 5.3 g

95. Fresh Peaches with Honey Vanilla Creme Fraiche

"This is a fancy, elegant little dessert that is deceivingly quick-and-easy to put together. Garnish with a sprig of mint for extra prettiness. A little sprinkle of cinnamon is a nice twist."

Serving: 2 | Prep: 10 m | Ready in: 10 m

Ingredients

- 1/4 cup creme fraiche
- 1 tablespoon honey
- 1 tablespoon vanilla sugar
- 2 large ripe peaches, diced

Direction

- Stir creme fraiche, honey, and vanilla sugar together in a bowl until smooth. Be sure to scrape the spoon often, as the honey tends to stick to it and harden.
- Divide diced peaches into 2 dessert bowls. Drizzle creme fraiche mixture over peaches and serve immediately.

Nutrition Information

- Calories: 191 calories
- Total Fat: 11.2 g
- Cholesterol: 41 mg
- Sodium: 16 mg
- Total Carbohydrate: 23.9 g
- Protein: 1.1 g

96. Fresh Southern Peach Cobbler

"I've been experimenting with cobbler for some time and this recipe is the final result. Loved by all. Use fresh Georgia peaches, of course!"

Serving: 4 | Prep: 20 m | Cook: 40 m | Ready in: 1 h

Ingredients

- 8 fresh peaches - peeled, pitted and sliced into thin wedges
- 1/4 cup white sugar
- 1/4 cup brown sugar
- 1/4 teaspoon ground cinnamon
- 1/8 teaspoon ground nutmeg
- 1 teaspoon fresh lemon juice
- 2 teaspoons cornstarch
- 1 cup all-purpose flour
- 1/4 cup white sugar
- 1/4 cup brown sugar
- 1 teaspoon baking powder
- 1/2 teaspoon salt
- 6 tablespoons unsalted butter, chilled and cut into small pieces
- 1/4 cup boiling water
- MIX TOGETHER:

- 3 tablespoons white sugar
- 1 teaspoon ground cinnamon

Direction

- Preheat oven to 425 degrees F (220 degrees C).
- In a large bowl, combine peaches, 1/4 cup white sugar, 1/4 cup brown sugar, 1/4 teaspoon cinnamon, nutmeg, lemon juice, and cornstarch. Toss to coat evenly, and pour into a 2 quart baking dish. Bake in preheated oven for 10 minutes.
- Meanwhile, in a large bowl, combine flour, 1/4 cup white sugar, 1/4 cup brown sugar, baking powder, and salt. Blend in butter with your fingertips, or a pastry blender, until mixture resembles coarse meal. Stir in water until just combined.
- Remove peaches from oven, and drop spoonfuls of topping over them. Sprinkle entire cobbler with the sugar and cinnamon mixture. Bake until topping is golden, about 30 minutes.

Nutrition Information

- Calories: 562 calories
- Total Fat: 17.6 g
- Cholesterol: 46 mg
- Sodium: 400 mg
- Total Carbohydrate: 99.4 g
- Protein: 3.5 g

97. Fresh Spiced Peach Jam

"Perfect for canning! This spiced peach spread is very rich to the taste. Use it on biscuits, bread, or French toast. It's truly a taste of fall! Store in a cool, dark area."

Serving: 60 | Prep: 20 m | Cook: 50 m | Ready in: 13 h 10 m

Ingredients

- 6 cups peeled and chopped fresh peaches
- 3 cups white sugar
- 3 tablespoons lemon juice

- 1/2 teaspoon ground cinnamon
- 1/2 teaspoon ground nutmeg
- 1/2 teaspoon ground allspice

Direction

- Heat five 12-ounce jars in simmering water until ready for use. Wash lids and rings in warm soapy water.
- Mix peaches, sugar, lemon juice, cinnamon, nutmeg, and allspice in a large pot. Bring to a boil; cook, stirring occasionally, until peaches are soft, about 15 minutes. Remove from heat.
- Mash peaches with an immersion blender or potato masher to desired size and texture. Return to the heat; continue cooking jam until thickened, about 10 minutes more.
- Pack jam into hot jars, filling to within 1/4 inch of the top. Wipe rims with a clean, damp cloth. Top with lids and screw on rings.
- Place a rack in the bottom of a large stockpot and fill halfway with water. Bring to a boil and lower in jars using a holder, placing them 2 inches apart. Pour in more boiling water to cover the jars by at least 1 inch. Bring the water to a rolling boil, cover the pot, and process for 10 minutes.
- Remove the jars from the stockpot and place onto a cloth-covered or wood surface, several inches apart, until cool, about 12 hours. Press the top of each lid with a finger, ensuring that lid does not move up or down and seal is tight.

Nutrition Information

- Calories: 43 calories
- Total Fat: 0 g
- Cholesterol: 0 mg
- Sodium: < 1 mg
- Total Carbohydrate: 10.9 g
- Protein: 0 g

98. Fricken Yummy

"This is a wonderful refreshing drink that will make you say, 'that's fricken yummy!'"

Serving: 1 | Prep: 1 m | Ready in: 1 m

Ingredients

- 1 (1.5 fluid ounce) jigger apple schnapps
- 1 (1.5 fluid ounce) jigger peach schnapps
- 4 fluid ounces lemon-lime flavored carbonated beverage

Direction

- Fill an 8 ounce glass with ice. Pour in apple and peach schnapps. Fill glass with lemon-lime soda; stir.

99. Fried Peach and Pancetta Pizza

"Growing up, I always loved when my family made pizza from scratch, but what I loved even more was what came after the meal. Any extra dough and scraps were rolled out, left to rise, fried, and sprinkled with sugar to create a simple, but delicious donut-like treat.

Here we're doing a savory twist, using the same technique to make a pizza featuring ricotta, pancetta, and peaches. Garnish with extra sprig of thyme if desired."

Serving: 4 | Prep: 20 m | Cook: 30 m | Ready in: 1 h

Ingredients

- 8 ounces pancetta bacon, thickly sliced
- 1 teaspoon olive oil, or as needed
- 12 ounces pizza dough, or more to taste, cut into quarters
- 1 tablespoon all-purpose flour, or as needed
- 1 cup olive oil, or as needed
- 1/2 cup ricotta cheese
- 2 teaspoons chopped fresh thyme, or to taste
- ground black pepper to taste
- 20 slices fresh peach
- 1/4 cup freshly grated Parmigiano-Reggiano cheese, or to taste
- 4 teaspoons extra-virgin olive oil, or to taste

Direction

- Preheat an oven to 475 degrees F (245 degrees C). Line baking sheets with aluminum foil.
- Sprinkle pancetta into a cold skillet and drizzle 1 teaspoon olive oil over pancetta. Cook and stir pancetta over medium heat until browned and caramelized, 5 to 10 minutes. Remove pan from heat and cool pancetta in the oil in the skillet.
- Place 1 dough quarter on a work surface and lightly dust with flour; roll into a 1/8-inch-thick irregularly shaped crust. Stretch dough with your hands to an even thickness; let rest on the work surface for 5 minutes. Repeat with remaining dough.
- Heat about 1 cup olive oil, reaching about 1/2-inch depth, in a heavy cast iron skillet over medium-high heat. Fry each piece of dough until browned and cooked through, about 2 minutes per side. The first side will be lighter than the second side. Drain the crusts on paper towels.
- Transfer pizza crusts, lighter-side up, to prepared baking sheets. Spread about 2 tablespoons ricotta cheese onto each crust using the back of a spoon. Sprinkle about 1/2 teaspoon fresh thyme over ricotta layer. Sprinkle pancetta over the ricotta-thyme layer; season with black pepper. Nestle about 5 peach slices onto each pizza, working around the pancetta pieces. Sprinkle 1 tablespoon Parmesan-Reggiano cheese over each pizza. Drizzle about 1 teaspoon extra-virgin olive oil over Parmesan-Reggiano layer.
- Bake in the preheated oven until cheese is melted and peaches are lightly browned and tender, 12 to 15 minutes. Cool pizzas for 5 to 10 minutes on the baking sheet.

Nutrition Information

- Calories: 504 calories
- Total Fat: 25.8 g

- Cholesterol: 34 mg
- Sodium: 1098 mg
- Total Carbohydrate: 46.3 g
- Protein: 19.8 g

100. Frozen Fruit and Juice Cups

"This frozen treat makes a perfect summertime snack for the kids and adults alike. Packed with healthy fruits, it's a nutritious way to cool off on a hot day. It's simple enough that the kids can help you make them."

Serving: 24 | Prep: 20 m | Ready in: 8 h 20 m

Ingredients

- 2 ripe peaches - peeled, pitted, and chopped
- 2 bananas, sliced
- 1 1/2 cups seedless red grapes
- 1 cup fresh blueberries
- 1 cup sliced fresh strawberries
- 100 (3-ounce) bathroom plastic cups
- 1 (64 fluid ounce) bottle tropical juice blend (such as V8 Splash®)

Direction

- Toss peaches, bananas, grapes, blueberries, and strawberries together in a large bowl.
- Fill plastic cups halfway with peach mixture. Top with tropical juice, leaving some room at the top for expansion. Freeze until solid, 8 hours to overnight.

Nutrition Information

- Calories: 45 calories
- Total Fat: 0.1 g
- Cholesterol: 0 mg
- Sodium: 17 mg
- Total Carbohydrate: 11.5 g
- Protein: 0.3 g

101. Fruit Crepe Kebabs

"This is a fun sweet crepe recipe which is easy enough for the entire family to get creative with. I picked specific fruit for this recipe, but any fruit that fits on a kebab is an option. Kids love this. You can drizzle strawberry and/or chocolate syrup or sprinkle confectioners' sugar over the finished product. Top with whipped cream if desired."

Serving: 8 | Prep: 30 m | Cook: 30 m | Ready in: 1 h

Ingredients

- 1 1/2 cups milk
- 3 egg yolks
- 2 tablespoons vanilla extract
- 1 1/2 cups all-purpose flour
- 2 tablespoons white sugar
- 1/2 teaspoon salt
- cooking spray
- 5 tablespoons melted butter
- Fruit:
- 1 pound strawberries
- 2 bananas, cut into bite-sized pieces
- 2 peaches, cut into bite-sized pieces
- 2 kiwifruits, peeled and cut into bite-sized pieces
- skewers

Direction

- Mix milk, egg yolks, and vanilla extract together in a large bowl. Stir in flour, sugar, and salt until well blended.
- Heat a crepe pan over medium heat. Coat with cooking spray. Pour about 1/4 cup batter into the pan and tip the spread batter to the edges. Cook until bubbles form on the top and edges are dry, 2 to 3 minutes. Flip and cook until other side is browned and edges are golden, 1 to 2 minutes more. Repeat with remaining batter.
- Let crepes cool. Cut lengthwise into strips 1 to 2 inches wide. Wrap strawberries, bananas, peaches, and kiwi in the crepe strips and thread wrapped fruits onto skewers.

Nutrition Information

- Calories: 275 calories

- Total Fat: 10.4 g
- Cholesterol: 100 mg
- Sodium: 221 mg
- Total Carbohydrate: 39.1 g
- Protein: 5.9 g

102. Fruit Smoothies from Aunt Sues Honey

"Get your daily fruits and vegetables and fuel up your body with a different color smoothie every day of the week. Check out the variations in the notes."

Serving: 2 | Prep: 5 m | Ready in: 5 m

Ingredients

- Red Smoothie:
- 1 3/4 cups soy or almond milk
- 1/2 frozen banana
- 1 cup frozen strawberries
- 1 cup frozen peach slices
- 1 cup frozen raspberries
- 2 tablespoons Aunt Sue's® Raw Unfiltered Honey

Direction

- Blend all ingredients together, very slowly increasing speed from low to high. Blend for 1 1/2 minutes at high.

Nutrition Information

- Calories: 388 calories
- Total Fat: 4.1 g
- Cholesterol: 0 mg
- Sodium: 116 mg
- Total Carbohydrate: 84.1 g
- Protein: 8.7 g

103. Fruity Chicken Salsa

"A great, fruity accompaniment for chicken breasts. Viva la salsa!"

Serving: 4

Ingredients

- 1/2 cup fresh diced kiwi fruit
- 3/4 cup fresh diced peaches
- 1 jalapeno pepper, seeded and chopped
- 1/2 cup cucumber - peeled, seeded and chopped
- 1/4 cup diced sweet onion
- 1 teaspoon lemon juice
- salt and pepper to taste

Direction

- In a large nonporous glass bowl combine the kiwi, peaches/nectarines/apricots, jalapeno chile pepper, cucumber, onion, lemon juice, salt and pepper. Mix all together. Cover bowl and refrigerate overnight.

Nutrition Information

- Calories: 27 calories
- Total Fat: 0.2 g
- Cholesterol: 0 mg
- Sodium: 2 mg
- Total Carbohydrate: 6.4 g
- Protein: 0.5 g

104. Fruity Chili

"This is a sweet spin on an American favorite."

Serving: 8 | Prep: 20 m | Cook: 15 m | Ready in: 35 m

Ingredients

- 2 (14 ounce) cans tomato sauce
- 2 (15 ounce) cans kidney beans, rinsed and drained
- 2 tablespoons chili powder
- 1 tablespoon white sugar
- 1 pinch cayenne pepper (optional)

- 1 pound ground beef
- 2 tablespoons chili powder
- 1 tablespoon white sugar
- 1 pinch cayenne pepper (optional)
- 1 teaspoon cooking oil
- 1/2 red onion, chopped
- 1 banana pepper, chopped
- 1 apple - peeled, cored, and chopped
- 1 peach - peeled, pitted, and chopped

Direction

- Combine the tomato sauce, kidney beans, 2 tablespoons chili powder, 1 tablespoon sugar, and cayenne pepper in a large sauce pan; bring to a simmer over low heat.
- Place a large skillet over medium-high heat; place the ground beef in the skillet; season with 2 tablespoons chili powder, 1 tablespoon sugar, and the cayenne pepper; cook until brown; add to the sauce mixture.
- Heat the oil in a small skillet over medium-high heat; cook the onion in the oil until slightly browned; add to the sauce mixture, along with the apple, peach, and banana pepper. Allow to simmer another 1 to 2 minutes until hot.

Nutrition Information

- Calories: 259 calories
- Total Fat: 8.5 g
- Cholesterol: 34 mg
- Sodium: 820 mg
- Total Carbohydrate: 30.8 g
- Protein: 17.1 g

105. Fruity Oatmeal Bake

"A yummy, warm, and filling dish for breakfast or brunch that is very easy to prepare. Serve with additional milk if desired."

Serving: 8 | Prep: 20 m | Cook: 35 m | Ready in: 55 m

Ingredients

- cooking spray
- 3 cups quick-cooking oats
- 1 cup packed brown sugar
- 1/4 cup honey wheat germ
- 2 teaspoons baking powder
- 1 teaspoon salt
- 1/2 teaspoon ground cinnamon
- 1 cup milk
- 1/2 cup butter, melted
- 2 eggs, lightly beaten
- 3/4 cup chopped tart apple
- 1/3 cup chopped peach
- 1/3 cup blueberries

Direction

- Preheat oven to 350 degrees F (175 degrees C). Grease an 8-inch baking dish with cooking spray.
- Combine oats, brown sugar, wheat germ, baking powder, salt, and cinnamon in a large bowl.
- Whisk milk, melted butter, and eggs together in a bowl. Pour over oat mixture; mix until blended. Fold in apple, peach, and blueberries.
- Pour mixture into the prepared baking dish.
- Bake in the preheated oven until a toothpick inserted into the center comes out clean, 35 to 40 minutes. Cut into squares.

Nutrition Information

- Calories: 372 calories
- Total Fat: 15.6 g
- Cholesterol: 74 mg
- Sodium: 532 mg
- Total Carbohydrate: 52.9 g
- Protein: 7.4 g

106. Fruity Tart

"Cutting up all the fruit takes a bit of time, but the rest is easy as pie. Use any fruit of your liking."

Serving: 8 | Prep: 20 m | Cook: 20 m | Ready in: 2 h 40 m

Ingredients

- 1 (9 inch) pie crust, baked
- 1 (4.6 ounce) package non-instant vanilla pudding mix
- 3 cups milk
- 1/2 cup fresh strawberries, sliced
- 1/2 cup fresh blueberries
- 1 cup fresh peaches, pitted and sliced
- 1/2 cup fresh raspberries
- 1 cup kiwi, sliced
- 1/4 cup any flavor fruit jam

Direction

- Combine pudding mix and milk in a medium saucepan. Cook according to package directions. Pour pudding into pastry shell and refrigerate until cool and firm. Arrange fruit on top of pudding layer.
- Place jam in a small saucepan over low heat, stirring occasionally until runny. Using a pastry brush, coat fruit with jam. Now hide in the closet and eat the whole thing yourself.

Nutrition Information

- Calories: 245 calories
- Total Fat: 7.3 g
- Cholesterol: 7 mg
- Sodium: 265 mg
- Total Carbohydrate: 41.2 g
- Protein: 4.3 g

107. Fuzzy Italian Navel

"This is soooo Goood! Peach and orange intermingle with a touch of carbonation!"

Serving: 1 | Prep: 1 m | Ready in: 1 m

Ingredients

- 1 (1.5 fluid ounce) jigger grenadine syrup
- 2 (1.5 fluid ounce) jiggers peach schnapps
- 1 cup orange juice
- 2 fluid ounces carbonated water

Direction

- Measure grenadine and peach schnapps into a glass of ice. Fill with orange juice to within 1 inch of the glass rim; top with carbonated water.

108. Fuzzy Navel Shake

"This shake is a refreshing no-alcohol alternative with all the great taste. Try the Fuzzy Navel recipe from Carnation Breakfast Essentials today!"

Serving: 2 | Prep: 5 m | Ready in: 5 m

Ingredients

- 1 cup orange juice
- 1/2 cup fresh or frozen sliced peaches
- 1/2 medium banana
- 1/4 cup plain fat-free yogurt
- 1 packet Classic French Vanilla Flavor CARNATION BREAKFAST ESSENTIALS® LIGHT START™ Complete Nutritional Drink

Direction

- Place juice, peaches, banana, yogurt and Carnation Breakfast Essentials Drink in blender; cover. Blend until smooth.

Nutrition Information

- Calories: 111 calories
- Total Fat: 0.3 g
- Cholesterol: 3 mg

- Sodium: 61 mg
- Total Carbohydrate: 23.2 g
- Protein: 5.1 g

109. Fuzzy Navel Slush

"This is a great slush for those who enjoy the drink by the same name."

Serving: 30 | Prep: 10 m | Ready in: 10 m

Ingredients

- 9 cups water
- 1 1/2 cups white sugar (optional)
- 1 (12 fluid ounce) can frozen orange juice concentrate
- 1 (12 fluid ounce) can frozen lemonade concentrate
- 1 pint peach schnapps
- 1 (2 liter) bottle lemon-lime flavored carbonated beverage

Direction

- In a large freezer container, combine water and sugar. Stir until sugar is dissolved. Stir in orange juice concentrate, lemonade concentrate and peach schnapps. Cover and freeze for 4 hours or overnight.
- To serve, fill glass 3/4 of the way full with slush, then top off with lemon-lime soda, and stir.

110. Fuzzy Navel Smoothie AlcoholFree

"I was trying to mimic a more healthy version of the Jamba Juice® 'Coldbuster' smoothie. After experimenting I came up with this and decided it is closer to a fuzzy-navel-type smoothie. Our family loves our new own version of the cold-buster!"

Serving: 4 | Prep: 10 m | Ready in: 10 m

Ingredients

- 2 fresh peaches - peeled, pitted, and diced
- 12 ice cubes
- 1 cup orange juice, or more to taste
- 1 (6 ounce) container orange yogurt
- 2 tablespoons frozen orange juice concentrate

Direction

- Blend peaches in a blender until smooth. Add ice cubes, orange juice, orange yogurt, and orange juice concentrate; blend until desired consistency is reached.

Nutrition Information

- Calories: 105 calories
- Total Fat: 0.5 g
- Cholesterol: 3 mg
- Sodium: 27 mg
- Total Carbohydrate: 22.7 g
- Protein: 2.4 g

111. GA Peach Pound Cake

"This Georgia peach pound cake can also be made with other fruits such as apple or cherry."

Serving: 16 | Prep: 20 m | Cook: 1 h 10 m | Ready in: 1 h 30 m

Ingredients

- 1 cup butter or margarine, softened
- 2 cups white sugar
- 4 eggs
- 1 teaspoon vanilla extract

- 3 cups all-purpose flour
- 1 teaspoon baking powder
- 1/2 teaspoon salt
- 2 cups fresh peaches, pitted and chopped

Direction

- Preheat oven to 325 degrees F (165 degrees C). Butter a 10 inch tube pan and coat with white sugar.
- In a large bowl, cream together the butter and sugar until light and fluffy. Add the eggs one at a time, beating well with each addition, then stir in the vanilla. Reserve 1/4 cup of flour for later, and sift together the remaining flour, baking powder and salt. Gradually stir into the creamed mixture. Use the reserved flour to coat the chopped peaches, then fold the floured peaches into the batter. Spread evenly into the prepared pan.
- Bake for 60 to 70 minutes in the preheated oven, or until a toothpick inserted into the cake comes out clean. Allow cake to cool in the pan for 10 minutes, before inverting onto a wire rack to cool completely.

Nutrition Information

- Calories: 307 calories
- Total Fat: 13 g
- Cholesterol: 77 mg
- Sodium: 196 mg
- Total Carbohydrate: 44.1 g
- Protein: 4.1 g

112.Georgia Peach Homemade Ice Cream

"This is the best peach ice cream you'll ever eat!!!"

Serving: 32 | Prep: 15 m | Ready in: 1 h

Ingredients

- 2 1/2 pounds fresh peaches - peeled, pitted and chopped

- 1/2 cup white sugar
- 1 pint half-and-half cream
- 1 (14 ounce) can sweetened condensed milk
- 1 (12 fluid ounce) can evaporated milk
- 1 teaspoon vanilla extract
- 2 cups whole milk, or as needed

Direction

- Puree peaches with the sugar and half-and-half in batches in a blender or food processor.
- In a gallon ice cream freezer container, mix together the peach mixture, sweetened condensed milk, evaporated milk, and vanilla. Pour in enough whole milk to fill the container to the fill line, about 2 cups.
- Follow the manufacturer's instructions to freeze the ice cream.

Nutrition Information

- Calories: 106 calories
- Total Fat: 4.5 g
- Cholesterol: 16 mg
- Sodium: 42 mg
- Total Carbohydrate: 14.1 g
- Protein: 2.8 g

113.Georgia Spiced Peaches

"This is an old, old recipe from relatives in Georgia."

Serving: 100

Ingredients

- 19 pounds firm ripe peaches
- 7 pounds white sugar
- 2 cups distilled white vinegar
- 1 quart water
- 24 whole cloves
- 3 tablespoons crushed cinnamon stick

Direction

- Peel peaches and set aside. In a large pot over medium high heat, boil sugar, vinegar and water until the syrup is moderately thick.
- Add cloves, cinnamon and peaches. Bring to boil stirring occasionally until the peaches can be pierced to the pit with a fork.
- Fill sterilized canning jars with peaches. Continue boiling syrup until heavy and add to peaches to cover.
- In a large stock pot, pour water half way to top with boiling water. Using a holder, carefully lower jars into pot. Leave a 2-inch space between jars. Add more boiling water to cover them, about 2 inches above the tops. Bring to a boil and cover, processing for 35 minutes. Remove jars from pot. Put jars on a wood or cloth surface, several inches apart and allow to cool. Jars will be sealed.

Nutrition Information

- Calories: 140 calories
- Total Fat: 0 g
- Cholesterol: 0 mg
- Sodium: 4 mg
- Total Carbohydrate: 36 g
- Protein: 0 g

---

114. German Pear Pancake

"This delicious German-style pancake is traditionally made with apples, but pears are a delightful variation. Serve with maple syrup or creme fraiche."

Serving: 8 | Prep: 15 m | Cook: 35 m | Ready in: 50 m

Ingredients

- 2 large firm pears, cored and cut into 1/8-inch-thick slices
- 1/2 cup white sugar, divided
- 2 tablespoons lemon juice
- 1 1/2 teaspoons lemon zest
- 1/4 cup butter, sliced
- 6 large eggs
- 1 cup whole milk
- 1 teaspoon pure vanilla extract
- 1/2 teaspoon kosher salt
- 1 cup all-purpose flour
- 1 tablespoon confectioners' sugar, or to taste

Direction

- Toss pear slices with 1/4 cup white sugar, lemon juice, and lemon zest to coat.
- Arrange butter in a 12-inch cast-iron skillet and place on the center rack of the oven. Heat oven to 400 degrees F (200 degrees C). Remove skillet from oven once the butter has just melted, 3 to 5 minutes.
- Beat eggs in a large bowl until frothy; add milk, 1/4 cup white sugar, vanilla extract, and salt and mix until just combined. Sift flour into egg mixture and stir until batter is just mixed.
- Stir pear slices into the melted butter and spread into a single layer. Pour batter over pears.
- Bake in the preheated oven until pancake is set in the middle, the sides have risen, and the bottom is browned, 28 to 30 minutes. Top pancake with confectioners' sugar.

Nutrition Information

- Calories: 265 calories
- Total Fat: 10.7 g
- Cholesterol: 158 mg
- Sodium: 227 mg
- Total Carbohydrate: 35.5 g
- Protein: 7.6 g

---

115. GingerPeach Cake

"A tangy, moist, peachy cake!"

Serving: 12 | Prep: 25 m | Cook: 50 m | Ready in: 2 h 30 m

Ingredients

- 2 cups cake flour
- 4 tablespoons baking powder

- 1 teaspoon ground cinnamon
- 1/2 teaspoon ground nutmeg
- 1/4 teaspoon salt
- 1/4 cup unsalted butter, softened
- 1/2 cup white sugar
- 2 eggs
- 2 teaspoons vanilla extract
- 1 teaspoon lemon zest
- 1 tablespoon sour cream
- 1/2 cup milk
- 6 fresh mint leaves, thinly sliced
- 2 fresh basil leaves, thinly sliced
- 1 tablespoon grated fresh ginger root
- 6 fresh peaches - peeled, pitted and chopped

Direction

- Preheat an oven to 350 degrees F (175 degrees C). Grease a 10-inch Bundt pan.
- Sift together the cake flour, baking powder, cinnamon, nutmeg, and salt. Cream the butter and sugar with an electric mixer until light and fluffy. Add the eggs one at a time, beating well. Beat in the vanilla and lemon zest. Add half of the flour mixture and beat on medium speed to combine. Blend in the sour cream and milk; stir in the remaining flour mixture. Fold in the mint, basil, ginger, and peaches and mix until thoroughly combined. Pour the batter into the prepared pan.
- Bake in the preheated oven until browned and a toothpick inserted in the cake comes out clean, 50 to 60 minutes. Let the cake cool in the pan for 10 minutes, then turn it out onto a wire rack to cool completely.

Nutrition Information

- Calories: 178 calories
- Total Fat: 5.4 g
- Cholesterol: 43 mg
- Sodium: 580 mg
- Total Carbohydrate: 29.3 g
- Protein: 3.4 g

116. GingerPeach Jam

"This peach jam has a bit of a bite from the ginger, a nice combination."

Serving: 64 | Prep: 10 m | Cook: 25 m | Ready in: 35 m

Ingredients

- 4 1/2 cups fresh peaches - peeled, pitted and chopped
- 1/4 cup finely chopped crystallized ginger
- 1 (1.75 ounce) package powdered fruit pectin
- 6 cups white sugar
- 1/2 teaspoon butter

Direction

- Bring peaches, ginger, and pectin to a boil in a large saucepan over medium heat. Stir in the sugar and butter; cook and stir until the sugar is dissolved. Return to a boil, stirring constantly for 1 minute more. Remove from heat, and skim off any foam with a spoon.
- Sterilize the jars and lids in boiling water for at least 5 minutes. Pack the peach jam into the hot, sterilized jars, filling the jars to within 1/4 inch of the top. Run a knife or a thin spatula around the insides of the jars after they have been filled to remove any air bubbles. Wipe the rims of the jars with a moist paper towel to remove any food residue. Top with lids, and screw on rings.
- Place a rack in the bottom of a large stockpot and fill halfway with water. Bring to a boil over high heat, then carefully lower the jars into the pot using a holder. Leave a 2 inch space between the jars. Pour in more boiling water if necessary until the water level is at least 1 inch above the tops of the jars. Bring the water to a full boil, cover the pot, and process for 10 minutes.
- Remove the jars from the stockpot and place onto a cloth-covered or wood surface, several inches apart, until cool. Once cool, press the top of each lid with a finger, ensuring that the seal is tight (lid does not move up or down at all). Store in a cool, dark area.

Nutrition Information

- Calories: 76 calories
- Total Fat: 0 g
- Cholesterol: < 1 mg
- Sodium: < 1 mg
- Total Carbohydrate: 19.6 g
- Protein: 0 g

117. Gingersnap Fresh Peach Pie

"A gingersnap cookie crust with fresh peaches. I made this recipe, well, because I could not find one and believed it should exist. Hope you enjoy."

Serving: 10 | Prep: 30 m | Cook: 45 m | Ready in: 1 h 45 m

Ingredients

- 1/3 cup butter, melted
- 40 gingersnap cookies, crushed
- 3 fresh peaches - peeled, pitted, and mashed
- 1/4 cup all-purpose flour
- 2 tablespoons brown sugar
- 1/2 teaspoon ground cinnamon
- 1/2 teaspoon ground nutmeg
- 4 fresh peaches - peeled, pitted, and sliced
- 1/4 teaspoon lemon juice
- 1 1/2 tablespoons butter, melted
- 1/3 cup white sugar

Direction

- Preheat oven to 350 degrees F (175 degrees C).
- Combine gingersnaps and 1/3 cup butter in a bowl; press cookie mixture into a 9-inch baking dish to make a crust.
- Mix mashed peaches with flour, brown sugar, cinnamon, and nutmeg in a large bowl until well blended. Gently fold sliced peaches and lemon used into mashed peach mixture. Pour peaches into prepared crust, lightly pressing the peaches down.
- Bake in the preheated oven until bubbly, about 40 minutes. Stir white sugar and 1 1/2

tablespoons butter in a small bowl; drizzle butter syrup over peach filling.
- Preheat the oven's broiler.
- Return pie to the oven and broil until syrup is caramelized, 5 to 10 minutes. Let pie cool before serving.

Nutrition Information

- Calories: 252 calories
- Total Fat: 12.3 g
- Cholesterol: 21 mg
- Sodium: 154 mg
- Total Carbohydrate: 34.5 g
- Protein: 1.5 g

118. Grandma Dees Apricot Ham Glaze

"Great complement to a holiday ham."

Serving: 80 | Prep: 5 m | Cook: 10 m | Ready in: 15 m

Ingredients

- 2 (15 ounce) cans sliced peaches, drained
- 1 (10 ounce) jar apricot preserves
- 1/4 cup orange liqueur
- 1/4 cup bourbon whiskey (such as Wild Turkey ®)
- 1 1/2 teaspoons ground cinnamon
- 1/2 teaspoon ground cloves
- 1/4 teaspoon ground nutmeg
- 1/4 teaspoon ground allspice

Direction

- Combine peaches and apricot jam in a saucepan over medium-low heat.
- Stir orange liqueur, bourbon, cinnamon, cloves, nutmeg, and allspice into the peach mixture; bring to a boil, stirring until flavors combine and glaze thickens, about 5 minutes. Remove from heat and serve warm.

Nutrition Information

- Calories: 18 calories
- Total Fat: 0 g

- Cholesterol: 0 mg
- Sodium: 2 mg
- Total Carbohydrate: 3.9 g
- Protein: 0.1 g

119. Grandma Ruths Peach Dump Cobbler

"Super easy, kid-friendly recipe that anyone can make. Can use any seasonal fruit as desired. Been making this recipe since I was about ten years old when taught by my grandma. We usually used peaches or blackberries, but you could certainly use any seasonal fruit you like."

Serving: 6 | Prep: 10 m | Cook: 20 m | Ready in: 30 m

Ingredients

- 1/2 cup butter
- 2 cups all-purpose flour
- 1 cup white sugar
- 1 cup milk
- 1 pinch baking powder
- 1 pinch ground cinnamon
- 2 cups sliced fresh peaches, or as desired

Direction

- Preheat oven to 350 degrees F (175 degrees C).
- Place butter in a 9x13-inch baking dish and place in preheating oven until butter melts.
- Whisk flour, sugar, milk, baking powder, and cinnamon together in a bowl until batter is smooth. Pour batter into prepared baking dish and top batter with peaches.
- Bake in the preheated oven until browned around the edges and a toothpick inserted into the center of the cobbler comes out clean, about 20 minutes.

Nutrition Information

- Calories: 448 calories
- Total Fat: 16.6 g
- Cholesterol: 44 mg
- Sodium: 146 mg
- Total Carbohydrate: 69.8 g
- Protein: 5.8 g

120. Grandma Sals Peach Kuchen

"Peaches and custard baked to a chewy, gooey perfection on a tender cookie crust. Can be made all year with canned peaches. Delicious hot with ice cream or alone cold."

Serving: 12 | Prep: 20 m | Cook: 45 m | Ready in: 1 h 5 m

Ingredients

- 2 cups all-purpose flour
- 1/4 teaspoon baking powder
- 1/2 teaspoon salt
- 1 cup white sugar, divided
- 1/2 cup butter
- 6 fresh peaches - peeled, pitted and halved
- 1 teaspoon ground cinnamon
- 2 egg yolks
- 1 cup heavy cream

Direction

- Preheat the oven to 400 degrees F (200 degrees C).
- Sift the flour, baking powder, salt and 2 tablespoons of sugar into a large bowl. Cut in butter by pinching between your fingers until the mixture resembles coarse cornmeal. Press into the bottom and up the sides of a 9x13 inch baking dish. Place the peach halves cut side up on top of the crust in a nice pattern. Mix together the remaining sugar and cinnamon; sprinkle over the peach halves.
- Bake for 15 minutes in the preheated oven. While the peaches are baking, whisk together the egg yolks and cream in a medium bowl. Pour over the peaches after the 15 minutes are up.
- Reduce the oven's temperature to 350 degrees F (175 degrees C). Return the dish to the oven, and bake for 30 to 40 minutes, until golden brown.

Nutrition Information

- Calories: 298 calories

- Total Fat: 16 g
- Cholesterol: 82 mg
- Sodium: 170 mg
- Total Carbohydrate: 36.4 g
- Protein: 3.1 g

121.Grandmas Peach French Toast

"My mother gave me this to use at my mother group. Everyone loved it so I decided to post it and share the great blend of peaches and French toast. Smells great when cooking."

Serving: 8 | Prep: 9 h | Cook: 45 m | Ready in: 9 h 45 m

Ingredients

- 1 cup packed brown sugar
- 1/2 cup butter
- 2 tablespoons water
- 1 (29 ounce) can sliced peaches, drained
- 12 (3/4 inch thick) slices day-old French bread
- 5 eggs
- 1 tablespoon vanilla extract
- 1 pinch ground cinnamon, or to taste

Direction

- In a saucepan, stir together the brown sugar, butter and water. Bring to a boil, then reduce heat to low, and simmer for 10 minutes, stirring frequently.
- Pour the brown sugar mixture into a 9x13 inch baking dish, and tilt the dish to cover the entire bottom. Place peaches in a layer over the sugar coating, then top with slices of French bread. In a medium bowl, whisk together the eggs and vanilla. Slowly pour over the bread slices to coat evenly. Sprinkle cinnamon over the top. Cover and refrigerate for 8 hours or overnight.
- Remove the dish from the refrigerator about 30 minutes before baking to come to room temperature. Preheat the oven to 350 degrees F (175 degrees C).
- Bake for 25 to 30 minutes in the preheated oven, or until the bread is golden brown. Spoon out portions to serve.

Nutrition Information

- Calories: 362 calories
- Total Fat: 15 g
- Cholesterol: 147 mg
- Sodium: 276 mg
- Total Carbohydrate: 51.3 g
- Protein: 7.2 g

122. Grandmothers Peach Fuzz

"This is a fantastic rum based drink that my grandmother made for me. It cannot be made virgin, the rum is the key ingredient! The peach skins add a lovely bit of color. Canned peaches do not work as well."

Serving: 2 | Prep: 10 m | Cook: 5 m | Ready in: 15 m

Ingredients

- 3/4 cup spiced rum
- 1 (6 ounce) can frozen limeade concentrate
- 3 large ripe peaches, halved and pitted with skins on
- 2 cups ice cubes
- 1 teaspoon white sugar, or to taste (optional)

Direction

- Place the rum, limeade concentrate, and peaches into the container of a blender. Blend until smooth. Add the ice, and blend until finely ground, sweeten with sugar, if desired. Pour into margarita glasses, and enjoy!

123. Great Grandmas Peach Cobbler

"This was my great grandma's recipe from the 40's and earlier. Its so easy to make. I remember this being my favorite dessert from when I was a child. This is delicious when hot and served with ice cream or I enjoy it cold by itself. Enjoy!"

Serving: 8 | Prep: 10 m | Cook: 45 m | Ready in: 55 m

Ingredients

- 1 (29 ounce) can sliced peaches in juice, drained, reserving juice
- 1 cup self-rising flour
- 1 cup white sugar
- 1 egg
- 1/2 cup butter, melted

Direction

- Preheat oven to 350 degrees F (175 degrees C).
- Arrange peach slices in a 9-inch round baking dish. Pour about half the reserved peach juice on top; discard remaining juice. Beat egg, flour, and sugar in a bowl until combined; pour over peaches. Drizzle melted butter over flour mixture.
- Bake in preheated oven until golden brown, about 45 minutes.

Nutrition Information

- Calories: 307 calories
- Total Fat: 12.3 g
- Cholesterol: 54 mg
- Sodium: 293 mg
- Total Carbohydrate: 48.4 g
- Protein: 3.1 g

124. Green Halloween Punch

"I told my daughter's friends that this green non-alcoholic Halloween punch was 'insect juice' and added a whole bunch of plastic insects. It turned out to be a big hit. I had an extra-big spider that wouldn't swim, so I placed a bowl upside-down into the punch container and sat the insect on top."

Serving: 24 | Prep: 5 m | Ready in: 5 m

Ingredients

- 32 fluid ounces orange juice
- 32 fluid ounces pineapple juice
- 32 fluid ounces peach juice
- 3 drops green food coloring
- plastic insects
- 32 ounces club soda, or more as needed

Direction

- Combine orange juice, pineapple juice, and peach juice in a large glass or plastic bowl. Add a few drops of green food coloring so it turns bright green. Float plastic spiders and insects in the bowl. Add soda water right before serving.

Nutrition Information

- Calories: 63 calories
- Total Fat: 0.1 g
- Cholesterol: 0 mg
- Sodium: 5 mg
- Total Carbohydrate: 15.4 g
- Protein: 0.6 g

125. Gregs Hot Peach Pie

"Homemade crust, fresh peaches and a little habanero make a pie with the perfect combination of sweet and spicy."

Serving: 8 | Prep: 20 m | Cook: 50 m | Ready in: 1 h 40 m

Ingredients

- 1 1/2 cups all-purpose flour

- 1/2 teaspoon salt
- 9 tablespoons cold unsalted butter, cut into 1/4-inch cubes
- 3 tablespoons ice-cold peach nectar, or as needed
- 4 large fresh peaches - peeled, pitted and chopped
- 6 large fresh peaches - peeled, pitted, and sliced
- 3 habanero peppers, seeded and minced (wear gloves), or to taste
- 1/3 cup all-purpose flour
- 1 cup white sugar
- 1/4 cup unsalted butter, softened

Direction

- Place 1 1/2 cup of flour and the salt into the work bowl of a food processor, and pulse briefly once or twice to combine. Add 9 tablespoons of chilled unsalted butter, and pulse 4 or 5 times, a few seconds per time, until the mixture looks like coarse crumbs. With the machine running, drizzle the peach nectar into the dough, 1 tablespoon at a time, until the dough gathers itself into a crumbly mass. Transfer the dough into a bowl, form into a ball, and wrap it in plastic wrap. Refrigerate to hydrate the dough, about 30 minutes.
- Preheat oven to 350 degrees F (175 degrees C).
- Place the 4 chopped peaches into the food processor, and pulse to puree, about 1 minute. Add the minced habanero peppers, 1 teaspoon at a time, and puree until smooth. Place the remaining 6 sliced peaches into a bowl, and toss lightly with the habanero puree.
- In a bowl, mix 1/3 cup of flour, the white sugar, and 1/4 cup of softened unsalted butter until it forms a crumbly mixture; set the streusel aside.
- Cut the dough in half, and roll each half into a circle about 10 inches in diameter. Fit one dough circle into a 9-inch pie dish. Pour the peach-habanero filling into the bottom pie crust, and sprinkle with the crumbly sugar streusel. Fit the top crust onto the pie, and

crimp with a fork to seal the edges. Cut several slits into the top crust for venting steam.
- Bake in the preheated oven until the crust is golden brown and the filling is bubbling and thickened, about 50 minutes.

Nutrition Information

- Calories: 412 calories
- Total Fat: 19 g
- Cholesterol: 50 mg
- Sodium: 156 mg
- Total Carbohydrate: 57.9 g
- Protein: 3.3 g

126. Grilled Balsamic Peaches

"This is a perfect summer side dish paired with grilled pork tenderloin."

Serving: 4 | Prep: 10 m | Cook: 4 m | Ready in: 14 m

Ingredients

- 4 peaches, halved and pitted
- 1 tablespoon olive oil
- salt and ground black pepper to taste
- 1/4 teaspoon Cajun seasoning
- 1 tablespoon balsamic vinegar
- 1 tablespoon chopped Italian flat leaf parsley
- 4 sprigs Italian flat leaf parsley, for garnish

Direction

- Preheat grill for high heat for 10 minutes.
- Place olive oil in a bowl. Add peach halves and toss to evenly coat with olive oil. Season with salt and pepper.
- Cook the peaches, flesh side down, on preheated grill until slightly charred, 4 to 5 minutes. Remove from the grill and dust with Cajun seasoning. Cut halves into 1 inch-thick slices. Place halves in a bowl; add vinegar and parsley, tossing peaches to coat evenly. Place on a serving platter and garnish with sprigs of parsley.

Nutrition Information

- Calories: 43 calories
- Total Fat: 3.6 g
- Cholesterol: 0 mg
- Sodium: 47 mg
- Total Carbohydrate: 2.5 g
- Protein: 0.9 g

127. Grilled Chicken with Peach Sauce

"My neighbor made this dish at a barbecue and I had to have the recipe. It is so easy and you will be surprised what a wonderful flavor the peaches give to the chicken!"

Serving: 8 | Prep: 15 m | Cook: 25 m | Ready in: 40 m

Ingredients

- 8 skinless, boneless chicken breast halves
- 1 pinch salt and ground black pepper to taste
- 2 cups peach preserves
- 3 tablespoons extra-virgin olive oil
- 2 tablespoons soy sauce
- 1 tablespoon finely chopped garlic
- 1 tablespoon Dijon mustard
- 4 ripe peaches, halved and pitted

Direction

- Preheat grill for medium heat and lightly oil the grate. Season chicken breast halves with salt and black pepper.
- Stir peach preserves, olive oil, soy sauce, garlic, and mustard in a bowl; season with salt and black pepper. Reserve about 1/2 cup peach sauce.
- Place chicken on preheated grill; cook until golden brown, 6 to 7 minutes, then flip chicken. Continue cooking for 5 to 6 minutes. Brush both sides of the chicken with peach sauce. Cook until no longer pink in the center and the juices run clear, 4 to 5 more minutes. An instant-read thermometer inserted into the center should read at least 165 degrees F (74 degrees C).
- Arrange peach halves cut side down on the grill. Grill for 2 minutes, flip, and brush with reserved 1/2 cup peach sauce. Continue to grill until peaches are tender, 3 to 4 minutes more.

Nutrition Information

- Calories: 406 calories
- Total Fat: 7.9 g
- Cholesterol: 67 mg
- Sodium: 333 mg
- Total Carbohydrate: 59.3 g
- Protein: 24.8 g

128. Grilled Fruit Gorgonzola Salad

"This salad can be eaten in any season using available fruit but is probably best in summer when the selection of pit fruits is at its best. The warm sweetness of the fruit complements the melting lightly pungent creaminess of the cheese and bitter greens."

Serving: 4 | Prep: 15 m | Cook: 10 m | Ready in: 25 m

Ingredients

- 1/3 ripe pineapple, peeled, cored, and cut into 1-inch pieces
- 2 firm ripe peaches or nectarines
- 1 Anjou pear
- 1 tablespoon oil
- Freshly ground black pepper
- 1/3 pound crumbled Gorgonzola cheese
- 15 leaves fresh basil, chopped
- 10 sprigs Italian flat leaf parsley, chopped
- 2 cups arugula leaves, chopped
- 1 tablespoon olive oil (optional)

Direction

- Preheat an outdoor grill for medium heat and lightly oil grate.

- Cut the peaches in half, removing the pit. Keeping the skin on the pear, cut straight down one side, then the opposite, leaving the core. Cut the two remaining sides off of the core (the pieces will not be even).
- Brush a small amount of oil on the pineapple, peaches, and pear to prevent them from sticking to the grill. Sprinkle all sides of the fruit with pepper. Place the fruit flesh side down on the grill and cook for 10 minutes, turning as needed, until soft and caramelized.
- When the fruit is cooked, remove from the grill and place on a serving platter. Sprinkle with crumbled cheese and top with chopped basil, parsley and arugula. Drizzle with olive oil if desired. Serve hot.

Nutrition Information

- Calories: 317 calories
- Total Fat: 18.4 g
- Cholesterol: 41 mg
- Sodium: 424 mg
- Total Carbohydrate: 29.3 g
- Protein: 11.3 g

129. Grilled Peach Bourbon Smash

"Peaches are incredibly delicious, especially caramelized on the grill and muddled with your favorite bourbon, grilled lemon, and mint. Strain over ice, make a toast to good times, and enjoy this totally smashing summer refreshment with a good friend."

Serving: 2 | Prep: 15 m | Cook: 5 m | Ready in: 23 m

Ingredients

- 1 large peach – halved, stone removed, and skin on
- 1/2 lemon
- 1/4 cup white sugar
- 5 leaves fresh mint
- 2 fluid ounces simple syrup
- 3 fluid ounces bourbon (such as Bulleit®)
- ice

- 4 fluid ounces ginger ale, or as needed

Direction

- Preheat an outdoor grill for medium-high heat and lightly oil the grate. When the grill is hot, close lid and allow to heat, 5 minutes.
- Place peach halves and lemon, cut-side down, in sugar until coated. Place on the grill; cook until fruits are soft, about 5 minutes. Cool on a cutting board, about 1 minute. Cut peach into slices with a knife; reserve 2 for garnish.
- Place remaining peach, mint leaves, and simple syrup into a cocktail shaker; juice lemon into the shaker. Gently muddle with a cocktail muddler. Pour in bourbon and ice, cover, and shake until the outside of the shaker has frosted. Strain into a chilled glass; top off with ginger ale, and garnish with grilled peach slices and lemon.

Nutrition Information

- Calories: 317 calories
- Total Fat: 0.1 g
- Cholesterol: 0 mg
- Sodium: 16 mg
- Total Carbohydrate: 56.1 g
- Protein: 0.4 g

130. Grilled Peach Cobbler

"A simple and tasty finish to a barbeque in the summertime. Your kids can play around with the toppings."

Serving: 8 | Prep: 10 m | Cook: 6 m | Ready in: 16 m

Ingredients

- 4 ripe peaches, halved and pitted
- 1 tablespoon vegetable oil
- 8 scoops vanilla ice cream
- 1/2 cup graham cracker crumbs, or to taste

Direction

- Preheat an outdoor grill for medium-high heat.
- Lightly brush each peach half with vegetable oil.
- Place peaches cut-side down on the grill; cook until tender, 5 to 6 minutes. Flip and continue cooking, 1 to 2 minutes more. Transfer to individual serving bowls.
- Top each peach half with 1 scoop vanilla ice cream and 1 tablespoon graham cracker crumbs before serving.

Nutrition Information

- Calories: 100 calories
- Total Fat: 4.9 g
- Cholesterol: 9 mg
- Sodium: 49 mg
- Total Carbohydrate: 13.1 g
- Protein: 1.3 g

131.Grilled Peach Salad with Spinach and Raspberries

"Right before your grilled entree comes off the grill, throw some peaches on for the salad. The caramelization adds a dimension of flavor and appearance to the peaches. Put them on a bed of fresh spinach, add raspberries and a good vinaigrette, and some almonds, too, for crunch."

Serving: 4 | Prep: 20 m | Cook: 5 m | Ready in: 25 m

Ingredients

- 1/4 cup extra-virgin olive oil
- 1/4 cup balsamic vinegar
- 1/2 clove garlic, minced
- 1/2 teaspoon Dijon mustard
- 1 pinch salt and freshly ground black pepper
- salt and pepper to taste
- 2 fresh peach, sliced into 8 pieces
- 1 tablespoon avocado oil
- 8 ounces fresh spinach
- 6 ounces fresh raspberries
- 1/4 cup sliced blanched almonds

Direction

- Preheat an outdoor grill for medium heat and lightly oil the grate.
- Combine olive oil, balsamic vinegar, garlic, mustard, salt, and pepper in a small container with a lid. Cover and shake vigorously to combine dressing ingredients. Set aside.
- Brush peach slices lightly with avocado oil. Place peaches, cut-side down, onto the grill; cook until grill marks form, 1 to 2 minutes. Turn each slice and cook until grill marks form, 1 to 2 minutes more. Remove from grill
- Divide spinach between 4 salad plates. Top each salad with 4 grilled peach slices. Evenly distribute raspberries and top with some almonds. Drizzle each salad evenly with dressing.

Nutrition Information

- Calories: 218 calories
- Total Fat: 17.5 g
- Cholesterol: 0 mg
- Sodium: 143 mg
- Total Carbohydrate: 13.6 g
- Protein: 3.3 g

132. Grilled Peaches

"This is a very simple, yet delicious end to a grilled meal. Peaches are grilled with a balsamic glaze, then served up with crumbled blue cheese. A sophisticated, yet extremely simple recipe. Perfect for summer entertaining!"

Serving: 4 | Prep: 20 m | Cook: 18 m | Ready in: 38 m

Ingredients

- 3 tablespoons white sugar
- 3/4 cup balsamic vinegar
- 2 teaspoons freshly ground black peppercorns
- 2 large fresh peaches with peel, halved and pitted
- 2 1/2 ounces blue cheese, crumbled

Direction

- In a saucepan over medium heat, stir together the white sugar, balsamic vinegar, and pepper. Simmer until liquid has reduced by one half. It should become slightly thicker. Remove from heat, and set aside.
- Preheat grill for medium-high heat.
- Lightly oil the grill grate. Place peaches on the prepared grill, cut side down. Cook for about 5 minutes, or until the flesh is caramelized. Turn peaches over. Brush the top sides with the balsamic glaze, and cook for another 2 to 3 minutes.
- Transfer the peach halves to individual serving dishes, and drizzle with remaining glaze. Sprinkle with crumbled blue cheese.

Nutrition Information

- Calories: 147 calories
- Total Fat: 5.2 g
- Cholesterol: 13 mg
- Sodium: 262 mg
- Total Carbohydrate: 21.4 g
- Protein: 4.1 g

133. Grilled Peaches and Cream

"This is an easy grilled peach dessert! I use a honey nut flavored cream cheese spread and it's wonderful! Drizzle a little extra honey after they're grilled and they're perfect!"

Serving: 8 | Prep: 15 m | Cook: 8 m | Ready in: 23 m

Ingredients

- 4 peaches, halved and pitted
- 2 tablespoons clover honey
- 1 cup soft cream cheese with honey and nuts
- 1 tablespoon vegetable oil

Direction

- Preheat a grill for medium-high heat.
- Brush peaches with a light coating of oil. Place pit side down onto the grill. Grill for 5

minutes, or until the surfaces have nice grill marks. Turn the peaches over, and drizzle with a bit of honey. Place a dollop of the cream cheese spread in the place where the pit was. Grill for 2 to 3 more minutes, or until the filling is warm. Serve immediately.

Nutrition Information

- Calories: 139 calories
- Total Fat: 10.2 g
- Cholesterol: 32 mg
- Sodium: 135 mg
- Total Carbohydrate: 11.6 g
- Protein: 1.1 g

134. Grilled Peaches and Ice Cream

"Warm, sweet peaches combine with cool, creamy ice cream to make a treat worth waiting all year for."

Serving: 8 | Prep: 15 m | Cook: 15 m | Ready in: 30 m

Ingredients

- 4 fresh ripe peaches
- Vegetable oil for brushing
- 8 scoops ice cream, such as Market Pantry Vanilla Bean or Sea Salt Caramel Pretzel Ice Cream

Direction

- Heat grill to medium-high. Cut peaches in half; remove pits. Brush cut sides with oil. Place cut-sides down on grill. Grill 3 to 4 minutes until grill marks appear. Brush tops with oil, turn over and move to indirect heat. Grill about 10 minutes longer until warm and tender.
- Serve warm peach halves topped with ice cream.

Nutrition Information

- Calories: 65 calories

- Total Fat: 3.4 g
- Cholesterol: 9 mg
- Sodium: 19 mg
- Total Carbohydrate: 7.9 g
- Protein: 0.7 g

135. Grilled Peaches with Gingersnaps

"A light summertime dessert. The gingersnaps give a little crunch and add some snap."

Serving: 2 | Prep: 10 m | Cook: 10 m | Ready in: 20 m

Ingredients

- 1 firm peach, halved and pitted
- 1 teaspoon canola oil
- 2 tablespoons brown sugar
- 4 scoops vanilla fat-free frozen yogurt
- 2 gingersnap cookies, crumbled

Direction

- Preheat an outdoor grill for high heat, and lightly oil the grate. Brush peach halves with canola oil.
- Place peach halves on the preheated grill. Grill until tender and peach is warmed through, about 10 minutes. Place the hot peach on a plate skin-side down. Sprinkle with brown sugar, allowing the sugar to melt. Alternatively, use a small torch to caramelize the sugar. Serve each peach half with 2 scoops of vanilla frozen yogurt and gingersnap cookie crumbles sprinkled on top.

Nutrition Information

- Calories: 155 calories
- Total Fat: 3.4 g
- Cholesterol: 2 mg
- Sodium: 66 mg
- Total Carbohydrate: 28.5 g
- Protein: 2.8 g

136. Grilled Prosciutto and Peach Flatbread Pizza

"Soft naan topped with a light spread of ricotta, topped with sweet peaches, salty prosciutto, a little basil, and a drizzle of honey balsamic reduction - all grilled to perfection!"

Serving: 4 | Prep: 15 m | Cook: 29 m | Ready in: 44 m

Ingredients

- 1 cup balsamic vinegar
- 1/4 cup honey
- 1/2 teaspoon lemon juice
- 1/4 teaspoon black pepper
- 2 naan bread
- 4 ounces ricotta cheese
- 2 fresh peaches, sliced
- 1 (3 ounce) package prosciutto, torn into pieces
- 3 tablespoons thinly sliced fresh basil

Direction

- Combine balsamic vinegar, honey, lemon juice, and pepper in a small saucepan. Bring to a boil over high heat; reduce to low. Simmer until mixture has reduced down to 1/3 cup, about 15 minutes.
- Preheat an outdoor grill for medium-high heat and lightly oil the grate.
- Grill naan until faint char marks appear, 2 to 3 minutes. Spread ricotta cheese over the charred side. Top with peaches and prosciutto. Sprinkle with basil. Drizzle with balsamic reduction.
- Return flatbreads to the grill. Grill with the cover on, until the cheese is melted and the bottom of the flatbread begins to char, about 7 minutes.

Nutrition Information

- Calories: 355 calories
- Total Fat: 10.7 g
- Cholesterol: 33 mg
- Sodium: 625 mg
- Total Carbohydrate: 53.4 g

- Protein: 12.8 g

137. Grilled Salmon with Curried Peach Sauce

"This salmon steak is grilled with a sweet, simple peach sauce. It can also be baked."

Serving: 2 | Prep: 15 m | Cook: 15 m | Ready in: 30 m

Ingredients

- 2 fresh peaches, peeled and diced
- 1/4 cup honey
- 1 teaspoon curry powder
- salt and pepper to taste
- 2 salmon steaks

Direction

- Preheat an outdoor grill for medium-high heat, and lightly oil grate.
- Stir together the peaches, honey, and curry powder in a small saucepan over medium heat. Bring to a simmer, and cook until the peaches break down, and the sauce thickens, about 10 minutes. Season to taste with salt and pepper.
- Season the salmon steaks with salt and pepper, and cook on the preheated grill until the fish flakes easily with a fork, 5 to 10 minutes per side depending on the thickness of the steaks. Pour the peach sauce over the salmon to serve.

Nutrition Information

- Calories: 468 calories
- Total Fat: 18.6 g
- Cholesterol: 100 mg
- Sodium: 106 mg
- Total Carbohydrate: 41.5 g
- Protein: 34.1 g

138. Habanero Sauce

"A milder sweet-spicy habanero sauce, but can be made hotter by adding more habaneros. I chop the peppers and garlic in a mini food processor to ensure there are no large chunks in the sauce. It goes great on anything, but mostly we eat it as a dip/salsa with tortilla chips."

Serving: 25 | Prep: 15 m | Ready in: 15 m

Ingredients

- 6 habanero peppers, seeded and chopped, or to taste
- 4 cloves garlic, minced
- 1 (15 ounce) can sliced peaches, drained
- 1/4 cup dark molasses
- 1/4 cup honey
- 1/4 cup brown sugar
- 1 cup distilled white vinegar
- 2 tablespoons spicy brown mustard (such as Gulden's®)
- 2 tablespoons paprika
- 1 tablespoon kosher salt
- 1 tablespoon black pepper
- 1 tablespoon ground cumin
- 1/2 teaspoon ground coriander
- 1/2 teaspoon ground ginger
- 1/2 teaspoon ground allspice
- 1 teaspoon liquid smoke flavoring

Direction

- Place the habanero peppers and garlic into a blender. Puree until the peppers are finely chopped. Add the peaches, molasses, honey, brown sugar, vinegar, mustard, paprika, salt, black pepper, cumin, coriander, ginger, allspice, and liquid smoke. Continue to puree until smooth.

Nutrition Information

- Calories: 43 calories
- Total Fat: 0.4 g
- Cholesterol: 0 mg
- Sodium: 250 mg
- Total Carbohydrate: 10.3 g
- Protein: 0.4 g

139. Halloween Fruit Snacks

"If you are concerned that your kids eat too many sweets during Halloween, try these non-candy snacks. Dried and fresh fruit like apricots, mangoes, and grapes are so much more appealing when they look at you!"

Serving: 12 | Prep: 30 m | Ready in: 30 m

Ingredients

- 4 ounces dried apricots
- 4 ounces dried peaches
- 1/2 pound seedless green grapes, halved
- 2 tablespoons confectioners' sugar
- 1 teaspoon water, or as needed
- 1/4 cup small candy eyeballs

Direction

- Arrange apricots and peaches on a platter. Skewer a few grapes on a toothpick vertically and the last one horizontally (for the head).
- Mix confectioners' sugar with water to make a thin, slightly sticky icing. Use icing to glue 2 candy eyeballs on each piece of fruit and on the horizontal "head" of the grape caterpillar.

Nutrition Information

- Calories: 83 calories
- Total Fat: 1 g
- Cholesterol: < 1 mg
- Sodium: 3 mg
- Total Carbohydrate: 19.1 g
- Protein: 0.8 g

140. Healthier Southern Peach Cobbler

"This healthier version lets you enjoy sweetness from the peaches, not added sugar."

Serving: 4 | Prep: 20 m | Cook: 40 m | Ready in: 1 h

Ingredients

- 8 fresh peaches - peeled, pitted, and sliced into thin wedges
- 2 tablespoons brown sugar
- 1/4 teaspoon ground cinnamon
- 1/8 teaspoon ground nutmeg
- 1 teaspoon fresh lemon juice
- 2 teaspoons cornstarch
- 1 cup whole wheat pastry flour
- 1/4 cup white sugar
- 1/4 cup brown sugar
- 1 teaspoon baking powder
- 1/2 teaspoon salt
- 6 tablespoons unsalted butter, chilled and cut into small pieces
- 1/4 cup boiling water
- 2 tablespoons brown sugar
- 1 teaspoon ground cinnamon

Direction

- Preheat oven to 425 degrees F (220 degrees C).
- Combine peaches, 2 tablespoons brown sugar, 1/4 teaspoon cinnamon, nutmeg, lemon juice, and cornstarch in a large bowl. Toss to coat evenly, and pour into a 2-quart baking dish.
- Bake in the preheated oven for 10 minutes.
- Meanwhile, combine flour, white sugar, 1/4 cup brown sugar, baking powder, and salt in a large bowl. Blend in butter with your fingertips or a pastry blender until mixture resembles coarse meal. Stir in water until just combined.
- Remove peaches from oven, and drop spoonfuls of flour mixture over them.
- Mix together 2 tablespoons brown sugar and 1 teaspoon ground cinnamon. Sprinkle entire cobbler with the sugar and cinnamon mixture. Bake until topping is golden, about 30 minutes.

Nutrition Information

- Calories: 446 calories
- Total Fat: 17.7 g
- Cholesterol: 46 mg
- Sodium: 431 mg
- Total Carbohydrate: 71 g
- Protein: 3.3 g

141. Honeyed Peach Pancake Syrup

"This sweet syrup is also great on ice cream!"

Serving: 24 | Prep: 20 m | Cook: 20 m | Ready in: 1 h 45 m

Ingredients

- 6 cups thickly sliced peaches with peels
- 3 cups water
- 1 cup honey, or more to taste
- 3 tablespoons freshly squeezed lemon juice, or to taste

Direction

- Combine peaches and water in a nonreactive 3-quart pot. Bring to a boil. Reduce heat and simmer until peaches are soft and have colored the liquid, 20 to 25 minutes. Strain peaches and their juice through a fine-mesh sieve set over a bowl. Let peaches stand, occasionally giving them a gentle press with the back of a spoon, 5 minutes. Discard peach solids.
- Return strained juice to pot. Stir in honey to taste. Bring to a boil. Skim off and discard any foam that appears on top. Taste and add lemon juice to adjust sweetness. Pour hot syrup into clean half-pint jars or bottles, leaving 1/2 inch headspace and using wide-mouth jars if freezing. Wipe rims clean with a damp paper towel.

- Let cool completely (about 1 hour). Apply clean lids. Store in fridge up to 3 weeks or in freezer up to 6 months.

Nutrition Information

- Calories: 51 calories
- Total Fat: 0 g
- Cholesterol: 0 mg
- Sodium: 3 mg
- Total Carbohydrate: 13.8 g
- Protein: 0.1 g

142. HoneySpiced Peaches

"Serve up a taste of summer any time of year when you preserve fresh, ripe peaches with honey and spices."

Serving: 24

Ingredients

- 8 pounds peaches
- 1 cup sugar
- 4 cups water
- 2 cups honey
- 1 1/2 teaspoons whole allspice
- 3/4 teaspoon whole cloves
- 3 sticks cinnamon
- 3 Ball® or Kerr® Quart (32 oz) Jars with lids and bands

Direction

- Prepare boiling water canner. Heat jars and lids in simmering water until ready to use. Do not boil. Set bands aside.
- Wash, peel and pit peaches. Leave peaches in halves or cut into slices, if desired. Treat fruit to prevent browning.
- Combine sugar, water and honey. Cook until sugar dissolves. Add peaches in syrup one layer at a time and cook for 3 minutes.
- Pack hot peaches into hot jars leaving 1/2 inch headspace. Add 1/2 tsp allspice, 1/4 tsp cloves and 1 stick cinnamon to each jar.

- Ladle hot syrup over peaches leaving 1/2 inch headspace. Remove air bubbles. Wipe rim. Center hot lid on jar. Apply band and adjust until fit is fingertip tight.
- Process filled jars in a boiling water canner for 25 minutes, adjusting for altitude. Remove jars and cool. Check lids for seal after 24 hours. Lid should not flex up and down when center is pressed.

Nutrition Information

- Calories: 148 calories
- Total Fat: 0 g
- Cholesterol: 0 mg
- Sodium: 7 mg
- Total Carbohydrate: 38.9 g
- Protein: 0.1 g

143. Huckleberry Peach Cobbler

"This cobbler combines huckleberries and peaches. Blueberries can be substituted if huckleberries aren't available. It's great served warm with vanilla ice cream. This cobbler works great with either fresh or frozen fruits."

Serving: 6 | Prep: 30 m | Cook: 30 m | Ready in: 1 h 15 m

Ingredients

- 2 cups huckleberries
- 3 cups sliced peaches
- 1/4 cup cornstarch
- 2/3 cup white sugar
- 2 tablespoons butter
- 1 cup all-purpose flour
- 2 teaspoons baking powder
- 1/4 cup white sugar
- 1/4 teaspoon salt
- 1/4 cup rolled oats
- 1 teaspoon grated lemon zest
- 1/4 teaspoon ground cinnamon
- 1/4 cup butter
- 1/2 cup milk

Direction

- Preheat oven to 400 degrees F (200 degrees C).
- If you're using frozen fruit, thaw and drain it before proceeding. Combine fruit in an ungreased 2-quart casserole dish. Mix the cornstarch and 2/3 cup sugar, and toss with fruit mixture. Dot with 2 tablespoons butter and set aside.
- Sift the flour, baking powder, sugar, and salt into a bowl. Stir in the oats, lemon zest, and cinnamon. Cut in 1/4 cup butter until it's the size of small peas. Stir in milk to form a stiff batter. Spoon dollops of cobbler batter over the fruit in the casserole dish; the batter may not entirely cover the fruit.
- Bake in the preheated oven until the fruit is bubbling and the topping is golden brown, about 30 minutes. Allow to cool about 15 minutes. Serve warm.

Nutrition Information

- Calories: 385 calories
- Total Fat: 12.5 g
- Cholesterol: 32 mg
- Sodium: 314 mg
- Total Carbohydrate: 66.1 g
- Protein: 3.8 g

144. Indian Summer Raspberry Peach Sangria

"Love at first sip!"

Serving: 8 | Prep: 10 m | Ready in: 10 m

Ingredients

- 1 (750 milliliter) bottle red wine
- 24 fluid ounces raspberry-flavored soda water
- 1/2 cup peach schnapps
- 1/2 cup pomegranate juice
- 1/2 cup fresh lemon juice
- 1 cup fresh raspberries
- 2 peaches, sliced

- 2 lemons, sliced
- 1 orange, sliced
- 4 cups ice cubes, or as desired (optional)

Direction

- Stir red wine, raspberry-flavored soda water, peach schnapps, pomegranate juice, and lemon juice together in a large pitcher or punch bowl; add raspberries, peach slices, lemon slices, and orange slices. Float ice cubes in the beverage to chill.

Nutrition Information

- Calories: 175 calories
- Total Fat: 0.2 g
- Cholesterol: 0 mg
- Sodium: 12 mg
- Total Carbohydrate: 21.5 g
- Protein: 0.8 g

145. Jackies Fresh Peach Cobbler

"An old fashion recipe from a collection of my mother's favorites. With a dash of nutmeg the aroma will take you back to grandma's kitchen."

Serving: 12 | Prep: 15 m | Cook: 45 m | Ready in: 1 h

Ingredients

- 1/2 cup butter, melted
- 2 large peaches, peeled and sliced
- 1 1/2 cups white sugar, divided
- 1 cup all-purpose flour
- 2 teaspoons baking powder
- 1/4 teaspoon salt
- 1 pinch ground nutmeg
- 3/4 cup milk

Direction

- Preheat oven to 375 degrees F (190 degrees C). Pour butter into an 8-inch square baking dish.
- Combine peaches and 3/4 cup sugar together in a bowl. Whisk flour, remaining sugar,

baking powder, salt, and nutmeg together in a bowl; stir in milk just until batter is combined. Pour batter over butter and top with peaches.
- Bake in the preheated oven until cobbler is golden brown, 45 to 50 minutes.

Nutrition Information

- Calories: 216 calories
- Total Fat: 8.1 g
- Cholesterol: 22 mg
- Sodium: 192 mg
- Total Carbohydrate: 35.3 g
- Protein: 1.7 g

146. Jersey Summer Salsa

"A quick, simple recipe utilizing all of New Jersey's favorite summer produce: tomatoes, peaches, and corn. Easily adjusted to suit your fancy in terms of sweet/spicy. A favorite in my house, where the saying goes 'the spicier the better,' and this salsa has the taste of sweet peaches in the background."

Serving: 16 | Prep: 15 m | Cook: 5 m | Ready in: 20 m

Ingredients

- 2 ears fresh corn, husked
- 1 large fresh tomato, chopped
- 1 large fresh peach, pitted and chopped
- 1 red onion, chopped
- 6 pepperoncini peppers, chopped
- 1 tablespoon green chile pepper, chopped
- garlic salt to taste

Direction

- Bring a large pot of water to a boil. Boil the corn 5 minutes, or until kernels are tender. Drain corn, cool, and cut kernels from cob.
- In a food processor, pulse the tomato, peach, red onion, pepperoncini peppers, green chile pepper, and garlic salt until chunky. Transfer to a bowl, and mix in the corn.

Nutrition Information

- Calories: 19 calories
- Total Fat: 0.2 g
- Cholesterol: 0 mg
- Sodium: 245 mg
- Total Carbohydrate: 4.1 g
- Protein: 0.6 g

147. Juicy Peach Crisp

"This recipe takes the simplicity of fresh peaches and turns them into a scrumptious dessert!"

Serving: 6 | Prep: 15 m | Cook: 45 m | Ready in: 1 h

Ingredients

- 6 fresh peaches - peeled, pitted, and sliced
- 1/2 teaspoon almond extract
- 1 cup all-purpose flour
- 1 cup white sugar
- 1/4 cup brown sugar
- 1/2 teaspoon ground cinnamon
- 1/4 teaspoon salt
- 1/2 cup butter

Direction

- Preheat an oven to 375 degrees F (190 degrees C), and grease an 8 inch square baking dish.
- Place the peaches in the bottom of the baking dish, and sprinkle them with almond extract.
- In a bowl, combine the flour, sugar, brown sugar, cinnamon, and salt. Cut the butter into the flour mixture with a pastry cutter until the mixture resembles crumbs.
- Sprinkle the flour mixture in an even layer over the top of the peaches, and bake in the preheated oven for about 45 minutes, until the peaches are bubbling and the topping is browned.

Nutrition Information

- Calories: 401 calories
- Total Fat: 15.6 g
- Cholesterol: 41 mg
- Sodium: 213 mg
- Total Carbohydrate: 64.4 g
- Protein: 2.4 g

148. Jump Rope Pie

"'Apples, peaches, pears and plums; tell me when your birthday comes!' How many times did I play this skipping game as a child, and never thought to combine those fruits until now. It's such a fresh-tasting combination of flavours. Great on its own, or enjoy a slice with a scoop of vanilla ice cream or a dollop of whipped cream."

Serving: 8 | Prep: 30 m | Cook: 50 m | Ready in: 1 h 20 m

Ingredients

- 1 recipe pastry for a double crust 9-inch pie
- 1 cup white sugar
- 3 tablespoons all-purpose flour, or more as needed
- 1/2 teaspoon ground cinnamon
- 1 pinch freshly grated nutmeg
- 2 cups peeled, cored and sliced apples
- 1 cup peeled, pitted and sliced peaches
- 1 cup peeled, cored and sliced pears
- 1 cup pitted and sliced plums
- 1 teaspoon grated fresh ginger root
- 1 tablespoon lemon juice

Direction

- Preheat oven to 425 degrees F (220 degrees C). Line a 9-inch pie plate with pastry.
- Whisk sugar, flour, cinnamon, and nutmeg together in a small bowl; sprinkle 1/4 cup of sugar mixture over pastry in pie plate.
- Stir apples, peaches, pears, plums, and ginger together in a bowl; sprinkle with lemon juice and stir to distribute. Place fruit mixture in pie plate; sprinkle with remaining sugar mixture. Cover with pastry, pinch to seal top and bottom crusts together, and cut a few slits in

top pastry with a sharp knife. Alternatively, cover with a lattice crust.

- Bake in the preheated oven for 15 minutes; reduce temperature to 350 degrees F (180 degrees C) and continue baking until crust is golden and filling has thickened, about 35 minutes. Cool completely before serving.

Nutrition Information

- Calories: 376 calories
- Total Fat: 15.1 g
- Cholesterol: 0 mg
- Sodium: 235 mg
- Total Carbohydrate: 58.4 g
- Protein: 3.4 g

149. Just Peachy Bread

"A quick bread that's moist and yummy for the tummy! Easy and tasty."

Serving: 20 | Prep: 15 m | Cook: 55 m | Ready in: 1 h 15 m

Ingredients

- 1 (29 ounce) can sliced peaches with juice
- 6 tablespoons sugar
- 2 cups all-purpose flour
- 1 teaspoon baking powder
- 1 teaspoon baking soda
- 1/4 teaspoon salt
- 1 teaspoon ground cinnamon
- 1 1/2 cups sugar
- 1/2 cup butter flavored shortening
- 2 eggs
- 1 teaspoon vanilla extract
- 1 cup chopped pecans

Direction

- Preheat oven to 325 degrees F (165 degrees C). Grease and flour two 9x5 inch loaf pans.
- Place peaches, peach juice and 6 tablespoons sugar in a blender; puree until smooth.

- In a large bowl, sift together flour, baking powder, baking soda, salt and cinnamon. In a large bowl, cream together the shortening and 1 1/2 cups sugar. Stir in the eggs one at a time, beating well with each addition, then stir in the vanilla. Blend this mixture into the flour mixture, alternately with the peach puree; stir just to combine. Fold in the nuts. Pour batter into prepared pans.
- Bake at 325 degrees for 55 to 60 minutes, or until a toothpick inserted into the center of a loaf comes out clean. Cool 10 minutes in pans; turn out on rack and let cool completely.

Nutrition Information

- Calories: 229 calories
- Total Fat: 9.9 g
- Cholesterol: 19 mg
- Sodium: 119 mg
- Total Carbohydrate: 33.9 g
- Protein: 2.7 g

150. Kelleys Peach Cobbler

"Serve with whipped cream or vanilla ice cream to put this over-the-top!"

Serving: 8 | Prep: 15 m | Cook: 45 m | Ready in: 1 h

Ingredients

- 1/2 cup butter, melted
- 1 (16 ounce) package frozen peach slices
- 2/3 cup white sugar
- 1/2 cup water
- 1 cup all-purpose flour
- 1 cup white sugar
- 1/2 cup milk
- 1 1/2 teaspoons baking powder
- 1/4 teaspoon salt

Direction

- Preheat oven to 350 degrees F (175 degrees C). Spread melted butter in a 2-quart baking dish.

- Heat peaches, 2/3 cup sugar, and water in a saucepan over medium-high heat, stirring occasional, until slightly thickened, about 5 minutes; remove from heat.
- Mix flour, 1 cup sugar, milk, baking powder, and salt in a bowl until batter is combined; pour over melted butter in baking dish. Arrange peaches over the batter and pour any remaining liquid on top.
- Bake in preheated oven until golden brown, 40 to 45 minutes.

Nutrition Information

- Calories: 348 calories
- Total Fat: 12 g
- Cholesterol: 32 mg
- Sodium: 253 mg
- Total Carbohydrate: 60.2 g
- Protein: 2.6 g

151.Kikis Spiced Habanero Peach Jam

"I developed this recipe when I was low on funds one holiday season and needed an inexpensive gift for family and friends. I now make several batches every years at several peoples request. It has become a huge hit at bake sales as well. Don't be afraid of the fact that it has habanero peppers in the recipe. The heat is very subtle and just adds to the flavor of the jam. It's also great spread over a block of cream cheese served with crackers for an easy appetizer for parties. Try it instead of sugar in your baked bean recipe and you will not be disappointed."

Serving: 80 | Prep: 20 m | Cook: 30 m | Ready in: 7 d s50 m

Ingredients

- 3 1/2 pounds fresh peaches - peeled, pitted, and chopped
- 6 tablespoons lemon juice
- 1 vanilla bean, halved lengthwise and seeds scraped out
- 1 teaspoon ground cinnamon
- 1 teaspoon ground allspice
- 1/2 teaspoon ground nutmeg
- 1/2 teaspoon ground cardamom
- 2 habanero peppers, stemmed and seeded
- 2 (3 ounce) pouches liquid pectin
- 5 cups white sugar
- 2 cups packed brown sugar

Direction

- Put peaches in a Dutch oven or soup pot; stir in lemon juice, vanilla bean, cinnamon, allspice, nutmeg, and cardamom.
- Place habanero peppers in a blender; top peppers with peach mixture. Blend until mostly smooth; transfer mixture back to the Dutch oven. Stir pectin into peach-habanero pepper mixture; bring to a full rolling boil. Quickly stir white sugar and brown sugar into mixture; return to a boil, stirring constantly, until sugar is dissolved, about 2 minutes.
- Sterilize the jars and lids in boiling water for at least 5 minutes. Pack jam into the hot, sterilized jars, filling the jars to within 1/4 inch of the top. Run a knife or a thin spatula around the insides of the jars after they have been filled to remove any air bubbles. Wipe the rims of the jars with a moist paper towel to remove any food residue. Top with lids, and screw on rings.
- Place a rack in the bottom of a large stockpot and fill halfway with water. Bring to a boil and lower jars into the boiling water using a holder. Leave a 2-inch space between the jars. Pour in more boiling water if necessary to bring the water level to at least 1 inch above the tops of the jars. Bring the water to a rolling boil, cover the pot, and process for 15 minutes.
- Remove the jars from the stockpot and place onto a cloth-covered or wood surface, several inches apart, until cool. Once cool, press the top of each lid with a finger, ensuring that the seal is tight (lid does not move up or down at all). Store in a cool, dark area, and wait 1 to 2 weeks before opening for best results.

Nutrition Information

- Calories: 75 calories

- Total Fat: 0 g
- Cholesterol: 0 mg
- Sodium: 2 mg
- Total Carbohydrate: 19.2 g
- Protein: 0 g

152. Layered CheddarFruit Salad

"Everyone loves those layered salads; here's a fruit one! My personal preference is that this salad be served well-chilled so I make sure all fruit is chilled when I assemble it. Then it can then be served right away."

Serving: 6 | Prep: 15 m | Ready in: 45 m

Ingredients

- 1/2 cup mayonnaise
- 1/2 cup sour cream
- 1 tablespoon honey
- 1 1/2 cups shredded Cheddar cheese, divided
- 4 cups shredded lettuce
- 3 cups fresh peaches - peeled, pitted, and sliced
- 3 cups sliced fresh strawberries
- 3 cups seedless grapes

Direction

- In a small bowl whisk the mayonnaise, sour cream and honey together.
- In a large bowl toss 1 cup of the cheese with the lettuce.
- In a 2 1/2 quart glass bowl, layer half of the lettuce mixture, peaches, remaining lettuce mixture, strawberries, grapes and remaining cheese. Spread mayonnaise mixture over the top or serve on the side. Chill well before serving.

Nutrition Information

- Calories: 402 calories
- Total Fat: 28.7 g
- Cholesterol: 45 mg
- Sodium: 299 mg
- Total Carbohydrate: 30.2 g

- Protein: 9.2 g

153. Lazy Peach Cobbler

"Very easy cobbler. Designed for the laid back person looking for a recipe that tastes like it took a lot of work. Great for other fruits too, enjoy the easy life!"

Serving: 12 | Prep: 10 m | Cook: 25 m | Ready in: 35 m

Ingredients

- 1/2 cup margarine
- 2 cups all-purpose flour
- 1 cup white sugar
- 1 teaspoon baking powder
- 1 (29 ounce) can sliced peaches, juice reserved

Direction

- Preheat oven to 350 degrees F (175 degrees C). Once oven reaches desired temperature, melt margarine in a glass 9x13 baking pan.
- In a large bowl, combine flour, sugar and baking powder. Pour reserved peach juice into dry ingredients and stir until smooth. Remove glass pan from oven and pour batter in starting in the center; batter will then spread itself over entire pan. Add peaches by placing them in center of pan; allow them to spread on their own.
- Bake cobbler in preheated oven for 20 to 25 minutes, or until brown on top. Do not overcook.

Nutrition Information

- Calories: 237 calories
- Total Fat: 7.7 g
- Cholesterol: 0 mg
- Sodium: 121 mg
- Total Carbohydrate: 40.6 g
- Protein: 2.7 g

154. Lemon Peach Parfaits

"These parfaits not only look amazing, but they are wonderfully cool, sweet and tangy. Sliced peaches are layered with pound cake and a light lemon sauce before being chilled and topped with a dollop of sweetened whipped cream. They will make you want to have dessert first!"

Serving: 6 | Prep: 10 m | Cook: 15 m | Ready in: 1 h 25 m

Ingredients

- 2 (10 ounce) packages frozen sliced peaches, thawed
- 2 tablespoons brown sugar
- 1/4 cup white sugar
- 2 tablespoons all-purpose flour
- 2 teaspoons grated lemon zest
- 1/4 teaspoon salt
- 1/3 cup lemon juice
- 1 cup boiling water
- 2 egg yolks
- 2 tablespoons butter
- 1 (10.75 ounce) loaf prepared pound cake, cubed
- 1 cup sweetened whipped cream

Direction

- Place peach slices into a large bowl, and sprinkle with brown sugar. Stir to coat, and set aside.
- In a medium metal bowl, stir together the white sugar, flour, lemon zest and salt. Whisk in the lemon juice until the mixture is smooth. Gradually whisk in the boiling water.
- In a smaller bowl, whisk the yolks together. Gradually whisk in about 1/2 cup of the hot lemon mixture. Then whisk the yolk mixture back into the larger bowl. Set the bowl over a pan of simmering water. Cook, stirring frequently until the mixture is thick enough to coat the back of a metal spoon. Remove from the heat and whisk in the butter. Set aside.
- In each parfait glass, make a layer of pound cake cubes, about 1/2 cup. Top with about 2 tablespoons of lemon sauce, then 1/4 cup of peach slices. Repeat the layers one more time.

Top with 1 tablespoon of the lemon sauce. Refrigerate for at least 1 hour to be sure it is thoroughly chilled. Top each parfait with a dollop of whipped cream before serving.

Nutrition Information

- Calories: 423 calories
- Total Fat: 17.6 g
- Cholesterol: 197 mg
- Sodium: 346 mg
- Total Carbohydrate: 64.6 g
- Protein: 4.9 g

155. Little Anns Peach and Blueberry Pie

"The very best peach pie you will find. The blueberries make the difference."

Serving: 8 | Prep: 20 m | Cook: 45 m | Ready in: 1 h 5 m

Ingredients

- 1 pastry for a double-crust 9-inch pie
- 3 cups sliced peaches
- 1 cup blueberries
- 2 tablespoons lemon juice
- 1 cup white sugar
- 2 tablespoons quick-cooking tapioca
- 1/2 teaspoon salt
- 2 tablespoons butter, cut into pieces
- 1 egg yolk, beaten

Direction

- Preheat oven to 425 degrees F (220 degrees C). Place one pie crust on the bottom of a pie plate.
- Toss peach slices and blueberries in a large bowl with lemon juice. Combine sugar, tapioca, and salt in a small bowl; pour over peach mixture and toss to coat. Transfer to prepared pie plate and scatter butter pieces over fruit. Cover pie with remaining crust; press and seal the top and bottom crusts.

- Cut several slits in the top crust to allow steam to escape, then brush with egg yolk.
- Bake in preheated oven until golden brown, 45 to 50 minutes.

Nutrition Information

- Calories: 386 calories
- Total Fat: 18.4 g
- Cholesterol: 33 mg
- Sodium: 403 mg
- Total Carbohydrate: 53.2 g
- Protein: 3.3 g

156. Mamas TexasStyle Peach Cobbler

"This is very traditional southern comfort food always cooked in a big bowl. My grandmother passed down her 'cobbler bowl' to me that she got from her grandmother."

Serving: 6 | Prep: 10 m | Cook: 50 m | Ready in: 1 h

Ingredients

- 1 cup self-rising flour
- 1 cup white sugar
- 1 cup milk
- 1 cup butter, melted
- 1 (28 ounce) can sliced cling peaches in heavy syrup

Direction

- Preheat oven to 350 degrees F (175 degrees C).
- Mix self-rising flour and sugar in a bowl. Stir milk into the flour mixture.
- Pour melted butter in an oven-safe bowl. Pour flour mixture over melted butter. Layer peaches in heavy syrup atop flour mixture. Do not stir!
- Bake in preheated oven until peaches are bubbly and crust is lightly browned, 50 to 60 minutes.

Nutrition Information

- Calories: 553 calories
- Total Fat: 31.7 g
- Cholesterol: 85 mg
- Sodium: 504 mg
- Total Carbohydrate: 66 g
- Protein: 4.6 g

157. Mango Peach and Pineapple Salsa

"This fruity and spicy salsa is yummy on just about everything from chips to barbequed chicken, tacos, and even tofu! By the way, pineapple mojitos are a great accompaniment!"

Serving: 16 | Prep: 20 m | Ready in: 1 h 20 m

Ingredients

- 2 mangos, peeled, seeded and chopped
- 2 small peaches, halved, pitted, and cut into 1/2-inch dice
- 1 cup diced fresh pineapple
- 4 tomatoes, chopped
- 1 white onion, diced
- 1 red bell pepper, diced
- 1 yellow bell pepper, diced
- 1 cup chopped fresh cilantro, or to taste
- 1 clove garlic, minced
- 1 small jalapeno pepper, minced
- 2 tablespoons lime juice
- 1 teaspoon salt
- 2 tablespoons white sugar, or to taste
- 3/4 cup water

Direction

- Place the mango, peach, pineapple, tomato, onion, red pepper, yellow pepper, and cilantro in a mixing bowl. Stir in the garlic, jalapeno, lime juice, salt, sugar, and water. Cover and refrigerate at least 1 hour before serving.

Nutrition Information

- Calories: 40 calories
- Total Fat: 0.2 g
- Cholesterol: 0 mg
- Sodium: 150 mg
- Total Carbohydrate: 9.8 g
- Protein: 0.8 g

158. MangoPeach Preserves

"This was adapted from Peach Preserves (on this site, thank you Kevin!). I changed some of the amounts and ingredients. Full of flavor, and you leave the peach skin on so it's a cinch to make! There are chunks of fruit, so if you want a smoother texture, add a couple more peaches before cooking and strain with a mesh strainer before adding sugar. As with all preserves, a little time consuming, but worth every minute..."

Serving: 56 | Prep: 10 m | Cook: 50 m | Ready in: 1 h

Ingredients

- 7 ripe unpeeled peaches, pitted and coarsely chopped
- 3 cups chopped fresh mango
- 2 3/4 cups white sugar
- 1 (1.75 ounce) package powdered fruit pectin

Direction

- Place 1/2 the peaches in a large saucepan and crush until mostly mashed. Add the remaining peaches and mangos. Bring to a boil over medium-low heat. Cook until mostly liquid, 20 to 30 minutes.
- Pour peach-mango mixture into a bowl and measure 5 1/4 cups back into the pan. For a thicker mixture, use only 5 cups. Add sugar to the pan and bring to a boil over medium heat. Gradually stir in pectin and bring back to a boil. Boil for 1 minute; immediately remove from heat.
- Pour preserves into hot, sterilized jars, filling to within 1/4 inch of the top. Run a clean knife or thin spatula around the insides of the jars to

remove any air bubbles. Wipe rims with a moist paper towel to remove any residue. Top with lids and screw on rings.

- Place a rack in the bottom of a large canning pot and fill halfway with water. Bring to a boil and lower jars 2 inches apart into the boiling water using a holder. Pour in more boiling water to cover jars by at least 1 inch. Bring to a rolling boil, cover, and process for 5 minutes.

Nutrition Information

- Calories: 42 calories
- Total Fat: 0 g
- Cholesterol: 0 mg
- Sodium: < 1 mg
- Total Carbohydrate: 10.8 g
- Protein: 0 g

159. Mascarpone Stuffed French Toast with Peaches

"Lemon zest and mascarpone stuffed into thick white bread slices, dipped in batter, pan fried, and smothered in fresh peach sauce. I love this recipe for breakfast but it could be fancy enough for dessert too."

Serving: 8 | Prep: 35 m | Cook: 25 m | Ready in: 1 h

Ingredients

- 8 fresh peaches
- 1/2 cup sugar
- 4 pinches ground nutmeg
- 1/2 teaspoon ground cinnamon
- 4 Mexican bolillo rolls
- 1 cup mascarpone cheese
- 6 tablespoons confectioners' sugar
- 1 lemon, zested
- 6 eggs
- 3/4 cup milk
- 1/2 teaspoon vanilla extract
- 2 teaspoons butter, or as needed
- 2 teaspoons vegetable oil, or as needed

Direction

- Peel peaches, remove pits, and slice into a heavy saucepan, catching all the juices. Stir in sugar, nutmeg, and cinnamon, and cook over medium heat until bubbly. Continue cooking, stirring occasionally, until the sauce reaches a syrupy consistency, about 10 minutes. Remove from heat.
- Meanwhile, cut off and discard the ends of the bolillo rolls. Slice the rolls into 1 1/4-inch-thick slices. Lay each slice of bread on a board, and with a sharp knife held parallel to the board, cut a pocket into each slice, leaving three sides intact. Set aside.
- Stir together the mascarpone, confectioners' sugar, and lemon zest until smooth. Scoop this mixture into a small plastic bag. Cut off one corner of the bag, and pipe as much filling into the pocket in each slice of bread as will fit without overflowing.
- Whisk together the eggs, milk, and vanilla in a shallow bowl. Melt butter with oil over medium heat in a large nonstick skillet. Dip each stuffed piece of bread into the batter, add to the skillet, and cook until browned on both sides. Serve hot with the warm peach sauce.

Nutrition Information

- Calories: 456 calories
- Total Fat: 20.4 g
- Cholesterol: 180 mg
- Sodium: 92 mg
- Total Carbohydrate: 56.3 g
- Protein: 12.7 g

160. Microwave Peach Plum Butter

"This is a peach plum jam that is easy to make and tastes great. You can freeze it and put it on ice cream."

Serving: 16 | Prep: 10 m | Cook: 15 m | Ready in: 2 h 25 m

Ingredients

- 1 cup finely chopped, peeled peaches
- 1 cup pitted, chopped plums
- 1 tablespoon water
- 1/2 teaspoon ground cinnamon
- 1/2 teaspoon ground ginger
- 1/2 cup granular no-calorie sucralose sweetener (such as Splenda®)

Direction

- Combine peaches, plums, and water in a microwave-safe glass or ceramic bowl. Heat in the microwave on high in 3 minute intervals, stirring between heating, until mixture is very thick, about 15 minutes. Stir in the cinnamon, ginger, and sweetener. Pour fruit butter into a jar. Cover and refrigerate until ready to use.

Nutrition Information

- Calories: 7 calories
- Total Fat: 0 g
- Cholesterol: 0 mg
- Sodium: < 1 mg
- Total Carbohydrate: 1.8 g
- Protein: 0.1 g

161. Minty Peach Chicken Salad

"Great for a summer luncheon or without the chicken as a salsa! Use a slotted spoon to serve on lettuce-lined plates."

Serving: 4 | Prep: 20 m | Ready in: 50 m

Ingredients

- 3 fresh peaches - peeled, pitted, and cubed
- 2 cups cubed cooked chicken breast
- 1 cucumber, seeded and chopped

- Dressing:
- 1/4 cup white wine vinegar
- 1/4 cup minced fresh mint
- 1/3 cup white sugar
- 1 tablespoon lemon juice
- 1/4 teaspoon salt
- 1/8 teaspoon ground black pepper
- 3 dashes hot sauce, or to taste
- 2 avocados - peeled, pitted, and cubed

Direction

- Combine peaches, chicken, and cucumber in a large bowl.
- Blend vinegar, mint, sugar, lemon juice, salt, pepper, and hot sauce in a blender until vinaigrette is smooth. Drizzle vinaigrette over peach mixture; toss to coat. Cover bowl with plastic wrap and refrigerate until chilled, at least 30 minutes. Fold avocado into salad before serving.

Nutrition Information

- Calories: 385 calories
- Total Fat: 20 g
- Cholesterol: 52 mg
- Sodium: 222 mg
- Total Carbohydrate: 32.7 g
- Protein: 21.8 g

- 1 banana, sliced
- 1/2 cup raisins
- 1/4 cup water
- 1/2 cup rolled oats
- 1/4 cup brown sugar
- 1/2 cup all-purpose flour
- 1/2 teaspoon ground cinnamon
- 1 pinch salt
- 1/4 cup butter

Direction

- Preheat oven to 350 degrees F (175 degrees C).
- Combine apples, peaches, banana, raisins and water in a 7x11 baking dish.
- In medium bowl, combine oats, brown sugar, flour, cinnamon and salt. Cut in butter with two knives or pastry blender until mixture resembles coarse crumbs. Sprinkle over fruit.
- Bake in preheated oven 35 to 45 minutes, until topping starts to brown. Serve warm.

Nutrition Information

- Calories: 160 calories
- Total Fat: 5 g
- Cholesterol: 12 mg
- Sodium: 53 mg
- Total Carbohydrate: 29 g
- Protein: 1.7 g

162. Mixed Fruit Crisp

"I found this recipe calling for only apples or peaches, but found it worked wonderfully with any fruit you have available. Please experiment! If using primarily apples, try a bit of shredded cheddar cheese, sprinkled on top of crumble topping the last 10 minutes of baking. Tastes wonderful with vanilla ice cream."

Serving: 10 | Prep: 15 m | Cook: 45 m | Ready in: 1 h

Ingredients

- 3 Granny Smith apples - peeled, cored and sliced
- 4 fresh peaches - peeled, pitted, and sliced

163. Moist Peach Pound Cake

"This is a delicious, moist, feel-good cake."

Serving: 20 | Prep: 15 m | Cook: 1 h 5 m | Ready in: 1 h 20 m

Ingredients

- 3 cups all-purpose flour
- 1/2 teaspoon salt
- 1/4 teaspoon baking soda
- 1 (29 ounce) can peaches, drained and mashed
- 1/2 cup sour cream

- 1 cup butter, softened
- 3 cups white sugar
- 6 eggs
- 1 teaspoon vanilla extract
- 1 teaspoon almond extract

Direction

- Preheat oven to 350 degrees F (175 degrees C). Grease and sugar two 9x5-inch loaf pans.
- Combine flour, salt, and baking soda in a bowl. Mix mashed peaches and sour cream in another bowl.
- Beat butter and sugar with an electric mixer in a large bowl until light and fluffy. Add eggs one at a time, allowing each egg to blend into the butter mixture before adding the next. Beat in vanilla extract and almond extract with the last egg. Pour in the flour mixture alternately with the peach mixture, mixing until just incorporated.
- Bake in preheated oven until a toothpick inserted into the center comes out clean, about 65 minutes. Cool in the pans for 10 minutes before removing to cool completely on a wire rack.

Nutrition Information

- Calories: 310 calories
- Total Fat: 11.9 g
- Cholesterol: 83 mg
- Sodium: 165 mg
- Total Carbohydrate: 48.9 g
- Protein: 4.2 g

---

164. Momma Alices Cold Peach Souffle

"This cold souffle is like eating a cloud. So light, fluffy, and absolutely delicious! If peaches aren't your thing, this dish can also be made with crushed pineapple, canned pears, 4 bananas, or any other kind of fruit!"

Serving: 8 | Prep: 25 m | Cook: 3 m | Ready in: 3 h 3 m

Ingredients

- 1 (16 ounce) can peaches, drained and syrup reserved
- 1 (.25 ounce) envelope unflavored gelatin
- 4 eggs, separated
- 1/4 cup cold water
- 1 tablespoon lemon juice
- 1/8 teaspoon almond extract
- 1/8 teaspoon salt
- 1/2 cup white sugar
- 2 cups heavy whipping cream

Direction

- Pour reserved peach syrup into a measuring cup. Add enough cold water to make 1 cup. Pour into the top of a double boiler. Sprinkle in gelatin; let stand, about 5 minutes.
- Beat egg yolks and 1/4 cup cold water together in a bowl. Stir into gelatin mixture. Cook, stirring constantly, over simmering water, until gelatin dissolves and sauce thickens, 3 to 5 minutes. Remove from heat.
- Stir lemon juice, almond extract, and salt into the sauce. Refrigerate until cooled.
- Place drained peaches in a blender; blend until smooth. Stir into the gelatin mixture and refrigerate until mixture mounds up slightly.
- Beat egg whites in a glass, metal, or ceramic bowl until foamy. Gradually add sugar, continuing to beat until stiff, glossy peaks form. Fold into peach mixture.
- Beat heavy cream in a chilled glass or metal bowl with a chilled whisk until stiff peaks form. Fold into peach mixture. Pour into a large dish and chill until set, 2 1/2 to 3 hours.

Nutrition Information

- Calories: 318 calories
- Total Fat: 24.5 g
- Cholesterol: 175 mg
- Sodium: 98 mg
- Total Carbohydrate: 21 g
- Protein: 5.5 g

165. Moose River Hummers

"151 rum is layered over schnapps, and lit to produce a dazzling flame. Blow the flame out before drinking!"

Serving: 1 | Prep: 1 m | Ready in: 1 m

Ingredients

- 1/2 (1.5 fluid ounce) jigger peach schnapps
- 1/2 (1.5 fluid ounce) jigger 151 proof rum

Direction

- Pour schnapps into a shot glass. Hold a teaspoon just above the schnapps, and slowly pour 151 rum onto the spoon, letting it run in a separate layer on top of schnapps.
- Hold the glass away from face, and light the rum with the flame of a match or lighter. Let it burn for 15 seconds. Blow out the flame, and drink it in one gulp.

166. Moringa Coconut Smoothie

"This moringa coconut smoothie, made with bananas, peaches, and almond butter, is a great on-the-go breakfast that will keep you going until lunch."

Serving: 2 | Prep: 10 m | Ready in: 10 m

Ingredients

- 2 bananas
- 1 cup sliced frozen peaches
- 1/3 cup coconut milk
- 1 tablespoon moringa powder
- 1 tablespoon almond butter
- 1 cup water

Direction

- Layer bananas, peaches, coconut milk, moringa powder, and almond butter in a blender; add water. Blend mixture until very smooth, at least 1 minute.

Nutrition Information

- Calories: 252 calories
- Total Fat: 13.2 g
- Cholesterol: 0 mg
- Sodium: 48 mg
- Total Carbohydrate: 34.7 g
- Protein: 4 g

167. Moroccan Peach Roasted Chicken

"A true crowd pleaser, this sweet chicken is very juicy and goes very well with white rice. I have modified it from an original Djedjad recipe which calls for apricots."

Serving: 6 | Prep: 25 m | Cook: 35 m | Ready in: 1 h

Ingredients

- 1/4 cup margarine or butter
- 1/4 cup honey
- 1 teaspoon rose water
- 1 teaspoon salt
- ground black pepper to taste
- 4 pounds bone-in chicken pieces, with skin
- 1 pound fresh peaches, pitted and sliced
- 1 tablespoon white sugar
- 1/2 cup toasted slivered almonds (optional)

Direction

- Preheat the oven to 425 degrees F (220 degrees C).
- In a glass measuring cup, combine the margarine, honey, rose water, salt and pepper. Heat in the microwave until margarine has melted, about 30 seconds. Place chicken in a

baking dish and pour the margarine mixture over it. Stir to coat the chicken completely. Place the dish of chicken into the oven.

- Cook uncovered in the preheated oven until chicken pieces have browned, about 15 minutes. Reduce the oven temperature to 350 degrees F (175 degrees C). Add the peaches to the dish and sprinkle with sugar. Continue to roast until chicken is cooked through, about 20 more minutes.
- Remove chicken pieces to a serving dish and pour the juices from the pan over them. Garnish with slivered almonds.

Nutrition Information

- Calories: 567 calories
- Total Fat: 34.9 g
- Cholesterol: 130 mg
- Sodium: 603 mg
- Total Carbohydrate: 19.1 g
- Protein: 42.9 g

168. My BottomUp Peach Cobbler

"This was the result of letting my 3 baby cousins 'help' me in the kitchen. The oldest was 4. Surprisingly this cobbler turned out pretty well. If a bit messy."

Serving: 8 | Prep: 5 m | Cook: 45 m | Ready in: 50 m

Ingredients

- 1/2 cup butter
- 1 cup white sugar
- 1 pinch ground nutmeg, or to taste
- 3/4 cup self-rising flour
- 3/4 cup milk
- 1 (28 ounce) can sliced peaches, with juice

Direction

- Preheat an oven to 350 degrees F (175 degrees C).
- Place the butter into an 8x8-inch baking dish, and place into the oven until melted. Stir the sugar, nutmeg, and self-rising flour together in

a mixing bowl. Stir in the milk until no lumps remain. Pour the batter over the melted butter in the baking dish. Do not stir. Spoon the sliced peaches over top; gently pour in the juice.

- Return to the oven, and bake until the batter has firmed and the cobbler has risen a bit, 35 to 45 minutes.

Nutrition Information

- Calories: 296 calories
- Total Fat: 12.1 g
- Cholesterol: 32 mg
- Sodium: 244 mg
- Total Carbohydrate: 46.3 g
- Protein: 2.7 g

169. My Peach Bread Pudding

"My husband reviewed numerous bread pudding recipes and came up with this version. Top with melted vanilla ice cream if desired."

Serving: 8 | Prep: 30 m | Cook: 1 h 15 m | Ready in: 1 h 45 m

Ingredients

- 2 cups finely sliced peaches
- 1/4 cup all-purpose flour
- 1/4 cup white sugar
- 1/4 cup rum
- 1 tablespoon ground cinnamon
- 1 pinch nutmeg
- 1 cup milk
- 1 cup heavy whipping cream
- 1/4 cup butter
- 1 cup white sugar
- 2/3 cup brown sugar
- 4 eggs
- 2 teaspoons ground cinnamon
- 1 teaspoon vanilla extract
- 1/4 teaspoon salt
- 1/4 teaspoon ground nutmeg
- 3 cups stale bread cubes, crusts removed

Direction

- Preheat oven to 400 degrees F (200 degrees C).
- Mix peaches, flour, 1/4 cup white sugar, rum, 1 tablespoon cinnamon, and 1 pinch nutmeg together in a baking dish.
- Bake in the preheated oven until peaches are tender and bubbling, about 30 minutes. Remove and set peaches aside.
- Reduce oven temperature to 350 degrees F (175 degrees C). Grease a 1 1/2-quart casserole dish.
- Stir milk and heavy cream together in a saucepan over medium heat; heat until just warmed and a film forms over top of mixture, about 5 minutes. Remove from heat; stir in butter until melted. Cool mixture to lukewarm.
- Combine 1 cup white sugar, brown sugar, eggs, 2 teaspoons cinnamon, vanilla extract, salt, and 1/4 teaspoon nutmeg in a bowl; beat with an electric mixer at medium speed until combined, 1 minute. Slowly pour milk mixture into sugar mixture; stir to combine. Add bread cubes; stir gently. Fold in cooked peaches.
- Pour batter into prepared casserole dish.
- Bake in the preheated oven until pudding is bubbling and center is set, 45 to 50 minutes. Serve warm.

Nutrition Information

- Calories: 451 calories
- Total Fat: 20.4 g
- Cholesterol: 151 mg
- Sodium: 267 mg
- Total Carbohydrate: 58.5 g
- Protein: 6.3 g

170. Nanas Southern Pickled Peaches

"Old Southern favorite. Great on picnics with cucumber sandwiches or at Sunday supper."

Serving: 32 | Prep: 1 h | Cook: 25 m | Ready in: 1 h 25 m

Ingredients

- 4 cups sugar
- 1 cup white vinegar
- 1 cup water
- 2 tablespoons whole cloves
- 4 pounds fresh clingstone peaches, blanched and peeled
- 5 (3 inch) cinnamon sticks

Direction

- Combine the sugar, vinegar and water in a large pot, and bring to a boil. Boil for 5 minutes. Press one or two cloves into each peach, and place into the boiling syrup. Boil for 20 minutes, or until peaches are tender.
- Spoon peaches into sterile jars and top with liquid to 1/2 inch from the rim. Put one cinnamon stick into each jar. Wipe the rims with a clean dry cloth, and seal with lids and rings. Process in a hot water bath for 10 minutes to seal, or consult times recommended by your local extension.

Nutrition Information

- Calories: 110 calories
- Total Fat: 0 g
- Cholesterol: 0 mg
- Sodium: 3 mg
- Total Carbohydrate: 28.3 g
- Protein: 0.1 g

171. No Bake Peach Pie

"This recipe is perfect for a hot Summer's day!"

Serving: 8 | Prep: 10 m | Cook: 10 m | Ready in: 3 h 20 m

Ingredients

- 1/2 cup water
- 2/3 cup white sugar
- 3 tablespoons cornstarch
- 1 tablespoon butter
- 6 fresh peaches, peeled, pitted, and sliced
- 1 (9 inch) graham cracker pie crust

Direction

- Stir together the water, sugar, cornstarch, and butter in a small saucepan over medium-high heat. When the mixture has come to a boil, add a few slices of the peaches, then lower heat to medium-low and simmer for 5 minutes until thick and smooth. Remove from the heat, and allow to cool completely.
- Place the remaining peach slices into the pie crust, and spread the sauce all over them, covering completely. Refrigerate for at least 3 hours, or until firm before serving.

Nutrition Information

- Calories: 230 calories
- Total Fat: 8 g
- Cholesterol: 4 mg
- Sodium: 162 mg
- Total Carbohydrate: 39.2 g
- Protein: 1.1 g

172. No Skill Fruit Tart

"Just like a seasonal fruit pie--wonderful for people who have trouble making the perfect crust. My favorite is blackberries with peaches, but you can use pretty much any seasonal fruit that you love. This one's a no-brainer!"

Serving: 6 | Prep: 15 m | Cook: 30 m | Ready in: 45 m

Ingredients

- 2 cups all-purpose flour
- 1/2 teaspoon salt
- 1 cup shortening
- 1/2 cup cold water
- 3 tablespoons sugar
- 2 tablespoons cornstarch
- 2 cups sliced fresh peaches
- 1 cup fresh blackberries

Direction

- Preheat the oven to 450 degrees F (220 degrees C).
- In a medium bowl, stir together the flour and salt. Cut in shortening by rubbing between your fingers until the mixture resembles oatmeal. Gradually stir in water until dough is just wet enough to hold together. Knead briefly, just so the dough holds together without crumbling. Place in the refrigerator while preparing the fruit.
- In a medium bowl, stir together the sugar and cornstarch. Add the peaches and blackberries, and toss gently to coat. Set aside.
- Roll out the crust dough into a rough circle about the size of a dinner plate, and place on a flat baking sheet. Pile the fruit into a level mound in the center of the dough, leaving 1 to 2 inches of exposed dough around the edge. Throw out any juices that may have accumulated in the fruit bowl. Fold the dough up over the fruit - the edges should cover some of the fruit and berries, but not reach the center of the tart.
- Bake for 25 to 30 minutes in the preheated oven, until the fruit is bubbly and the crust is golden brown. Let cool completely before cutting into wedges and serving.

Nutrition Information

- Calories: 509 calories
- Total Fat: 34.7 g
- Cholesterol: 0 mg
- Sodium: 197 mg
- Total Carbohydrate: 45.4 g
- Protein: 4.7 g

173. Okanagan Peach Soup

"A smooth and very tasty soup served either chilled or hot! Best when the peaches are locally grown, ideally in late summer. Garnish with candied peach slices for a special touch. If coconut milk is not available to you, heavy cream can be used instead."

Serving: 5 | Prep: 30 m | Cook: 1 h | Ready in: 1 h 30 m

Ingredients

- 4 cloves garlic
- 1 tablespoon olive oil
- 2 1/4 cups fresh peaches - peeled, pitted and chopped
- 1/2 cup diced onion
- 1 tablespoon curry powder
- 1/8 teaspoon ground turmeric
- 1/4 cup packed brown sugar
- 1/4 cup Chardonnay wine
- 1 cup vegetable broth or stock
- 1/2 cup coconut milk
- salt and ground black pepper to taste

Direction

- Preheat oven to 275 degrees F. (135 degrees C). Roast garlic cloves on a baking sheet for about 30 minutes, or until golden but not burnt.
- Heat the oil in a medium saucepan over medium heat, sweat the onions and peaches until softened. Season with curry powder, turmeric, roasted garlic, and sugar. Cook over medium to low heat until caramelized, about 30 minutes. Deglaze the pan with Chardonnay wine, then stir in the vegetable stock.

- Remove from heat, and puree the soup in a blender or food processor, and strain through a fine sieve. Stir in the coconut milk, and season with salt and pepper. Reheat if desired, before serving.

Nutrition Information

- Calories: 156 calories
- Total Fat: 7.8 g
- Cholesterol: 0 mg
- Sodium: 103 mg
- Total Carbohydrate: 19.4 g
- Protein: 1.2 g

174. Old Fashioned Peach Cobbler

"I was searching for a peach cobbler recipe that reminded me of the yummy dessert I ate as a young girl in Southeast Missouri. No shortcuts here. Fresh peaches and homemade crust...but worth every minute! Absolutely delicious served warm with vanilla ice cream! Never any leftovers with this dessert!"

Serving: 18 | Prep: 30 m | Cook: 1 h 10 m | Ready in: 2 h 10 m

Ingredients

- 2 1/2 cups all-purpose flour
- 3 tablespoons white sugar
- 1 teaspoon salt
- 1 cup shortening
- 1 egg
- 1/4 cup cold water
- 3 pounds fresh peaches - peeled, pitted, and sliced
- 1/4 cup lemon juice
- 3/4 cup orange juice
- 1/2 cup butter
- 2 cups white sugar
- 1/2 teaspoon ground nutmeg
- 1 teaspoon ground cinnamon
- 1 tablespoon cornstarch
- 1 tablespoon white sugar
- 1 tablespoon butter, melted

Direction

- In a medium bowl, sift together the flour, 3 tablespoons sugar, and salt. Work in the shortening with a pastry blender until the mixture resembles coarse crumbs. In a small bowl, whisk together the egg and cold water. Sprinkle over flour mixture, and work with hands to form dough into a ball. Chill 30 minutes.
- Preheat oven to 350 degrees F (175 degrees C). Roll out half of dough to 1/8 inch thickness. Place in a 9x13 inch baking dish, covering bottom and halfway up sides. Bake for 20 minutes, or until golden brown.
- In a large saucepan, mix the peaches, lemon juice, and orange juice. Add 1/2 cup butter, and cook over medium-low heat until butter is melted. In a mixing bowl, stir together 2 cups sugar, nutmeg, cinnamon, and cornstarch; mix into peach mixture. Remove from heat, and pour into baked crust.
- Roll remaining dough to a thickness of 1/4 inch. Cut into half-inch-wide strips. Weave strips into a lattice over peaches. Sprinkle with 1 tablespoon sugar, and drizzle with 1 tablespoon melted butter.
- Bake in preheated oven for 35 to 40 minutes, or until top crust is golden brown.

Nutrition Information

- Calories: 338 calories
- Total Fat: 17.6 g
- Cholesterol: 26 mg
- Sodium: 177 mg
- Total Carbohydrate: 43.7 g
- Protein: 2.3 g

175. OldFashioned Peach Cream Pie

"This is an old recipe handed down to me by my grandmother. It's really one of the best pies I've ever tasted."

Serving: 8 | Prep: 20 m | Cook: 55 m | Ready in: 2 h 15 m

Ingredients

- 3/4 cup white sugar
- 2 tablespoons all-purpose flour
- 1/4 teaspoon salt
- 1 cup sour cream
- 1 egg, lightly beaten
- 1/2 teaspoon vanilla extract
- 2 cups sliced peaches
- 1 unbaked pie crust
- 1/3 cup all-purpose flour
- 1/3 cup white sugar
- 1 teaspoon ground cinnamon
- 1/4 cup butter, softened

Direction

- Preheat oven to 400 degrees F (200 degrees C).
- Whisk together the 3/4 cup sugar, the 2 tablespoons flour, and salt. Beat in the sour cream, egg, and vanilla. Stir in the sliced peaches. Pour the mixture into the pie crust.
- Bake in the preheated oven for 12 minutes. Reduce the oven temperature to 350 degrees F (175 degrees C), and continue baking until the filling is set, about 30 minutes. Remove from oven.
- Raise oven temperature to 400 degrees F (200 degrees C).
- Whisk together the 1/3 cup flour, 1/3 cup sugar, and cinnamon in a small bowl. Mix in the butter with a fork until mixture resembles coarse crumbs. Sprinkle the crumb topping evenly over the pie.
- Return the pie to the preheated oven and bake until topping is golden, about 10 minutes. Let pie cool slightly before slicing.

Nutrition Information

- Calories: 376 calories
- Total Fat: 19.9 g
- Cholesterol: 51 mg
- Sodium: 256 mg
- Total Carbohydrate: 46.3 g
- Protein: 3.9 g

176. Orange Peach Oat Smoothie

"Fresh peaches, orange juice, milk, yogurt, and oats are blended together for a breakfast that gets you out the door in a jiffy."

Serving: 2

Ingredients

- 1/4 cup Quaker® Oats (Quick or Old Fashioned, uncooked)
- 1/2 cup low-fat milk
- 1/3 cup plain yogurt
- 1/4 cup orange juice
- 1 teaspoon lemon juice
- 1/2 cup peaches
- 1 teaspoon honey
- 1/2 cup ice

Direction

- Place all ingredients in a blender and blend until smooth.

Nutrition Information

- Calories: 123 calories
- Total Fat: 2 g
- Cholesterol: 5 mg
- Sodium: 65 mg
- Total Carbohydrate: 21.2 g
- Protein: 5.9 g

177. Paleo Peach Crisp with Coconut and Slivered Almonds

"I always have frozen fruit and vegetables handy. Tonight I pulled out a 16-ounce bag of frozen peaches and decided to make this yummy paleo dessert. I hope you enjoy."

Serving: 4 | Prep: 10 m | Cook: 27 m | Ready in: 37 m

Ingredients

- 1 (16 ounce) package frozen peach slices
- 2 tablespoons coconut sugar, divided
- 1 1/2 cups almond flour
- 1/2 cup coconut flakes
- 1 teaspoon baking powder
- 1/2 teaspoon sea salt
- 3 tablespoons unsalted butter, cubed
- 1 teaspoon vanilla extract
- 1/4 cup slivered almonds
- 1 tablespoon coconut oil, melted

Direction

- Preheat oven to 350 degrees F (175 degrees C). Place peach slices in a baking dish.
- Thaw peaches in the preheating oven, about 5 minutes. Break apart and spread evenly in the baking dish. Sprinkle 1 tablespoon sugar on top.
- Combine remaining 1 tablespoon coconut sugar, almond flour, coconut flakes, baking powder, and salt in a food processor; pulse about 5 times until mixed. Add butter and vanilla extract; pulse a few more times until crumbly. Pour over peaches.
- Scatter slivered almonds over flour mixture. Drizzle coconut oil on top.
- Bake in the preheated oven until golden brown, 22 to 25 minutes.

Nutrition Information

- Calories: 630 calories
- Total Fat: 46.2 g
- Cholesterol: 23 mg
- Sodium: 356 mg
- Total Carbohydrate: 48.3 g
- Protein: 12.9 g

178. Paleo Peach Scones

"You may have noticed a few peach recipes lately! I am enjoying eating them and cooking with them! I hope you love my paleo peach scones as much as we do! I even spread a little almond butter on mine when they were warm."

Serving: 8 | Prep: 10 m | Cook: 20 m | Ready in: 35 m

Ingredients

- 2 cups almond flour
- 1/2 cup tapioca flour
- 1/2 cup coconut palm sugar, plus more for sprinkling
- 1/4 cup coconut flour
- 4 teaspoons baking powder
- 1 teaspoon sea salt
- 6 tablespoons cold unsalted butter, cut into cubes
- 2 large eggs at room temperature
- 1/3 cup unsweetened coconut cream
- 1/2 teaspoon vanilla extract
- 1/4 teaspoon ground cardamom
- 1/4 teaspoon freshly grated nutmeg
- 1 cup diced fresh peaches

Direction

- Preheat oven to 350 degrees F (175 degrees C). Line a baking sheet with parchment paper.
- Stir almond flour, tapioca flour, 1/2 cup coconut sugar, coconut flour, baking powder, and sea salt together in a bowl using a fork to break any lumps of baking powder. Cut butter into the flour mixture with a pastry cutter.
- Beat eggs, coconut cream, vanilla extract, cardamom, and nutmeg together in a separate bowl until smooth; pour into the flour mixture and stir with a spatula just until evenly moistened and sticky. Gently fold diced peach into the mixture.
- Shape the dough into a ball and move to the prepared baking sheet. Sprinkle coconut sugar over the top of the dough ball. Press dough into a somewhat flattened disc.

- Bake in preheated oven until surface is dried, about 10 minutes. Cut the disc into 8 wedges and continue baking until golden brown on top, 10 to 15 minutes more. Let cool on sheet for 5 minutes before moving to a wire rack to cool completely.

Nutrition Information

- Calories: 397 calories
- Total Fat: 28.8 g
- Cholesterol: 69 mg
- Sodium: 488 mg
- Total Carbohydrate: 29.8 g
- Protein: 8.7 g

179. Peach and Blueberry Cobbler

"The easiest dessert that everybody loves. I got the idea from my mom and she got it from my grandma. The thing I changed is, I don't use a cake mix. I use items from my pantry, and I add blueberries."

Serving: 6 | Prep: 10 m | Cook: 45 m | Ready in: 1 h 25 m

Ingredients

- 4 cups canned sliced peaches with juice
- 1 cup frozen blueberries
- 3/4 cup all-purpose flour
- 1/2 cup white sugar
- 1 teaspoon baking powder
- 1/2 cup butter

Direction

- Preheat oven to 400 degrees F (200 degrees C). Grease a 9x9-inch glass baking dish.
- Pour peaches into the prepared dish, and sprinkle the blueberries over the peaches. In a bowl, whisk the flour, sugar, and baking powder until thoroughly combined. With a pastry cutter, cut the butter into the flour mixture to make a crumble, and spread the crumble mixture over the fruit.

- Bake in the preheated oven until the fruit is bubbling and the topping is golden brown, 45 minutes to 1 hour. Allow to cool; filling will thicken as it cools.

Nutrition Information

- Calories: 344 calories
- Total Fat: 15.7 g
- Cholesterol: 41 mg
- Sodium: 197 mg
- Total Carbohydrate: 51.2 g
- Protein: 2.9 g

180. Peach and Cranberry Muffins

"A great way to use up peaches. Add cranberries for color and taste, and sprinkle brown sugar on top before baking, if desired."

Serving: 24 | Prep: 10 m | Cook: 25 m | Ready in: 45 m

Ingredients

- 3 cups all-purpose flour
- 1 tablespoon ground cinnamon
- 1 teaspoon baking soda
- 1 teaspoon salt
- 2 cups white sugar
- 1 1/4 cups applesauce
- 3 eggs, lightly beaten
- 2 cups peeled, pitted, and chopped peaches
- 1 1/2 (12 ounce) packages fresh cranberries
- 2 tablespoons brown sugar
- 2 tablespoons all-purpose flour

Direction

- Preheat oven to 375 degrees F (190 degrees C). Grease 24 muffin cups or line with paper muffin liners.
- Whisk 3 cups flour, cinnamon, baking soda, and salt together in a large bowl. Stir white sugar, applesauce, and eggs together in another bowl. Add sugar mixture to flour mixture and stir until batter is just combined.

Fold peaches and cranberries into batter. Spoon batter into prepared muffin cups.
- Stir brown sugar and 2 tablespoons flour together in a small bowl. Sprinkle brown sugar mixture over the tops of the muffins.
- Bake in the preheated oven until a toothpick inserted into the center of a muffin comes out clean, about 25 minutes. Cool for 10 minutes before transferring muffins to a wire rack to cool completely.

Nutrition Information

- Calories: 156 calories
- Total Fat: 0.8 g
- Cholesterol: 23 mg
- Sodium: 160 mg
- Total Carbohydrate: 35.1 g
- Protein: 2.6 g

181. Peach and Cream Cheese Torte

"This family favorite is too good to keep to ourselves."

Serving: 8 | Prep: 25 m | Cook: 35 m | Ready in: 1 h

Ingredients

- 1/2 cup butter
- 1/3 cup white sugar
- 3/4 cup all-purpose flour
- 2/3 cup chopped pecans
- 1/2 teaspoon vanilla extract
- 1 (8 ounce) package cream cheese
- 1 egg
- 1/4 teaspoon almond extract
- 1/4 cup white sugar
- 1/2 teaspoon vanilla extract
- 1 (28 ounce) can peach slices, drained
- 1/2 teaspoon ground cinnamon

Direction

- Preheat oven to 450 degrees F (230 degrees C).
- To make the crust, mix butter, 1/3 cup sugar, flour, pecans and 1/2 teaspoon vanilla extract

in a bowl. Press into the bottom of a 10-inch pie plate.

- Bake the crust in preheated oven for 5 minutes. Remove and allow to cool.
- Meanwhile, beat the cream cheese, egg, almond extract, 1/4 cup sugar, and 1/2 teaspoon vanilla extract in a bowl until smooth. Gently fold the peach slices into the cream cheese mixture. Spread the filling over the cooled crust. Sprinkle the cinnamon over the top.
- Bake in preheated oven for 10 minutes. Reduce heat to 325 degrees F (165 degrees C) and continue to cook for 20 to 25 minutes more.

Nutrition Information

- Calories: 422 calories
- Total Fat: 29.2 g
- Cholesterol: 85 mg
- Sodium: 178 mg
- Total Carbohydrate: 37.4 g
- Protein: 5.8 g

182. Peach and Escarole Salad

"One trick with escarole is to make sure you are using a sweet enough dressing to offset the bitterness. I accomplished that with a dressing of sherry and rice vinegar, and then, just to hedge my bets, I added some perfectly ripe peaches to the mix. The result was one of the best salads I've had in years."

Serving: 6 | Prep: 10 m | Ready in: 10 m

Ingredients

- 2 tablespoons olive oil
- 1 tablespoon rice vinegar
- 1 tablespoon sherry vinegar
- 1 teaspoon mayonnaise
- salt and ground black pepper to taste
- 1 small head escarole, cut into 1-inch ribbons
- 1 peach, sliced
- 4 ounces goat cheese, crumbled
- 1/2 cup toasted walnuts

Direction

- Whisk olive oil, rice vinegar, sherry vinegar, mayonnaise, salt, and black pepper in a bowl until smooth.
- Place escarole, peach slices, goat cheese, and walnuts in a large bowl; drizzle in vinegar mixture and toss to coat.

Nutrition Information

- Calories: 191 calories
- Total Fat: 17.3 g
- Cholesterol: 15 mg
- Sodium: 111 mg
- Total Carbohydrate: 4.2 g
- Protein: 6.1 g

183. Peach and Lavender Ice

"This lovely and sophisticated sorbet is great for cleansing the palate after a heavy meal. Even though it's mostly fruit, it does taste rather rich; so keep portions small. Freezing time is not included in this total, and will vary depending on your ice cream maker."

Serving: 24 | Prep: 5 m | Ready in: 4 h 5 m

Ingredients

- 2 pounds sliced frozen peaches, thawed
- 1 1/2 cups white sugar
- 1/2 cup dried lavender flowers
- 3 tablespoons lemon juice
- 3 cups water

Direction

- Puree peaches with sugar until smooth. Stir in lavender blossoms, and let stand at room temperature for 2 hours. Stir in lemon juice and water, then place into refrigerator and refrigerate until cold, about 2 hours.
- Freeze in a 6-quart ice cream maker according to manufacturer's instructions.

Nutrition Information

- Calories: 57 calories
- Total Fat: 0 g
- Cholesterol: 0 mg
- Sodium: 2 mg
- Total Carbohydrate: 14.5 g
- Protein: 0.1 g

184. Peach and Pineapple Sorbet

"This is the perfect peach sorbet! The peach and pineapple could be swapped with other fruits."

Serving: 6 | Prep: 10 m | Ready in: 30 m

Ingredients

- 3 peaches, peeled and diced
- 1 1/2 tablespoons orange juice
- 1/2 cup diced pineapple
- 1/2 cup simple syrup

Direction

- Combine the peaches and orange juice in a food processor; puree until smooth. Add the pineapple; puree again until smooth. Pour the simple syrup into the peach mixture; blend to combine.
- Pour mixture into an ice cream maker and freeze according to manufacturer's instructions.

Nutrition Information

- Calories: 63 calories
- Total Fat: 0 g
- Cholesterol: 0 mg
- Sodium: < 1 mg
- Total Carbohydrate: 16.3 g
- Protein: 0.1 g

185. Peach and Poppy Seed Bread

"Make use of peaches with this tasty bread. It comes out very moist."

Serving: 16 | Prep: 15 m | Cook: 30 m | Ready in: 55 m

Ingredients

- 1/2 cup applesauce
- 3/4 cup turbinado sugar
- 2 tablespoons honey
- 3 eggs
- 3 large peaches, peeled and chopped
- 1 teaspoon baking soda
- 1 teaspoon vanilla extract
- 1/4 teaspoon almond extract
- 2 tablespoons poppy seeds
- 2 cups whole wheat flour

Direction

- Preheat oven to 350 degrees F (175 degrees C). Prepare 2 9x5-inch bread pans with cooking spray.
- Stir the applesauce, sugar, honey and eggs together in a bowl; fold the chopped peaches into the applesauce mixture. Add the baking soda, vanilla extract, almond extract, poppy seeds, and flour; stir to combine into a batter. Pour about half of the batter into each of the prepared pans.
- Bake in the preheated oven until a toothpick inserted into the center comes out clean, 30 to 35 minutes. Cool in the pans for 10 minutes before removing to cool completely on a wire rack.

Nutrition Information

- Calories: 123 calories
- Total Fat: 1.7 g
- Cholesterol: 35 mg
- Sodium: 98 mg
- Total Carbohydrate: 24.7 g
- Protein: 3.5 g

186. Peach and Potato Coconut Curry

"This is a basic recipe that I created for my family during peach season. There are a lot of layers in this curry that build a rich, tangy taste. Serve with sour cream on top alongside naan bread and rice."

Serving: 6 | Prep: 40 m | Cook: 40 m | Ready in: 1 h 20 m

Ingredients

- 2 tablespoons grapeseed oil
- 1 large onion, chopped
- 3 cloves garlic, minced
- 1 tablespoon minced galangal root
- 1 tablespoon minced fresh ginger
- 1 tablespoon garam masala
- 1 teaspoon ground paprika
- 1 pinch chile powder, or to taste
- 3 potatoes, cut into 1/4-inch cubes
- 2 peaches, cut into 1/4-inch cubes
- 1 cup chopped tomato
- 2 tablespoons butter
- 1 tablespoon chopped fennel leaves
- 1 tablespoon chopped fresh oregano
- 1 lemon, juiced
- 2 cups chicken stock
- 1 cup coconut milk
- 1 tablespoon fish sauce
- 1 tablespoon chopped fresh basil
- 1 tablespoon chopped fresh mint
- 1 1/2 teaspoons salt
- 1 teaspoon freshly ground black pepper

Direction

- Heat oil in a large pot over medium heat. Cook and stir onion, garlic, galangal, ginger, garam masala, paprika, and chile powder in the hot oil until onion is browned, about 10 minutes.
- Stir potatoes, peaches, tomato, butter, fennel leaves, and oregano into the pot; bring to a simmer. Stir in lemon juice. Reduce heat to medium-low; add chicken stock, coconut milk, fish sauce, basil, mint, salt, and pepper.

Simmer until potatoes are tender, 25 to 30 minutes.

Nutrition Information

- Calories: 274 calories
- Total Fat: 17.1 g
- Cholesterol: 12 mg
- Sodium: 1131 mg
- Total Carbohydrate: 29.6 g
- Protein: 4.5 g

187. Peach Angel Food Cake

"This is a great tasting super easy (not to mention, low fat and low calorie) dessert!"

Serving: 14

Ingredients

- 1 (18.25 ounce) package angel food cake mix
- 1 (15 ounce) can diced peaches

Direction

- In a large bowl, combine cake mix, peaches and juice (do not add water). Mix well.
- Pour into tube pan or 2 loaf pans.
- Bake according to directions on cake package.
- If desired, serve with whipped topping.

Nutrition Information

- Calories: 146 calories
- Total Fat: 0 g
- Cholesterol: 0 mg
- Sodium: 319 mg
- Total Carbohydrate: 32.5 g
- Protein: 3.1 g

188. Peach Apple Salsa

"Great dish when peaches are plentiful!"

Serving: 6 | Prep: 20 m | Ready in: 3 h 20 m

Ingredients

- 1 cup diced peaches
- 1/2 cup diced apple
- 1/2 cup diced avocado
- 1/2 cup diced tomato
- 1/3 cup chopped green onion
- 1/4 cup chopped fresh cilantro
- 2 tablespoons lemon juice
- 2 tablespoons olive oil
- 1 teaspoon toasted sesame oil
- 1 teaspoon ground cumin
- 1 jalapeno pepper, seeded and minced
- salt and ground black pepper to taste

Direction

- Mix peaches, apple, avocado, tomato, green onion, cilantro, lemon juice, olive oil, sesame oil, cumin, jalapeno pepper, salt, and black pepper together in a bowl. Cover with plastic wrap and refrigerate for flavors to blend, at least 3 hours.

Nutrition Information

- Calories: 86 calories
- Total Fat: 7.3 g
- Cholesterol: 0 mg
- Sodium: 5 mg
- Total Carbohydrate: 5.6 g
- Protein: 0.7 g

189. Peach Avocado Salsa

"Fresh peaches with creamy avocado, bell pepper, onions, and jalapeno make a great summertime salsa. Use as a topper for grilled fish or chicken, or just dip tortilla chips in it. Not a fan of avocados? The salsa is just as great without it. The longer it can marinate, the better it is."

Serving: 4 | Prep: 20 m | Ready in: 50 m

Ingredients

- 2 fresh peaches - peeled, pitted, and diced
- 1 jalapeno pepper, seeded and minced
- 1/2 red onion, minced
- 1/2 red bell pepper, minced
- 1/4 cup chopped fresh cilantro, or to taste
- 2 cloves garlic, grated
- 1/2 lime, juiced
- 1/2 lemon, juiced
- salt and ground black pepper to taste
- 1 avocado - peeled, pitted, and diced

Direction

- Gently mix peaches, jalapeno pepper, red onion, red bell pepper, cilantro, garlic, lime juice, and lemon juice in a bowl; season with salt and black pepper.
- Cover bowl with plastic wrap and refrigerate at least 30 minutes. Fold avocado into the salsa to serve.

Nutrition Information

- Calories: 112 calories
- Total Fat: 7.5 g
- Cholesterol: 0 mg
- Sodium: 9 mg
- Total Carbohydrate: 12.6 g
- Protein: 1.7 g

190. Peach Banana Smoothie

"This is a delicious smoothie recipe that I stumbled upon while in the kitchen. It is a great treat on a warm summer day. Try vanilla yogurt for even more flavor."

Serving: 4 | Prep: 5 m | Ready in: 5 m

Ingredients

- 1 cup plain yogurt
- 1 (15.25 ounce) can peaches
- 2 bananas, sliced
- 1/4 cup orange juice
- 1/4 cup white sugar, or to taste
- 2 cubes ice

Direction

- Blend yogurt, peaches, bananas, orange juice, sugar, and ice in a blender on high until the ice is crushed and the smoothie is to your desired consistency.

Nutrition Information

- Calories: 194 calories
- Total Fat: 1.2 g
- Cholesterol: 4 mg
- Sodium: 48 mg
- Total Carbohydrate: 44.4 g
- Protein: 4.6 g

191. Peach Barbecue Sauce

"Sweet and spicy, this is a whole bunch tastier than your normal bottled barbecue sauce. I make this from late summer harvested fruits and vegetables and can it for use throughout the year and for holiday gifts. It is very mild, but that can be tweaked if you're so inclined."

Serving: 48 | Prep: 30 m | Cook: 1 h 30 m | Ready in: 10 h 35 m

Ingredients

- 7 large white peaches, peeled and pitted
- 5 large tomatoes, stems removed
- 1 large sweet onion, peeled
- 3 bell peppers - halved, seeded, and stems removed
- 10 cherry peppers - halved, seeded, and stems removed
- 5 jalapeno peppers - halved, seeded, and stems removed
- 4 cloves garlic, peeled
- 2 cups white sugar
- 1 cup apple cider vinegar
- 2 tablespoons liquid smoke flavoring
- 2 tablespoons herb seasoning (such as Bragg® Sprinkle Seasoning) (optional)
- 1 tablespoon mustard seeds
- 1 tablespoon canning salt
- 1 tablespoon cracked black pepper
- 2 teaspoons celery seeds
- 1/2 teaspoon ground ginger
- 1/2 teaspoon ground cinnamon
- 1 (6 ounce) can tomato paste
- 6 1-pint canning jars with lids and rings

Direction

- Place peaches, tomatoes, onion, bell peppers, cherry peppers, jalapeno peppers, garlic, sugar, vinegar, liquid smoke, herb seasoning, mustard seeds, salt, black pepper, celery seeds, ginger, and cinnamon in a large stockpot. Bring to a boil; cook and stir until peaches and vegetables begin to brown, scraping the bottom of pot frequently to keep from scorching, about 1 hour.
- Reduce heat and simmer mixture until softened and slightly reduced, 30 more minutes. Remove from heat.
- Puree mixture using a hand blender until well blended. Pour mixture, about 1 cup at a time, through a fine mesh strainer; press remaining sauce in strainer with a ladle to remove fibrous portions of tomato skins. The strained sauce should be glossy and thick. Stir in tomato paste and blend until smooth.
- Sterilize jars and lids in boiling water for at least 5 minutes. Pack the barbeque sauce into the hot sterilized jars, filling the jars to within 1/4 inch of the top. Run a knife or a thin spatula around the insides of the jars after they

have been filled to remove any air bubbles. Wipe the rims of the jars with a moist paper towel to remove any food residue. Top with lids and screw on rings.

- Place a rack in the bottom of a large stockpot and fill halfway with water. Bring to a boil and lower jars into the boiling water using a holder. Leave a 2-inch space between the jars. Pour in more boiling water if necessary to bring the water level to at least 1 inch above the tops of the jars. Bring the water to a rolling boil, cover the pot, and process for at least 30 minutes.

- Remove the jars from the stockpot and place onto a cloth-covered or wood surface, several inches apart, until cool. Once cool, press the top of each lid with a finger, ensuring that the seal is tight (lid does not move up or down at all). Store in a cool, dark area.

Nutrition Information

- Calories: 62 calories
- Total Fat: 0.8 g
- Cholesterol: 0 mg
- Sodium: 206 mg
- Total Carbohydrate: 13.5 g
- Protein: 0.8 g

---

192. Peach Beehives with Hard Sauce

"These wonderful beehives melt in your mouth! Make sure each peach is completely wrapped and sealed in the pie dough strips. This way the peach skin practically dissolves during baking. This dessert is delicious, rich and different, a treat your family and company will enjoy."

Serving: 4 | Prep: 20 m | Cook: 35 m | Ready in: 55 m

Ingredients

- 4 small ripe peaches, washed and dried
- 1 (9 inch) prepared, unbaked pie crust, thawed
- 1/4 cup butter
- 1/2 cup confectioners' sugar
- 1 teaspoon vanilla extract
- 1/4 teaspoon ground allspice
- 1 pinch salt
- 1/4 cup heavy cream

Direction

- Preheat oven to 375 degrees F (190 degrees C). Lightly grease the bottom of a shallow baking pan.

- Unroll the prepared pie crust onto a lightly floured surface, and cut into 1/2 inch wide strips. Place peach stem side down, and wrap strips of dough--over-lapping rows--around the fruit so it's completely covered. For ease, twirl the peach while holding the pastry in place and overlap rows. When completely wrapped, the peach will resemble a beehive. Make sure the entire peach is covered and sealed inside the crust. Repeat with remaining peaches. Arrange the wrapped peaches in a shallow baking pan.

- Bake peaches in preheated oven until crust turns golden brown, 35 to 40 minutes.

- Meanwhile, cream butter with 1/4 cup confectioners' sugar in a mixing bowl until light and fluffy. Beat in the vanilla extract, allspice, salt, and heavy cream until well blended. Stir in the remaining 1/4 cup confectioners' sugar.

- To serve, place baked peaches in serving bowls. Slice each peach in half and remove the pits. Spoon hard sauce over the peach halves.

Nutrition Information

- Calories: 444 calories
- Total Fat: 32 g
- Cholesterol: 51 mg
- Sodium: 322 mg
- Total Carbohydrate: 36.6 g
- Protein: 3.2 g

193. Peach Berry Cobbler

"The fresh taste of peaches combined with fresh blueberries, warm and slightly spicy, under a crunchy, soft biscuit topping. Serve warm with ice cream. Cinnamon may be used in place of nutmeg."

Serving: 8 | Prep: 15 m | Cook: 35 m | Ready in: 50 m

Ingredients

- 1 cup all-purpose flour
- 1/2 cup white sugar
- 1 1/2 teaspoons baking powder
- 1/2 cup milk
- 1/4 cup butter, softened
- 1/4 cup packed brown sugar
- 1 tablespoon cornstarch
- 1/2 cup cold water
- 3 cups fresh peaches - peeled, pitted, and sliced
- 1 cup fresh blueberries
- 1 tablespoon butter
- 1 tablespoon lemon juice
- 2 tablespoons coarse granulated sugar
- 1/4 teaspoon ground nutmeg

Direction

- Preheat oven to 350 degrees F (175 degrees C).
- In a medium bowl, stir together flour, 1/2 cup white sugar, and baking powder. Mix in milk and 1/4 cup butter until smooth.
- In a medium saucepan, stir together the brown sugar, cornstarch, and water. Mix in the peaches and blueberries. Cook and stir over medium heat until thick and bubbly. Mix in 1 tablespoon butter and lemon juice. Continue cooking until the butter melts. Pour into a 1 1/2 quart ungreased baking dish. Evenly spoon batter in mounds over the hot fruit. In a small bowl, mix the coarse sugar and nutmeg, and sprinkle over the batter.
- Place the baking dish on a shallow baking pan in the preheated oven. Bake cobbler for about 35 minutes, or until bubbly and a toothpick inserted into the crust comes out clean.

Nutrition Information

- Calories: 242 calories
- Total Fat: 7.7 g
- Cholesterol: 20 mg
- Sodium: 153 mg
- Total Carbohydrate: 41.9 g
- Protein: 2.4 g

194. Peach Blueberry Pie

"This recipe comes from the mortician's side of the family. I was wary at first because I had never heard of the combination of peaches and blueberries. I was quickly swayed after trying it and now believe that this is one of the best pies ever!"

Serving: 8 | Prep: 15 m | Cook: 45 m | Ready in: 1 h

Ingredients

- 1 pastry for a double-crust 9-inch pie
- 3 cups sliced peaches
- 1 cup blueberries
- 2 tablespoons fresh lemon juice
- 1 cup white sugar
- 2 tablespoons quick-cooking tapioca
- 1/2 teaspoon salt
- 2 tablespoons margarine, cut into pieces

Direction

- Preheat oven to 425 degrees F (220 degrees C). Place one pie crust into a pie plate.
- Toss peaches and blueberries in a bowl with lemon juice. Mix sugar, tapioca, and salt in a small bowl and add to peach mixture; stir to combine. Allow fruit to rest for 15 minutes, then transfer to prepared pie plate. Scatter margarine pieces over fruit and brush the edge of the pie with water. Cover pie with remaining crust; press and seal the top and bottom crusts.
- Bake in preheated oven until crust is golden brown and fruit is bubbly 45 to 50 minutes.

Nutrition Information

- Calories: 378 calories
- Total Fat: 17.7 g
- Cholesterol: 0 mg
- Sodium: 412 mg
- Total Carbohydrate: 53.1 g
- Protein: 3 g

195. Peach Bow Tie Salad

"This easy, yet gourmet, salad has spinach, peaches, romaine, bow tie pasta, and a poppy seed dressing. It's so delicious I could eat the entire recipe by myself! As a side salad this makes 12 to 18 servings, as a main dish salad it makes 5 to 9 servings."

Serving: 4 | Prep: 10 m | Cook: 15 m | Ready in: 25 m

Ingredients

- 1 cup farfalle (bow tie) pasta
- 10 ounces spinach
- 1 head romaine lettuce, roughly torn
- 2 peaches - peeled, pitted, and diced, or more to taste
- 3/4 cup poppy seed dressing (such as Briannas®)
- 2 cups diced cooked chicken (optional)

Direction

- Bring a large pot of lightly salted water to a boil. Cook the bow-tie pasta at a boil, stirring occasionally, until cooked through yet firm to the bite, about 12 minutes; drain and run under cold water to cool.
- Combine pasta, spinach, romaine lettuce, and peaches in a large bowl; add poppy seed dressing and toss to coat. Top salad with chicken.

Nutrition Information

- Calories: 444 calories
- Total Fat: 25.1 g
- Cholesterol: 68 mg

- Sodium: 427 mg
- Total Carbohydrate: 27.8 g
- Protein: 23.5 g

196. Peach Bread

"Use canned peaches to make this quick bread recipe for a cinnamon-accented loaf perfect for the holiday table."

Serving: 24 | Prep: 10 m | Cook: 1 h | Ready in: 1 h 10 m

Ingredients

- 3 eggs
- 2 cups white sugar
- 2 teaspoons vanilla extract
- 1 cup vegetable oil
- 2 cups diced canned peaches, drained
- 3 cups all-purpose flour
- 1 teaspoon baking powder
- 1 teaspoon salt
- 1 teaspoon baking soda
- 3 teaspoons ground cinnamon
- 1/2 cup chopped walnuts (optional)

Direction

- Preheat oven to 350 degrees F (175 degrees C). Grease and flour two 8 x 4 inch loaf pans.
- In a large bowl, beat the eggs lightly. Blend in the sugar, oil, and vanilla. Add flour, baking powder, baking soda, salt, and cinnamon; mix just to combine. Stir in the peaches and nuts. Pour batter into prepared pans.
- Bake for about 1 hour, or until a tester inserted in the center comes out clean.

Nutrition Information

- Calories: 238 calories
- Total Fat: 11.5 g
- Cholesterol: 23 mg
- Sodium: 180 mg
- Total Carbohydrate: 31.7 g
- Protein: 2.9 g

197. Peach Brulee

"Quick and easy peach dessert. Serve with whipped cream or vanilla ice cream."

Serving: 3 | Prep: 5 m | Cook: 2 m | Ready in: 7 m

Ingredients

- 1 (15 ounce) can peach halves, drained
- 1/4 cup packed brown sugar
- 1/4 teaspoon ground cinnamon
- 1/4 cup coarsely chopped pecans

Direction

- Preheat the broiler.
- Arrange peach halves, cut-side up in a shallow baking dish. In a small dish, stir together the brown sugar, cinnamon, and chopped pecans. Sprinkle the mixture over the peaches.
- Broil 3 inches from heat for 2 to 3 minutes, or until the topping is browned. Serve with whipped cream or vanilla ice cream.

Nutrition Information

- Calories: 200 calories
- Total Fat: 7.2 g
- Cholesterol: 0 mg
- Sodium: 11 mg
- Total Carbohydrate: 35.7 g
- Protein: 1.8 g

198. Peach Cake I

"Love those peaches!"

Serving: 10 | Prep: 20 m | Cook: 50 m | Ready in: 1 h 10 m

Ingredients

- 2/3 cup butter
- 1 cup white sugar
- 3/4 cup milk
- 1 cup all-purpose flour
- 1/4 teaspoon salt
- 2 teaspoons baking powder
- 1 (15 ounce) can sliced peaches

Direction

- Preheat oven to 350 degrees (175 degrees C). Lightly grease one 8 x 8-inch pan.
- Cream together the sugar and butter. Add the flour, milk, salt, and baking powder. Mix well and pour into prepared pan. Spread fruit evenly over the top of the batter and pour juice from canned peaches over top.
- Bake in at 350 degrees F (175 degrees C) for 50 minutes or until fully browned on top.

Nutrition Information

- Calories: 268 calories
- Total Fat: 12.8 g
- Cholesterol: 34 mg
- Sodium: 257 mg
- Total Carbohydrate: 37 g
- Protein: 2 g

199. Peach Cake II

"This is a recipe that my mother gave me several years ago, and we enjoy it often. I use canned peaches, but fresh would be nice."

Serving: 24

Ingredients

- 3 egg, beaten
- 1 3/4 cups white sugar
- 1 cup vegetable oil
- 2 cups all-purpose flour
- 1 teaspoon salt
- 1 teaspoon ground cinnamon
- 1 teaspoon baking soda
- 2 cups fresh peaches - peeled, pitted, and sliced
- 1/2 cup chopped pecans

Direction

- Preheat oven to 375 degrees F (190 degrees C). Grease and flour a 9x13 inch pan.
- In a large bowl, combine the eggs, sugar, oil, flour, salt, cinnamon, baking soda, peaches and pecans. Mix thoroughly by hand.
- Pour into prepared 9x13 inch pan and bake at 375 degrees F (190 degrees C) for 50 minutes or until done.

Nutrition Information

- Calories: 203 calories
- Total Fat: 11.5 g
- Cholesterol: 23 mg
- Sodium: 159 mg
- Total Carbohydrate: 23.6 g
- Protein: 2.1 g

200. Peach Clouds

"This is a very simple but elegant dessert. It must be made at least 8 hrs ahead of time, but oh so worth it. Serve with vanilla ice cream. Garnish with edible flowers or mint leaves. Simply elegant."

Serving: 6 | Prep: 20 m | Cook: 8 h | Ready in: 8 h 20 m

Ingredients

- 6 egg whites
- 1/4 teaspoon salt
- 1/2 teaspoon cream of tartar
- 1 1/2 cups white sugar
- 1 teaspoon vanilla extract
- 6 fresh peaches - peeled, pitted, and sliced

Direction

- Preheat oven to 450 degrees F (230 degrees C).
- Beat egg whites in clean, dry bowl with electric mixer for 2 minutes. Beat in salt and cream of tartar. Continue beating and pour in sugar, a few tablespoons at a time, until mixture is glossy and stiff peaks form. Fold in vanilla.

- Place in greased pie plate or spoon or pipe onto parchment-lined baking sheets.
- Place in preheated oven and turn oven off. Leave meringue in unopened oven 8 hours or overnight. To serve, place meringue on serving platter and arrange peaches on top.

Nutrition Information

- Calories: 237 calories
- Total Fat: 0 g
- Cholesterol: 0 mg
- Sodium: 156 mg
- Total Carbohydrate: 56.5 g
- Protein: 3.7 g

201. Peach Cobbler Cake

"Delicious and easy cobbler that can be made with many types of fruit. Only uses a few ingredients, but great for company! Serve warm with vanilla ice cream."

Serving: 10 | Prep: 15 m | Cook: 35 m | Ready in: 50 m

Ingredients

- 1 (18.25 ounce) package yellow cake mix, divided
- 1 (16 ounce) can sliced peaches in heavy syrup, drained in juice reserved
- 1 (10.5 ounce) can peaches in light syrup, drained and juice reserved
- 6 tablespoons cold butter, cut into pieces, or more to taste

Direction

- Preheat oven to 375 degrees F (190 degrees C).
- Spread 1/2 of the yellow cake mix into a 9x13-inch baking dish.
- Cut peaches from the larger can into large chunks and layer on top of the cake mix. Sprinkle butter over peach layer. Cover butter layer with remaining cake mix. Pour the reserved juice from both cans over cake mix mixture. Set the peaches from smaller can aside for another use.

- Bake in the preheated oven until cobbler is lightly browned, 35 to 40 minutes.

Nutrition Information

- Calories: 333 calories
- Total Fat: 13 g
- Cholesterol: 19 mg
- Sodium: 393 mg
- Total Carbohydrate: 53.6 g
- Protein: 2.7 g

202. Peach Cobbler CeliacFriendly

"Delicious peach cobbler that is celiac-friendly. Easy to make and very tasty."

Serving: 8 | Prep: 10 m | Cook: 30 m | Ready in: 40 m

Ingredients

- 1 cup buckwheat flour
- 1/2 cup brown sugar
- 1/4 cup white sugar
- 2 teaspoons baking powder
- 1 teaspoon vanilla extract
- 1/2 teaspoon salt
- 3/4 cup vanilla-flavored almond milk
- 6 tablespoons butter, melted
- 1 (28 ounce) can sliced peaches, drained
- 1 teaspoon ground cinnamon

Direction

- Preheat oven to 400 degrees F (200 degrees C). Grease a 9-inch baking dish.
- Combine flour, brown sugar, white sugar, baking powder, vanilla extract, and salt in a bowl; mix in almond milk and butter.
- Pour flour mixture into the prepared baking dish. Top with peaches. Sprinkle cinnamon on top.
- Bake in the preheated oven until the top is lightly browned and the peaches are bubbling, about 30 minutes.

Nutrition Information

- Calories: 265 calories
- Total Fat: 9.4 g
- Cholesterol: 23 mg
- Sodium: 351 mg
- Total Carbohydrate: 43.3 g
- Protein: 3.3 g

203. Peach Cobbler Dump Cake I

"Yellow cake mix and peaches canned in heavy syrup are the primary components in this simple dump cake recipe."

Serving: 24 | Prep: 10 m | Cook: 45 m | Ready in: 55 m

Ingredients

- 2 (16 ounce) cans peaches in heavy syrup
- 1 (18.25 ounce) package yellow cake mix
- 1/2 cup butter
- 1/2 teaspoon ground cinnamon, or to taste

Direction

- Preheat oven to 375 degrees F (190 degrees C).
- Empty peaches into the bottom of one 9x13 inch pan. Cover with the dry cake mix and press down firmly. Cut butter into small pieces and place on top of cake mix. Sprinkle top with cinnamon.
- Bake at 375 degrees F (190 degrees C) for 45 minutes.

Nutrition Information

- Calories: 155 calories
- Total Fat: 6.4 g
- Cholesterol: 11 mg
- Sodium: 171 mg
- Total Carbohydrate: 24.3 g
- Protein: 1.2 g

204. Peach Cobbler Dump Cake II

"If you love peaches, you will love this cake. My grandmother used to make it for Sunday dinner."

Serving: 12 | Prep: 5 m | Cook: 1 h | Ready in: 1 h 5 m

Ingredients

- 1 (29 ounce) can sliced peaches, drained, juice reserved
- 1 (6 ounce) package peach flavored Jell-O® mix
- 1 (18.25 ounce) package yellow cake mix
- 1/2 cup butter
- 1/2 cup water

Direction

- Preheat oven to 350 degrees F (175 degrees C).
- Place peaches in bottom of 9x13 cake pan. Sprinkle dry peach gelatin over peaches. Sprinkle dry cake mix over gelatin. Cut up butter and distribute over cake mix. Pour 1 cup of reserved peach juice and 1/2 cup of water over the top.
- Bake in the preheated oven for 60 minutes, or until the top is browned.

Nutrition Information

- Calories: 336 calories
- Total Fat: 12.7 g
- Cholesterol: 21 mg
- Sodium: 393 mg
- Total Carbohydrate: 53.8 g
- Protein: 3.7 g

205. Peach Cobbler I

"This is a yummy cobbler that is a favorite with our family of eight. You may use up to 5 cups of peaches."

Serving: 10 | Prep: 20 m | Cook: 50 m | Ready in: 1 h 10 m

Ingredients

- 1/2 cup butter, melted

- 4 cups fresh peaches - peeled, pitted, and sliced
- 2 tablespoons white sugar
- 1 cup white sugar
- 1/4 teaspoon salt
- 1 teaspoon baking powder
- 1 cup all-purpose flour
- 1 teaspoon ground cinnamon
- 1/2 cup milk

Direction

- Preheat oven to 350 degrees F (175 degrees C). Pour butter in to the bottom of a large casserole or 9 x 13 inch pan.
- In the prepared dish, toss together the peaches and 2 tablespoons sugar.
- In a mixing bowl, combine the 1 cup sugar, salt, baking powder, flour, cinnamon, and milk. Spoon batter over the peaches.
- Bake for 45 minutes in the preheated oven, or until top is golden brown.

Nutrition Information

- Calories: 234 calories
- Total Fat: 9.6 g
- Cholesterol: 25 mg
- Sodium: 180 mg
- Total Carbohydrate: 36.1 g
- Protein: 1.8 g

206. Peach Cobbler II

"This recipe is very old and was my grandmother's. This is a very delicious cobbler and can also be used with blueberries. Hope you enjoy this as our family has all these years."

Serving: 6 | Prep: 20 m | Cook: 45 m | Ready in: 1 h 10 m

Ingredients

- 3 fresh peaches - peeled, pitted, and sliced
- 1 teaspoon ground cinnamon
- 1 1/2 cups white sugar

- 1/2 cup shortening
- 1 cup white sugar
- 1 1/2 cups all-purpose flour
- 2 teaspoons baking powder
- 1/2 teaspoon salt
- 1 cup milk
- 2 cups boiling water
- 3 tablespoons butter

Direction

- Preheat oven to 350 degrees F (175 degrees C). Grease a 10x10-inch baking dish.
- Stir together peaches with cinnamon and 1 1/2 cups sugar. Set aside.
- In a medium bowl, cream together shortening and 1 cup sugar. Mix in flour, baking powder and salt alternately with milk. Pour into prepared pan. Top with peach mixture. Drop butter in boiling water and pour all over peaches.
- Bake in preheated oven 40 to 45 minutes, until golden brown.

Nutrition Information

- Calories: 672 calories
- Total Fat: 24 g
- Cholesterol: 19 mg
- Sodium: 376 mg
- Total Carbohydrate: 112.7 g
- Protein: 4.7 g

207. Peach Cobbler III

"An old fashioned fruit cobbler made with fresh or canned peaches. Delicious served with vanilla ice cream! If using canned peaches use juice from can instead of water."

Serving: 6

Ingredients

- 1/4 cup butter
- 1/2 cup white sugar
- 1 cup all-purpose flour
- 1/4 teaspoon salt

- 2 teaspoons baking powder
- 1/2 cup milk
- 2 cups fresh peaches, pitted and sliced
- 1/4 cup white sugar
- 1/4 teaspoon ground cinnamon
- 1 1/2 cups water

Direction

- Preheat oven to 375 degrees F (190 degrees C). Lightly butter a 9x9 inch glass baking pan.
- In a large bowl, cream the butter and 1/2 cup sugar.
- In a separate bowl, mix flour, salt and baking powder. Add to the creamed mixture alternately with the milk.
- Spread mixture evenly into baking dish.
- If using canned peaches, drain thoroughly, reserving the juice. Spoon fruit over batter.
- Sprinkle with cinnamon and 1/4 cup sugar. Pour fruit juice or water over the top.
- Bake at 375 degrees F (190 degrees C) for 45 to 55 minutes. During baking the fruit and juice go to the bottom and the batter rises.

Nutrition Information

- Calories: 262 calories
- Total Fat: 8.3 g
- Cholesterol: 22 mg
- Sodium: 324 mg
- Total Carbohydrate: 45 g
- Protein: 2.9 g

208. Peach Cobbler in a Mug

"Yum!"

Serving: 1 | Prep: 10 m | Cook: 2 m | Ready in: 12 m

Ingredients

- 1 tablespoon butter
- 2 tablespoons white sugar
- 2 tablespoons all-purpose flour
- 1 tablespoon nonfat dry milk powder

- 1/8 teaspoon baking powder
- 1/8 teaspoon ground cinnamon
- 1 pinch salt
- 2 tablespoons water
- 1 (4 ounce) container diced peaches, well drained

Direction

- Place butter into a microwave-safe cup and heat on high in microwave until melted, about 20 seconds.
- Combine sugar, flour, milk powder, baking powder, cinnamon, and salt in a small bowl; add water and stir. Transfer sugar mixture to the mug and stir with a fork until batter is well mixed. Add peaches to top of batter.
- Heat in the microwave on 70 percent power for 2 minutes. Let mug stand in the microwave for 1 minute more. Cool slightly.

Nutrition Information

- Calories: 333 calories
- Total Fat: 11.8 g
- Cholesterol: 32 mg
- Sodium: 343 mg
- Total Carbohydrate: 54.1 g
- Protein: 5.1 g

209. Peach Cobbler IV

"This peach cobbler is extremely easy to make, and can be enjoyed any time of year!"

Serving: 6

Ingredients

- 1/2 cup butter
- 1 cup self-rising flour
- 1 cup white sugar
- 1 cup milk
- 1 (16 ounce) can sliced peaches in heavy syrup

Direction

- Preheat oven to 350 degrees F (175 degrees C).
- Place butter or margarine in an 8X8 glass baking dish. Place dish in oven until butter is melted.
- In a medium bowl, combine flour and sugar. Mix well, then stir in milk. Spoon mixture into baking dish, on top of melted butter or margarine. Pour peaches over flour mixture.
- Bake in preheated oven for 50 to 60 minutes, until peaches are bubbly and crust is lightly browned.

Nutrition Information

- Calories: 417 calories
- Total Fat: 16.3 g
- Cholesterol: 44 mg
- Sodium: 396 mg
- Total Carbohydrate: 64.7 g
- Protein: 4.1 g

210. Peach Cobbler V

"This was handed down from my Grandmother. If they're in season, you can use 2 cups peeled and sliced fresh peaches. Yum!"

Serving: 8

Ingredients

- 1/2 cup butter
- 1 cup all-purpose flour
- 1 cup white sugar
- 1 teaspoon baking powder
- 1 cup milk
- 1 (21 ounce) can peach pie filling

Direction

- Preheat oven to 350 degrees F (175 degrees C). Place butter or margarine in a 9x13 inch pan and melt in oven while it is preheating.
- In a medium bowl, mix together flour, sugar, and baking powder. Stir in milk.

- Remove pan of melted butter or margarine from oven. Pour mixture into pan, but DO NOT STIR. Spread pie filling onto batter, without stirring.
- Bake in preheated oven for 50 to 60 minutes, until fruit is bubbly and batter is set and golden brown.

Nutrition Information

- Calories: 337 calories
- Total Fat: 12.3 g
- Cholesterol: 33 mg
- Sodium: 168 mg
- Total Carbohydrate: 54.2 g
- Protein: 3.5 g

211.Peach Cobbler VI

"This is a wonderful Southern recipe...very easy and tastes great!"

Serving: 8 | Prep: 15 m | Cook: 30 m | Ready in: 45 m

Ingredients

- 1 cup all-purpose flour
- 1/2 cup brown sugar
- 1/2 cup white sugar
- 2 teaspoons baking powder
- 1/2 teaspoon salt
- 1 teaspoon vanilla extract
- 3/4 cup milk
- 1/2 cup margarine, melted
- 1 (29 ounce) can sliced canned peaches, drained
- 1 teaspoon ground cinnamon

Direction

- Preheat oven to 400 degrees F (200 degrees C). Grease a 9x9-inch baking dish.
- In a large bowl, combine flour, brown sugar, white sugar, baking powder, salt, and vanilla. Pour milk into dry ingredients, and then stir in melted margarine. Mix thoroughly.

- Pour mixture into prepared baking pan. Arrange peaches on top and sprinkle with cinnamon. Bake in preheated oven until golden brown, about 30 minutes.

Nutrition Information

- Calories: 299 calories
- Total Fat: 11.9 g
- Cholesterol: 2 mg
- Sodium: 383 mg
- Total Carbohydrate: 46.8 g
- Protein: 3.2 g

212. Peach Cream Pie II

"I received this recipe years ago from Mrs. Brown from Brown's Berry Patch, Waterport, N.Y. It is great on a hot summer day."

Serving: 8

Ingredients

- 3/4 cup white sugar
- 2 tablespoons all-purpose flour
- 1/3 teaspoon ground nutmeg
- 1/3 teaspoon ground cinnamon
- 6 fresh peaches - pitted, skinned, and sliced
- 1 1/2 cups heavy whipping cream
- 1 recipe pastry for a 9 inch single crust pie

Direction

- Preheat oven to 400 degrees F (205 degrees C).
- In a small bowl, mix sugar, flour, nutmeg and cinnamon. Sprinkle a handful in the bottom of uncooked pie shell. Fill pie shell with sliced peaches, and sprinkle with remaining sugar mixture. Cover peaches with heavy cream; you may not need all the cream.
- Bake pie for 10 minutes. Reduce heat to 350 degrees F (175 degrees C), and bake for 50 minutes longer.

Nutrition Information

- Calories: 367 calories
- Total Fat: 24 g
- Cholesterol: 61 mg
- Sodium: 137 mg
- Total Carbohydrate: 36.4 g
- Protein: 2.5 g

Nutrition Information

- Calories: 295 calories
- Total Fat: 14.3 g
- Cholesterol: 20 mg
- Sodium: 67 mg
- Total Carbohydrate: 39.6 g
- Protein: 3.6 g

213. Peach Crisp III

"Very easy dessert with wholesome granola and oats for the topping. Not too sweet for those who prefer natural peach flavors. Good peaches make the difference, but you can use canned. Serve warm with fresh whipped cream."

Serving: 6 | Prep: 20 m | Cook: 30 m | Ready in: 50 m

Ingredients

- 1/2 cup quick cooking oats
- 1/2 cup honey-sweetened granola
- 3 tablespoons all-purpose flour
- 1/2 cup packed brown sugar
- 1/4 cup butter
- 5 cups fresh peaches - peeled, pitted, and sliced
- 1 tablespoon all-purpose flour
- 1 teaspoon ground cinnamon
- 1/2 teaspoon ground nutmeg
- 1/4 teaspoon ground allspice (optional)
- 1/4 cup chopped pecans (optional)

Direction

- Preheat oven to 375 degrees F (190 degrees C).
- In a medium bowl, combine the oats, granola, 3 tablespoons flour, and brown sugar. Cut in the 1/4 cup butter until crumbly.
- Place peach slices in an 8-inch square baking dish. Sprinkle with remaining 1 tablespoon flour. Scatter the oat mixture over the peaches. Sprinkle top with cinnamon, nutmeg, allspice, and pecans.
- Bake in preheated oven for 30 minutes, or until golden brown.

214. Peach Crisp with OatmealWalnut Topping

"I love fruit crisps. I created this recipe after picking a half-bushel of peaches with my family at a local orchard. The topping can be used on various other fruits as well. I served this with a scoop of vanilla ice cream. Enjoy!"

Serving: 6 | Prep: 20 m | Cook: 35 m | Ready in: 55 m

Ingredients

- 5 cups sliced fresh peaches
- 2 tablespoons instant tapioca
- 1/4 teaspoon almond extract
- 1/2 cup packed brown sugar, divided
- 1 3/4 cups all-purpose flour
- 1/2 cup old-fashioned rolled oats
- 1/3 cup chopped walnuts
- 6 tablespoons unsalted butter, melted and cooled

Direction

- Preheat oven to 375 degrees F (190 degrees C).
- Combine peaches, tapioca, almond extract, and 1/4 cup brown sugar in a bowl. Set mixture aside until tapioca pearls have softened, about 15 minutes. Whisk remaining 1/4 cup of brown sugar and flour in a separate bowl.
- Process rolled oats with walnuts in a food processor, pulsing a few times to grind to coarse crumbs; stir walnuts and oats into flour mixture. Drizzle topping mixture with melted butter and stir with a fork to create large crumbs of topping. Pour peaches and their

juice into an 8x8-inch baking dish; spread crumb topping atop peaches in an even layer.

- Bake in the preheated oven until topping is golden brown and the peaches are bubbling, 35 to 40 minutes. Serve slightly warm.

Nutrition Information

- Calories: 412 calories
- Total Fat: 16.6 g
- Cholesterol: 31 mg
- Sodium: 12 mg
- Total Carbohydrate: 60.9 g
- Protein: 5.8 g

215. Peach Crumble Cake

"This is a go-to recipe for me, and it's great for summer cookouts served with ice cream. Very quick and easy to make and most people have the ingredients in their pantries already. The more brown sugar you use on top, the more 'crumble' you will have."

Serving: 6 | Prep: 10 m | Cook: 30 m | Ready in: 40 m

Ingredients

- 2 (15 ounce) cans sliced peaches, peaches cut into thirds
- 1 (15.25 ounce) package yellow cake mix
- 3/4 cup butter, thinly sliced
- 3 cups brown sugar

Direction

- Preheat oven to 350 degrees F (175 degrees C).
- Pour peaches into a 9x13-inch baking dish. Spread cake mix in an even layer over peaches. Cover cake mix with butter slices and spread brown sugar over the top.
- Bake in the preheated oven until golden and bubbling, about 30 minutes.

Nutrition Information

- Calories: 852 calories
- Total Fat: 31.4 g
- Cholesterol: 62 mg

- Sodium: 662 mg
- Total Carbohydrate: 143.6 g
- Protein: 4.4 g

216. Peach Curd

"This is a variation on lemon curd, but made with peaches. We love it with scones or spread on toast or pound cake."

Serving: 48 | Prep: 20 m | Cook: 20 m | Ready in: 40 m

Ingredients

- 3 fresh peaches, halved and pitted
- 4 cups white sugar
- 2 eggs
- 4 egg yolks
- 1 tablespoon lemon juice
- 1 teaspoon rose water (optional)
- 3/4 cup butter

Direction

- Blend peach halves in a blender until smooth; transfer to a large bowl.
- Beat sugar, eggs, egg yolks, lemon juice, and rose water into peach puree until incorporated.
- Melt butter in the top of a double boiler over simmering water; stir peach mixture into melted butter, stirring constantly, until curd is thickened, 5 to 10 minutes.
- Sterilize jars and lids in boiling water for at least 5 minutes. Pack peach curd into the hot, sterilized jars, filling the jars to within 1/4 inch of the top. Run a knife or a thin spatula around the insides of the jars after they have been filled to remove any air bubbles. Wipe the rims of the jars with a moist paper towel to remove any food residue. Top with lids, and screw on rings.
- Place a rack in the bottom of a large stockpot and fill halfway with water. Bring to a boil and lower jars into the boiling water using a holder. Leave a 2-inch space between the jars. Pour in more boiling water if necessary to

bring the water level to at least 1 inch above the tops of the jars. Bring the water to a rolling boil, cover the pot, and process for 10 minutes.

- Remove the jars from the stockpot and place onto a cloth-covered or wood surface, several inches apart, until cool. Once cool, press the top of each lid with a finger, ensuring that the seal is tight (lid does not move up or down at all). Store in a cool dark area.

Nutrition Information

- Calories: 99 calories
- Total Fat: 3.5 g
- Cholesterol: 32 mg
- Sodium: 24 mg
- Total Carbohydrate: 17.1 g
- Protein: 0.5 g

217. Peach Curry Glazed Pork Chops

"The sweet yet spicy peach glaze makes any pork chops amazing, plus it's quick and easy!"

Serving: 4 | Prep: 15 m | Cook: 15 m | Ready in: 30 m

Ingredients

- 1/2 cup sliced syrup-packed peaches, drained, syrup reserved
- 3 tablespoons peach jam
- 2 tablespoons Dijon mustard
- 2 teaspoons curry powder
- 1 teaspoon honey
- 1 tablespoon vegetable oil
- 4 boneless pork chops
- 2 green onions, chopped
- 2 tablespoons chopped fresh cilantro

Direction

- In a bowl, mix the reserved peach syrup, peach jam, Dijon mustard, curry powder, and honey.

- Heat the vegetable oil in a skillet over medium heat, and cook the pork chops 8 minutes, or to desired doneness.
- Mix the green onions into the skillet, and cook 1 minute, until tender. Spoon the syrup mixture and peaches over the pork chops. Continue cooking until heated through. Sprinkle with cilantro to serve.

Nutrition Information

- Calories: 229 calories
- Total Fat: 10.2 g
- Cholesterol: 39 mg
- Sodium: 214 mg
- Total Carbohydrate: 19.2 g
- Protein: 15 g

218. Peach Custard Pie II

"A rich and wonderful summertime dessert. It makes peach season worth waiting for!"

Serving: 8

Ingredients

- 1 (9 inch) pie shell
- 4 eggs
- 1/2 cup white sugar
- 2 cups milk
- 1 teaspoon vanilla extract
- 4 fresh peaches - pitted, skinned, and sliced

Direction

- Preheat oven to 425 degrees F (220 degrees C).
- In a large mixing bowl, beat eggs and sugar together. Stir in milk and vanilla.
- Arrange peach slices in bottom of pastry-lined pie pan. Pour custard mixture over peaches.
- Bake in preheated oven for 10 minutes. Reduce heat to 350 degrees F (175 degrees C) and bake an additional 45 minutes, until custard is set and toothpick inserted in center comes out clean.

Nutrition Information

- Calories: 210 calories
- Total Fat: 8.9 g
- Cholesterol: 98 mg
- Sodium: 164 mg
- Total Carbohydrate: 26.4 g
- Protein: 5.9 g

219. Peach Dump Cake

"A friend gave me this recipe and it has always been a pleaser. This is a very quick and easy dessert. It's a recipe friends and family ask me to make for gatherings."

Serving: 12 | Prep: 10 m | Cook: 35 m | Ready in: 45 m

Ingredients

- 1 (29 ounce) can sliced peaches in heavy syrup, undrained
- 1 (18.25 ounce) box yellow cake mix
- 3/4 cup butter, sliced into pats, or more if needed

Direction

- Preheat oven to 350 degrees F (175 degrees C). Grease a 9x13-inch baking dish with margarine.
- Pour peaches and heavy syrup into the prepared baking dish. Spread cake mix evenly over peaches. Arrange butter pats in even rows on the cake mix.
- Bake in the preheated oven until top of cake is golden brown, 35 to 40 minutes.

Nutrition Information

- Calories: 318 calories
- Total Fat: 16.5 g
- Cholesterol: 31 mg
- Sodium: 367 mg
- Total Carbohydrate: 41.5 g
- Protein: 2.4 g

220. Peach Dumplings

"My dad used to make the best Peach Dumplings. Some people make them with a bread dough. My dad made his with a potato dough. The peach was wrapped in the dough and dropped into boiling water to cook. When they were served you would cut them up and sprinkle them with crushed vanilla wafers, sugar and melted butter. We ate them as a meal even though they sound like a dessert. Again, there are different ways to serve them: my friend's mother sprinkled hers with ricotta cheese and sugar."

Serving: 10 | Prep: 2 h | Cook: 20 m | Ready in: 2 h 20 m

Ingredients

- 8 potatoes - peeled and cubed
- 1 egg
- 5 cups all-purpose flour
- 10 firm ripe peaches
- 1 cup white sugar
- 1/2 cup butter, melted
- 1 (16 ounce) package vanilla wafers, crushed

Direction

- Place the potatoes in a pot with enough water to cover. Bring to a boil over medium-high heat, and cook until tender. Remove from heat, drain, and put through a ricer or mash.
- Place the riced potatoes onto a large clean work surface. Crack the egg over the top, then gradually work in the flour with your hands until you get a nice stiff dough. You may not need to use all of the flour, or you may need to use more. This could take as long as 30 minutes, or just seem like it. Let the dough rest for a minute before rolling.
- On a lightly floured surface, roll the dough out to 1/4 inch thickness. You may need to roll out 1/2 at a time. Cut the dough into 8x8 inch squares - larger or smaller depending on the size of your peaches. Wrap each peach in a square of dough, and pinch all of the seams to seal it in.
- Bring a large pot of water to a boil. Place the peach dumplings into the water. The peach should be as close to covered with the water as

it can get. We usually had 2 or 3 pots with boiling water because you can only fit about 3 to 4 peaches per pot. Boil for 20 minutes, rotating after 10 for even cooking. Remove from water using tongs or a large slotted spoon.

- To serve, place a peach dumpling onto a plate, and cut it up. Remove the pit, and sprinkle with melted butter, sugar and vanilla wafer crumbs.

Nutrition Information

- Calories: 761 calories
- Total Fat: 19.2 g
- Cholesterol: 43 mg
- Sodium: 225 mg
- Total Carbohydrate: 135.3 g
- Protein: 12.6 g

221. Peach Elderberry Coffee Cake

"This year around the farmland where I live we harvested over 20 pounds of wild elderberries. You can only make so many jars of jelly and so many pies, so I whipped this up one day and I thought I would share. Enjoy!"

Serving: 12 | Prep: 20 m | Cook: 35 m | Ready in: 55 m

Ingredients

- 1/2 cup butter
- 6 tablespoons butter
- 3/4 cup brown sugar
- 3/4 cup white sugar
- 2 eggs
- 2 tablespoons clover honey
- 1 tablespoon lemon juice
- 2 teaspoons vanilla extract
- 3 cups all-purpose flour
- 1 teaspoon ground cinnamon
- 1 teaspoon baking powder
- 1/2 teaspoon baking soda
- 1/2 teaspoon salt
- 1/2 cup milk
- 2 cups fresh elderberries

- 4 fresh peaches - peeled, pitted, and cubed
- Topping:
- 1 cup brown sugar
- 1/2 cup all-purpose flour
- 1/4 cup butter, cubed

Direction

- Preheat oven to 350 degrees F (175 degrees C). Grease a 9x13-inch baking dish.
- Beat 1/2 cup plus 6 tablespoons butter, 3/4 cup brown sugar, and white sugar together in a large bowl with an electric mixer until light and fluffy. Beat in eggs, honey, lemon juice, and vanilla extract until smooth.
- Sift 3 cups flour, cinnamon, baking powder, baking soda, and salt together in a separate bowl; beat into butter and sugar mixture until incorporated. Beat in milk until smooth batter forms. Fold in elderberries and peaches just until combined. Spread batter evenly into prepared baking dish.
- Whisk 1 cup brown sugar and 1/2 cup flour together in a separate bowl. Cut in 1/4 cup butter until mixture resembles coarse crumbs; sprinkle over batter.
- Bake in preheated oven until a toothpick inserted into the center comes out clean, 35 to 40 minutes.

Nutrition Information

- Calories: 494 calories
- Total Fat: 18.8 g
- Cholesterol: 78 mg
- Sodium: 340 mg
- Total Carbohydrate: 77.5 g
- Protein: 5.6 g

222. Peach Filled Cake

"This is a lovely cake to make when peaches are ripe. It is a lemon cake filled with fresh peach slices."

Serving: 16

Ingredients

- 3/4 cup butter, softened
- 1 cup white sugar
- 3 eggs
- 1 teaspoon lemon zest
- 2/3 cup milk
- 1 cup all-purpose flour
- 7/8 cup whole wheat flour
- 2 teaspoons baking powder
- 1/4 teaspoon salt
- 4 fresh peaches - pitted, skinned, and sliced
- 1/3 cup packed brown sugar
- 1/2 teaspoon ground cinnamon

Direction

- Bake at 350 degrees F (175 degrees C). Grease and flour one 8x10 inch cake pan.
- In a bowl, cream the butter or margarine with the granulated sugar. Beat in the eggs, then the lemon rind and milk.
- In another bowl, stir together the whole wheat flour, all-purpose flour, baking powder, and salt. Beat into the creamed mixture. Spread half the batter evenly into the prepared pan. Arrange the peach slices on top and sprinkle with the brown sugar combined with the ground cinnamon. Spread the remaining batter on top.
- Bake at 350 degrees F (175 degrees C) for 50 minutes. Let cake cool on a rack. Because this cake is so moist, it is easiest to serve it directly from the baking pan. It should be stored in the refrigerator. Makes 16 servings.

Nutrition Information

- Calories: 218 calories
- Total Fat: 10 g
- Cholesterol: 59 mg
- Sodium: 179 mg
- Total Carbohydrate: 30 g
- Protein: 3.3 g

223. Peach Finger Pie

"Peach pie in pick-up-able form! My grandmother has made this recipe for over 50 years and it has always been a favorite of mine. My kids LOVE this recipe! This pie is best in my opinion, when it is completely cooled."

Serving: 12 | Prep: 30 m | Cook: 45 m | Ready in: 3 h 15 m

Ingredients

- 4 cups all-purpose flour
- 2 tablespoons white sugar
- 1 pinch salt
- 1 1/2 cups vegetable shortening
- 1 egg
- cold water, or as needed
- 1 1/4 cups water, divided
- 1/4 cup cornstarch
- 3/4 cup white sugar
- 1/4 teaspoon salt (optional)
- 1 tablespoon lemon juice (optional)
- 4 cups fresh peaches - peeled, pitted, and sliced

Direction

- Mix together the flour, 2 tablespoons of sugar, and a pinch of salt in a large bowl. Cut the shortening into the flour mixture until the mixture resembles coarse crumbs. Beat the egg in a small bowl, and pour it into a 1-cup measuring cup. Pour in enough cold water to total 1 cup, and mix the water and egg into the dough. Mix the dough a few times with your fingers, until it holds together. Divide the dough in half.
- Preheat oven to 350 degrees F (175 degrees C).
- Whisk together 3/4 cup of water with the cornstarch in a bowl until smooth, and set aside. Mix 1/2 cup of water with 3/4 cup of sugar in a large saucepan until the sugar has dissolved, and bring to a boil. Whisk the

cornstarch mixture into the boiling sugar mixture until thickened and translucent, whisking constantly, about 1 minute; whisk in 1/4 teaspoon of salt and lemon juice, if desired. Combine with the sliced peaches.

- Roll half the crust out on a floured surface in a rectangle shape about 12 by 20 inches, and fit the pastry into a 10x15-inch jelly roll pan. Roll the second half of the crust out to the same size as the first crust. Pour the peach filling into the bottom crust, and place the top crust on the pie. Crimp and fold the edges to seal, and cut several slits into the top crust.
- Bake in the preheated oven until the crust is browned and the filling is bubbling, 45 minutes to 1 hour. Allow to cool completely to let the filling set up before slicing into squares to serve.

Nutrition Information

- Calories: 462 calories
- Total Fat: 26.4 g
- Cholesterol: 16 mg
- Sodium: 58 mg
- Total Carbohydrate: 51.6 g
- Protein: 4.9 g

224. Peach Gelee Candy

"This is an old fashioned, handcrafted candy that takes a little time and finesse to pull off. It's simple and sweet, but looks and tastes like something you're only suppose to enjoy a few times a year."

Serving: 25 | Prep: 10 m | Cook: 20 m | Ready in: 8 h 30 m

Ingredients

- 1 pound ripe peaches - peeled, pitted and sliced
- 1 tablespoon lime juice
- 2 cups white sugar, divided
- 3 tablespoons liquid pectin
- 1/2 cup white sugar, for sprinkling

Direction

- Line an 8x8-inch baking dish with plastic wrap.
- Combine peaches and lime juice in a blender. Puree until very smooth.
- Pour into a saucepan over medium heat, stir in 1/2 cup sugar, and bring to a boil. Cook, stirring continuously, until thickened, about 15 minutes.
- Stir in remaining 1 1/2 cups sugar and pectin. Using a thermometer, heat to 205 degrees F (96 degrees C) and cook, stirring continuously, for another 10 minutes. Remove from heat.
- Pour peach puree into the prepared baking dish. Shake gently and tap on the countertop to remove any air bubbles. Cover and refrigerate at least 8 hours or overnight.
- Sprinkle about half the 1/2 cup of sugar over a silicone baking mat and invert the peach gelee on top. Remove plastic wrap and sprinkle top with sugar. Trim off any uneven edges and cut gelee into 25 squares.

Nutrition Information

- Calories: 81 calories
- Total Fat: 0 g
- Cholesterol: 0 mg
- Sodium: < 1 mg
- Total Carbohydrate: 21 g
- Protein: 0 g

225. Peach Ice Cream

"A creamy, delicious Summertime treat! This recipe contains raw eggs. We recommend that pregnant women, young children, the elderly and the infirm do not consume raw eggs. "

Serving: 32 | Prep: 20 m | Ready in: 1 h 5 m

Ingredients

- 6 eggs, beaten
- 3 1/2 cups white sugar
- 10 fresh peaches, pitted and chopped

- 4 cups heavy cream
- 2 cups half-and-half cream
- 2 teaspoons vanilla extract
- 3/4 teaspoon salt

Direction

- In large bowl, mix together eggs and sugar until smooth; puree peaches in blender or food processor and stir 5 cups of puree into egg mixture. Stir in cream, half-and-half, vanilla and salt and mix well.
- Pour mixture into freezer canister of ice cream maker and freeze according to manufacturer's instructions.

Nutrition Information

- Calories: 229 calories
- Total Fat: 13.7 g
- Cholesterol: 81 mg
- Sodium: 86 mg
- Total Carbohydrate: 25.3 g
- Protein: 2.2 g

226. Peach Jam with Amaretto Liqueur

"Opinions differ how this jam tastes best. Some members of our family like it as a spread on toast, others add it to a bowl of natural yogurt. Both are very tasty."

Serving: 90 | Prep: 25 m | Cook: 5 m | Ready in: 30 m

Ingredients

- 4 1/2 cups finely chopped, peeled peaches
- 2 tablespoons lemon juice
- 3 cups sugar
- 1 (1.75 ounce) package fruit pectin (such as Sure-Jell® Pectin Light for less or no sugar)
- 1/3 cup amaretto liqueur, or more to taste

Direction

- Inspect 5 half-pint jars for cracks and rings for rust, discarding any defective ones. Immerse in simmering water until jam is ready. Wash new, unused lids and rings in warm soapy water.
- Mix peaches with lemon juice in a large pot immediately after chopping to prevent peaches from turning brown. Place pot over medium heat.
- Mix 1/4 cup of the sugar with pectin and add it to the pot with the peaches. Stir well. Slowly bring to a full rolling boil that does not stop bubbling when stirred. Add the remaining sugar and stir well, scraping the bottom of the pot, to fully dissolve the sugar. Cook for 1 minute, stirring constantly.
- Remove from heat and stir in amaretto liqueur.
- Ladle peach jam immediately into the prepared jars, filling to within 1/4 inch of the top. Run a clean knife or thin spatula around the insides of the jars to remove any air bubbles. Wipe rims with a moist paper towel to remove any spills. Top with lids and tightly screw on rings.
- Place a rack in the bottom of a large stockpot and fill halfway with water. Bring to a boil and lower jars 2 inches apart into the boiling water using a holder. Pour in more boiling water to cover jars by at least 1 inch. Bring to a rolling boil, cover, and process for 10 minutes.
- Remove the jars from the stockpot and place onto a cloth-covered or wood surface, several inches apart. Let rest for 24 hours without moving the jars. Gently press the center of each lid with a finger to ensure the lid does not move up or down. Remove the rings for storage and store in a cool, dark area.

Nutrition Information

- Calories: 31 calories
- Total Fat: 0 g
- Cholesterol: 0 mg
- Sodium: < 1 mg
- Total Carbohydrate: 7.5 g
- Protein: 0 g

227. Peach Kuchen

"This is my favorite recipe. It's quick, easy and delicious. I've made it with both canned or fresh peaches"

Serving: 12 | Prep: 10 m | Cook: 30 m | Ready in: 45 m

Ingredients

- 1/2 cup margarine
- 1/4 cup white sugar
- 1 egg
- 1 teaspoon vanilla extract
- 1 cup all-purpose flour
- 1/2 teaspoon baking powder
- 1/4 teaspoon salt
- 1 (29 ounce) can sliced peaches, drained
- 3 tablespoons white sugar
- 1 teaspoon ground cinnamon

Direction

- Preheat oven to 350 degrees F (175 degrees C). Grease and flour a 9 inch springform pan. Sift together the flour, baking powder and salt. Set aside.
- In a large bowl, cream together the butter and sugar until light and fluffy. Beat in the egg, then stir in the vanilla. Beat in the flour mixture. Spread dough with hands over the bottom and 1 inch up the sides of prepared springform pan. Arrange peach slices in a spoke pattern over the dough. Sprinkle with sugar and cinnamon.
- Bake in the preheated oven for 35 to 40 minutes, or until golden brown.

Nutrition Information

- Calories: 170 calories
- Total Fat: 8 g
- Cholesterol: 16 mg
- Sodium: 160 mg
- Total Carbohydrate: 23.4 g
- Protein: 2.1 g

228. Peach Monkey Bread

"A less-sweet monkey bread with peaches on top with dough made from scratch."

Serving: 6 | Prep: 20 m | Cook: 10 m | Ready in: 30 m

Ingredients

- 1 cup all-purpose flour
- 1 1/4 cups whole-wheat flour
- 1 tablespoon baking powder
- 2 1/2 teaspoons white sugar
- 1/2 teaspoon cream of tartar
- 1/4 teaspoon salt
- 1/3 cup vegetable oil
- 1/4 cup butter
- 2/3 cup milk
- 1/3 cup vegetable oil
- 1 1/2 cups chopped walnuts
- 1 fresh peach, cut into cubes
- 2/3 cup maple syrup
- 1 teaspoon ground cinnamon

Direction

- Preheat an oven to 450 degrees F (230 degrees C). Grease a 9-inch round pan.
- Mix all-purpose flour, whole-wheat flour, baking powder, sugar, cream of tartar, and salt together in a large bowl. Blend 1/3 cup vegetable oil and butter into the flour mixture until it looks like bread crumbs. Stir milk into the mixture to form a dough. Roll the dough into balls smaller than 1 inch in diameter and arrange into the prepared pan. Drizzle 1/3 cup vegetable oil over the dough.
- Sprinkle chopped walnuts over the dough; top with peach cubes. Stir maple syrup and cinnamon together in a small bowl; drizzle evenly over the peaches and walnuts.
- Bake in the preheated oven until the edges of the dough is golden brown, 10 to 12 minutes.

Nutrition Information

- Calories: 752 calories
- Total Fat: 52.2 g
- Cholesterol: 23 mg
- Sodium: 413 mg

- Total Carbohydrate: 66.6 g
- Protein: 11 g

229. Peach Muffins

"In my hurry to use up some peaches, I came up with this muffin recipe. It turned out so good, just like peach cobbler in a muffin, that I thought I'd share it with everyone! This is also really good bread! Just increase the baking time to 1 hour at 350 degrees F and use 2 loaf pans."

Serving: 16 | Prep: 25 m | Cook: 25 m | Ready in: 50 m

Ingredients

- 3 cups all-purpose flour
- 1 tablespoon ground cinnamon
- 1 teaspoon baking soda
- 1 teaspoon salt
- 1 1/4 cups vegetable oil
- 3 eggs, lightly beaten
- 2 cups white sugar
- 2 cups peeled, pitted, and chopped peaches

Direction

- Preheat oven to 400 degrees F (200 degrees C). Lightly grease 16 muffin cups.
- In a large bowl, mix the flour, cinnamon, baking soda, and salt. In a separate bowl, mix the oil, eggs, and sugar. Stir the oil mixture into the flour mixture just until moist. Fold in the peaches. Spoon into the prepared muffin cups.
- Bake 25 minutes in the preheated oven, until a toothpick inserted in the center of a muffin comes out clean. Cool 10 minutes before turning out onto wire racks to cool completely.

Nutrition Information

- Calories: 351 calories
- Total Fat: 18.2 g
- Cholesterol: 35 mg
- Sodium: 238 mg
- Total Carbohydrate: 44.3 g
- Protein: 3.6 g

230. Peach Pasta Salad

"This is a recipe that I have been making for years. It was always a favorite of my kids, and now the grandkids love it as well. Goes great at any summer barbecue. I sometimes use mangos instead of the peach. If fresh basil and thyme are available, the recipe is even better."

Serving: 8 | Prep: 25 m | Cook: 15 m | Ready in: 1 h 40 m

Ingredients

- 8 slices bacon
- 1/2 cup uncooked shell pasta
- 2 tablespoons white vinegar
- 1/4 cup white sugar
- 1 1/2 tablespoons dried basil
- 1 tablespoon dried thyme
- 4 cloves garlic, peeled
- 1 teaspoon salt
- 1 teaspoon curry powder
- 1/2 teaspoon ground black pepper
- 1 cup canola oil
- 4 peaches, peeled and cut into chunks
- 1/2 cup chopped fresh parsley
- 1/2 cup sliced celery
- 1/2 cup chopped red bell pepper
- 6 green onions, chopped

Direction

- Place the bacon in a large, deep skillet and cook over medium-high heat, turning occasionally, until evenly browned, about 10 minutes.
- Drain the bacon slices on a paper towel-lined plate. When cool, crumble the bacon and set aside.
- Fill a pot with lightly salted water and bring to a boil. Stir in the shell pasta and return to a boil; cook the pasta uncovered over medium heat, stirring occasionally, until cooked through but still slightly firm, about 13 minutes.

- Rinse pasta thoroughly in cold water several times to chill, and drain well.
- Place the vinegar, sugar, basil, thyme, garlic, salt, curry powder, and black pepper into the pitcher of a blender; blend on high speed until smooth. Reduce blender speed to low and slowly pour the canola oil into the blender to make a creamy dressing.
- Place the bacon, cooked pasta, peaches, parsley, celery, red bell pepper, and green onions into a large salad bowl and toss to combine.
- Pour the dressing over the salad and toss again to coat with dressing.
- Refrigerate salad for 1 hour before serving.

Nutrition Information

- Calories: 374 calories
- Total Fat: 32.2 g
- Cholesterol: 10 mg
- Sodium: 515 mg
- Total Carbohydrate: 17.6 g
- Protein: 5.1 g

231. Peach Pear Salsa

"A sweet and spicy topping for most grilled, baked, or broiled meats. It's especially tasty on grilled halibut and chicken."

Serving: 8 | Prep: 15 m | Cook: 15 m | Ready in: 30 m

Ingredients

- 1 tablespoon olive oil
- 1/2 red onion, diced
- 2 cloves garlic, minced
- 4 peaches - pitted and diced
- 1 pear - peeled, cored, and diced
- 1/4 cup honey
- 1 teaspoon curry powder
- salt and pepper to taste

Direction

- Heat the olive oil in a small skillet over medium-low heat; cook the onion and garlic in

the hot oil until translucent, about 5 minutes. Stir the peaches, pear, and honey into the onion and garlic mixture; allow to cook together for 2 minutes. Season with the curry powder, salt, and pepper. Continue cooking at a simmer until hot, 5 to 6 minutes.

Nutrition Information

- Calories: 76 calories
- Total Fat: 1.8 g
- Cholesterol: 0 mg
- Sodium: 3 mg
- Total Carbohydrate: 16 g
- Protein: 0.3 g

232. Peach Pecan Sweet Potatoes

"An easy, wonderful variation of a sweet potato recipe-- great for Thanksgiving, a side dish with Easter ham, or for any time of year!"

Serving: 8 | Prep: 30 m | Cook: 1 h 15 m | Ready in: 1 h 45 m

Ingredients

- 6 sweet potatoes, peeled and sliced 1/2 inch thick
- 1 (16 ounce) package frozen unsweetened peach slices, thawed
- 4 tablespoons butter, sliced into pats
- 1 tablespoon lemon juice
- 1/2 cup brown sugar
- 1/2 teaspoon ground ginger
- salt
- 1/4 cup coffee flavored liqueur (optional)
- 1/2 cup chopped pecans

Direction

- Preheat oven to 350 degrees F (175 degrees C). Lightly grease a 9x13-inch baking dish.
- Arrange half the sweet potatoes in the bottom of the prepared baking dish. Layer with half of the peach slices and dot with half the butter. Repeat layering with remaining sweet

potatoes and peach slices and sprinkle with lemon juice. Combine the brown sugar, ginger, and salt and mix well.

- Sprinkle the sugar mixture over the potatoes and peaches. Dot the casserole with remaining butter, and pour in the liqueur (see Cook's Note). Cover pan with aluminum foil.
- Bake in the preheated oven until sweet potatoes are tender, about 1 hour. Remove foil, sprinkle with pecans, and continue baking 10 to 15 minutes, until pecans are toasted and fragrant.

Nutrition Information

- Calories: 317 calories
- Total Fat: 10.8 g
- Cholesterol: 15 mg
- Sodium: 103 mg
- Total Carbohydrate: 50.9 g
- Protein: 2.6 g

233. Peach Pie

"Old fashioned peach pie using no eggs, my family's favorite."

Serving: 8 | Prep: 1 h | Cook: 45 m | Ready in: 1 h 45 m

Ingredients

- 10 fresh peaches, pitted and sliced
- 1/3 cup all-purpose flour
- 1 cup white sugar
- 1/4 cup butter
- 1 recipe pastry for a 9 inch double crust pie

Direction

- Mix flour, sugar and butter into crumb stage.
- Place one crust in the bottom of a 9 inch pie plate. Line the shell with some sliced peaches. Sprinkle some of the butter mixture on top of the peaches, then put more peaches on top of the crumb mixture. Continue layering until both the peaches and crumbs are gone.
- Top with lattice strips of pie crust.

- Bake at 350 degrees F (175 degrees C) for 45 minutes, or until crust is golden. Allow pie to cool before slicing. Best when eaten fresh.

Nutrition Information

- Calories: 425 calories
- Total Fat: 20.7 g
- Cholesterol: 15 mg
- Sodium: 280 mg
- Total Carbohydrate: 57 g
- Protein: 3.4 g

234. Peach Pie the Old Fashioned Two Crust Way

"This is a simple, quick, old fashioned, baked, two crust peach pie made with fresh peaches and simple ingredients. It's great during summer peach season."

Serving: 8 | Prep: 30 m | Cook: 45 m | Ready in: 1 h 15 m

Ingredients

- 1 (15 ounce) package pastry for a 9 inch double crust pie
- 1 egg, beaten
- 5 cups sliced peeled peaches
- 2 tablespoons lemon juice
- 1/2 cup all-purpose flour
- 1 cup white sugar
- 1/2 teaspoon ground cinnamon
- 1/4 teaspoon ground nutmeg
- 1/4 teaspoon salt
- 2 tablespoons butter

Direction

- Preheat the oven to 450 degrees F (220 degrees C).
- Line the bottom and sides of a 9 inch pie plate with one of the pie crusts. Brush with some of the beaten egg to keep the dough from becoming soggy later.

- Place the sliced peaches in a large bowl, and sprinkle with lemon juice. Mix gently. In a separate bowl, mix together the flour, sugar, cinnamon, nutmeg and salt. Pour over the peaches, and mix gently. Pour into the pie crust, and dot with butter. Cover with the other pie crust, and fold the edges under. Flute the edges to seal or press the edges with the tines of a fork dipped in egg. Brush the remaining egg over the top crust. Cut several slits in the top crust to vent steam.
- Bake for 10 minutes in the preheated oven, then reduce the heat to 350 degrees F (175 degrees C) and bake for an additional 30 to 35 minutes, until the crust is brown and the juice begins to bubble through the vents. If the edges brown to fast, cover them with strips of aluminum foil about halfway through baking. Cool before serving. This tastes better warm than hot.

Nutrition Information

- Calories: 428 calories
- Total Fat: 19.8 g
- Cholesterol: 31 mg
- Sodium: 358 mg
- Total Carbohydrate: 58.6 g
- Protein: 4.7 g

235. Peach Pie with Sour Cream

"This is my favorite pie recipe anywhere. Just make sure you use only fresh, high-quality sweet peaches."

Serving: 8 | Prep: 20 m | Cook: 1 h 15 m | Ready in: 1 h 35 m

Ingredients

- 1 1/4 cups all-purpose flour
- 1/2 cup butter, cut into chunks
- 1/2 teaspoon salt
- 2 tablespoons sour cream
- 4 fresh peaches - peeled, pitted, and sliced
- 3 egg yolks
- 2 tablespoons all-purpose flour
- 1/3 cup sour cream
- 1 cup white sugar

Direction

- Preheat oven to 425 degrees F (220 degrees C). Butter a 9-inch pie dish.
- Place 1 1/4 cups flour, butter, salt, and 2 tablespoons sour cream in a food processor; pulse until mixture comes together in a large ball. Press dough into prepared pie dish to form a crust.
- Bake in preheated hoven until golden brown, about 10 minutes. Remove pie crust from oven.
- Reduce oven heat to 350 degrees F (175 degrees C). Arrange peach slices in pie crust.
- Lightly beat egg yolks in a large bowl. Add in sugar, 1/3 cup sour cream, and 2 tablespoons flour; stir until well-mixed. Pour egg mixture over peaches. Cover pie with aluminum foil.
- Bake in preheated oven for 50 minutes; remove foil. Continue baking until peach filling is set, about 15 minutes more.

Nutrition Information

- Calories: 337 calories
- Total Fat: 16.1 g
- Cholesterol: 113 mg
- Sodium: 239 mg
- Total Carbohydrate: 45.2 g
- Protein: 3.8 g

236. Peach Pork Picante

"This one skillet dish is just peachy! Salsa, seasoning, pork and peach preserves all add up to one fruity, tangy treat."

Serving: 6 | Prep: 10 m | Cook: 20 m | Ready in: 30 m

Ingredients

- 1 pound boneless pork loin, cubed
- 1 (1 ounce) package taco seasoning mix
- 1 cup salsa

- 4 tablespoons peach preserves

Direction

- Season pork with taco seasoning. Heat oil in a large skillet over medium high heat. Add seasoned pork and sauté until browned, 5 to 7 minutes. Add salsa and peach preserves and mix well. Cover skillet and reduce heat. Let simmer gently for about 10 minutes and serve.

Nutrition Information

- Calories: 133 calories
- Total Fat: 3.4 g
- Cholesterol: 23 mg
- Sodium: 618 mg
- Total Carbohydrate: 15.1 g
- Protein: 9.9 g

237. Peach Preserves

"These fragrant preserves are simple to make, and may be stored. Toast and biscuits will never taste the same again!"

Serving: 64 | Prep: 20 m | Cook: 1 h | Ready in: 2 h

Ingredients

- 12 fresh peaches, pitted and chopped
- 4 1/2 cups white sugar
- 1 (2 ounce) package dry pectin

Direction

- Crush 1 cup chopped peaches in the bottom of a large saucepan. Add remaining peaches, and set pan over medium-low heat. Bring to a low boil, and cook for about 20 minutes or until peaches become liquid (my family likes a few bits of peach left).
- Pour peaches into a bowl, and then measure 6 cups back into the pan. Add sugar, and bring to a boil over medium heat. Gradually stir in dry pectin, and boil for 1 minute.
- Remove from heat after 1 minute, and transfer to sterilized jars. Process in hot water bath

canner for 10 minutes. Let cool, and place on shelf.

Nutrition Information

- Calories: 59 calories
- Total Fat: 0 g
- Cholesterol: 0 mg
- Sodium: < 1 mg
- Total Carbohydrate: 15.2 g
- Protein: 0 g

238. Peach Ripple Sherbet

"Vanilla ice cream with a ripple of fresh peaches."

Serving: 8 | Prep: 10 m | Ready in: 1 h

Ingredients

- 3 cups low-fat vanilla ice cream, divided
- 2 very ripe peaches, peeled and chopped
- 1 1/2 teaspoons lemon juice
- 2 drops almond extract (optional)

Direction

- Place ice cream in the refrigerator until softened to the texture of soft-serve ice cream, 20 to 30 minutes.
- Combine peaches, lemon juice, and almond extract in a blender. Add 1/2 cup softened ice cream; blend until smooth.
- Fold blended peach mixture into the remaining 2 1/2 cups softened ice cream, creating a marble effect. Cover and freeze until firm, 30 minutes to 1 hour.

Nutrition Information

- Calories: 89 calories
- Total Fat: 2.4 g
- Cholesterol: 13 mg
- Sodium: 38 mg
- Total Carbohydrate: 14.4 g
- Protein: 2.4 g

239. Peach Salad with Raspberry Vinaigrette

"Real light and refreshing either as starter or side salad. Easily doubles. I have used Parmesan instead of Asiago cheese. Nuts can be left out. I have also used pecans."

Serving: 4 | Prep: 10 m | Ready in: 10 m

Ingredients

- 1 (10 ounce) package fresh spinach
- 1/2 cup chopped almonds
- 1/3 cup sliced red onion
- 1/4 cup grated Asiago cheese
- 1/2 cup raspberry vinaigrette dressing
- salt and ground black pepper to taste
- 2 fresh peaches, sliced

Direction

- Combine spinach, almonds, onion, and Asiago cheese in a large bowl. Drizzle dressing over salad and season with salt and pepper. Add peaches and toss.

Nutrition Information

- Calories: 169 calories
- Total Fat: 8.2 g
- Cholesterol: 6 mg
- Sodium: 576 mg
- Total Carbohydrate: 19.8 g
- Protein: 6.4 g

240. Peach Salsa

"This sweet but zippy salsa is a great way to use summer fruits and vegetables. Try it on pork or chicken at your next cookout."

Serving: 128 | Prep: 30 m | Cook: 1 h 30 m | Ready in: 2 h

Ingredients

- 20 tomatoes, chopped
- 6 onions, finely chopped
- 5 fresh peaches - peeled, pitted and chopped
- 5 pears - peeled, cored and chopped
- 1 green bell pepper, finely chopped
- 1 red bell pepper, finely chopped
- 4 cups white sugar
- 1 cup distilled white vinegar
- 2 tablespoons salt
- 4 tablespoons pickling spice, wrapped in cheesecloth

Direction

- In a large saucepan, bring to a boil the tomatoes, onions, peaches, pears, green bell pepper, red bell pepper, sugar, vinegar and salt. Reduce heat. Place the pickling spice into the mixture. Stirring frequently, simmer 1 1/2 hours, or until volume is reduced by half.
- Discard spice bag. Transfer the mixture to sterile containers. Store in the refrigerator until use.

Nutrition Information

- Calories: 35 calories
- Total Fat: 0.1 g
- Cholesterol: 0 mg
- Sodium: 110 mg
- Total Carbohydrate: 8.9 g
- Protein: 0.3 g

241. Peach Salsa II

"Make the most of peach season with a few jars of this sweet peach salsa."

Serving: 28 | Prep: 1 h | Cook: 20 m | Ready in: 1 h 35 m

Ingredients

- 4 cups fresh peaches - peeled, pitted and chopped
- 1/2 cup chopped onion
- 1/2 cup chopped red bell pepper
- 4 jalapeno peppers, minced
- 1/4 cup chopped fresh cilantro
- 3 cloves garlic, minced

- 1 1/2 teaspoons ground cumin
- 1/4 cup distilled white vinegar
- 1 teaspoon grated lime zest
- 1/4 cup white sugar
- 1 (49 gram) package light fruit pectin crystals
- 3 1/2 cups white sugar
- canning jars

Direction

- Sterilize jars and lids.
- In a large saucepan, combine peaches, onion, pepper, cilantro, garlic, cumin, vinegar, and lime zest. Stir together pectin and 1/4 cup sugar. Bring to a boil, and stir in remaining 3 1/2 cups sugar. Boil for 1 minute, stirring constantly. Remove from heat, and stir for 5 minutes.
- Pour peach salsa into prepared jars, leaving 1/4 inch air space. Seal, and process in a boiling water bath for 15 minutes.

Nutrition Information

- Calories: 118 calories
- Total Fat: 0.1 g
- Cholesterol: 0 mg
- Sodium: 5 mg
- Total Carbohydrate: 30.2 g
- Protein: 0.1 g

242. Peach Salsa with Cilantro and Lime

"A sweet and tangy side dish that makes a great side dish, garnish, or party treat. The sugar helps a lot to bring out the flavor in the peaches while refrigerating."

Serving: 6 | Prep: 15 m | Ready in: 45 m

Ingredients

- 4 fresh peaches - peeled, pitted, and diced
- 1/4 red onion, finely chopped
- 1 tablespoon chopped fresh cilantro
- 1 lime, juiced

- 1 teaspoon white sugar

Direction

- Mix peaches, onion, and cilantro together in a large bowl; drizzle with lime juice. Sprinkle salsa with sugar; toss to coat. Refrigerate for 30 minutes before serving.

Nutrition Information

- Calories: 23 calories
- Total Fat: 0 g
- Cholesterol: 0 mg
- Sodium: 3 mg
- Total Carbohydrate: 5.7 g
- Protein: 0.1 g

243. Peach Sangria

"I love this homemade sangria that my Grandfather taught me to make when I was young wife. He told me he had learn to make when he was working down in Mexico in his younger days. It is easy but it does takes time to cure between steps. We have had mango sangria, peach-mango sangria, or pear-pineapple sangria. You can garnish with blueberries, mint leaves, or fresh peach slices if you would like."

Serving: 10 | Prep: 20 m | Ready in: 4 h 20 m

Ingredients

- 4 large fresh peaches - peeled, pitted, and sliced
- 1 cup hot water
- 1/2 cup light brown sugar
- 1 pinch ground cinnamon
- 2 1/2 cups dry white wine
- 1/2 cup triple sec liqueur
- 1 (750 milliliter) bottle sparkling white wine, chilled

Direction

- Blend peaches, hot water, brown sugar, and cinnamon in a blender or food processor until smooth. Transfer to a pitcher; stir in dry white wine and triple sec. Cover and chill in refrigerator for at least 4 hours.

- Strain peach mixture through a large cheesecloth-lined sieve; squeeze cloth to remove all the juices. Pour juice into a large pitcher; stir in sparkling white wine.

Nutrition Information

- Calories: 214 calories
- Total Fat: 0 g
- Cholesterol: 0 mg
- Sodium: 14 mg
- Total Carbohydrate: 23.4 g
- Protein: 0.1 g

244. Peach Sangria Rosa

"I am in love with this creation and so are all of my friends! It is the perfect combination of flavors, and the peach adds just the right touch."

Serving: 16 | Prep: 15 m | Ready in: 1 h 15 m

Ingredients

- 1 cup peach flavored syrup
- 4 sliced fresh ripe peaches
- 2/3 cup confectioners' sugar
- 6 cups chilled rose wine
- ice
- 6 cups chilled lemon-lime soda

Direction

- Stir together peach syrup, peaches, and sugar; let sit at room temperature for one hour.
- Pour peaches into large, one-gallon pitcher and stir in the wine. Add ice to glasses and fill about 3/4 full of sangria. Top with the lemon-lime soda. Enjoy!

245. Peach Sauce

"Make this up in advance for sourdough pancakes. I used Celestial Seasonings® tea. Substitute water for tea if you don't have it on hand. Chopped pecans might taste good in this, as well as brandy instead of vanilla."

Serving: 10 | Prep: 10 m | Cook: 15 m | Ready in: 30 m

Ingredients

- 1/2 cup cold peach-flavored tea
- 2 tablespoons cornstarch
- 4 cups diced peaches
- 1/2 cup white sugar
- 1/2 cup brown sugar
- 1/4 teaspoon grated nutmeg
- 2 teaspoons vanilla extract

Direction

- Whisk tea and cornstarch together in a small bowl; transfer to a saucepan. Add peaches; cook, stirring constantly, over medium heat until just boiling, 2 to 3 minutes. Stir in white sugar, brown sugar, and nutmeg; simmer over medium-low heat until sauce is thickened, about 10 minutes. Remove from heat and stir in vanilla extract. Let stand for 5 to 10 minutes to thicken.

Nutrition Information

- Calories: 103 calories
- Total Fat: 0 g
- Cholesterol: 0 mg
- Sodium: 6 mg
- Total Carbohydrate: 25.6 g
- Protein: 0 g

246. Peach Skillet Cake with Sorghum Flour

"You'll need a skillet to capture all the goodness of this dessert. Create the vanilla cake batter using gluten-free sorghum flour, arrange the peach slices on top and bake to a golden brown. A dollop of whipping cream adds to the yum factor."

Serving: 8 | Prep: 15 m | Cook: 30 m | Ready in: 45 m

Ingredients

- 1 1/4 cups gluten-free sorghum all-purpose flour
- 1 teaspoon baking powder
- 1/2 teaspoon baking soda
- 1/4 teaspoon salt
- 4 tablespoons butter, room temperature
- 2/3 cup granulated sugar
- 3 large eggs
- 1 teaspoon vanilla
- 1/3 cup low-fat buttermilk
- 2 fresh peaches, peeled and sliced (may use canned)
- 2 tablespoons cinnamon sugar for topping

Direction

- Preheat oven to 350 degrees F. Prepare a 10-inch, ovenproof skillet with cooking spray.
- Whisk together sorghum flour, baking powder, baking soda and salt. Set aside.
- In separate bowl, beat butter and sugar with a mixer on medium speed until light and fluffy. Add vanilla. Beat in eggs and buttermilk. Add dry ingredients and mix until blended.
- Pour batter into prepared skillet. Place peach slices in spiral fan on top. Sprinkle with cinnamon sugar. Bake until golden brown and a toothpick inserted in the center comes out clean, 30 to 35 minutes.
- The batter bakes up around the peaches. Let cool slightly before serving. Cake can be served as rustic dessert topped with whipped cream sweetened with sorghum syrup or as a breakfast cake.

Nutrition Information

- Calories: 241 calories
- Total Fat: 7.7 g
- Cholesterol: 85 mg
- Sodium: 291 mg
- Total Carbohydrate: 37.7 g
- Protein: 5.3 g

247. Peach Smoothie

"Canned peaches blended with ice cream, soy milk and orange juice."

Serving: 4 | Prep: 1 m | Ready in: 1 m

Ingredients

- 1 (15 ounce) can sliced peaches, drained
- 4 scoops vanilla ice cream
- 2 cups vanilla soy milk
- 1/4 cup orange juice

Direction

- In a blender, combine peaches, ice cream, soy milk and orange juice. Blend until smooth. Pour into glasses and serve.

Nutrition Information

- Calories: 152 calories
- Total Fat: 4.2 g
- Cholesterol: 9 mg
- Sodium: 75 mg
- Total Carbohydrate: 24.8 g
- Protein: 4.8 g

248. Peach Summer Cobbler

"I couldn't find a cobbler recipe that was exactly what I was looking for, so I threw this together. This is my first submitted recipe, so please be kind when ripping it to shreds!"

Serving: 12 | Prep: 30 m | Cook: 45 m | Ready in: 1 h 15 m

Ingredients

- Topping:
- 1 cup all-purpose flour
- 1/2 cup milk
- 1/2 cup butter, melted
- 1/2 cup packed brown sugar
- 1 tablespoon vanilla extract
- 1 teaspoon ground cinnamon
- 1 teaspoon baking powder
- Filling:
- 1/4 cup packed brown sugar
- 4 teaspoons all-purpose flour
- 1 1/2 teaspoons ground cinnamon
- 1 pinch ground allspice
- 3 tablespoons water
- 4 cups peeled and sliced fresh peaches
- 1 pinch white sugar, or more to taste

Direction

- Preheat oven to 350 degrees F (175 degrees C). Butter an 8-inch square baking dish.
- Mix 1 cup flour, milk, melted butter, 1/2 cup brown sugar, vanilla extract, 1 teaspoon cinnamon, and baking powder together in a bowl until batter is combined.
- Combine 1/4 cup brown sugar, 4 teaspoons flour, 1 1/2 teaspoons cinnamon, and allspice together in a bowl; add water and mix. Stir peaches into brown sugar filling. Spoon filling into the prepared baking dish. Spread batter over the filling; top with white sugar.
- Bake in the preheated oven until filling is bubbling and top is golden brown, 45 to 60 minutes.

Nutrition Information

- Calories: 182 calories

- Total Fat: 8 g
- Cholesterol: 21 mg
- Sodium: 105 mg
- Total Carbohydrate: 26 g
- Protein: 1.6 g

249. Peach Tartlets with Apricot Glaze

"This simple 3-ingredient dessert will save the day when you need to whip up something quick but impressive at the last minute. Substitute the peaches with any kind of fresh fruit, such as plums, nectarines, apples, or pears."

Serving: 18 | Prep: 10 m | Cook: 12 m | Ready in: 32 m

Ingredients

- 1 (17.3 ounce) package frozen puff pastry, thawed
- 3/4 cup apricot preserves, divided
- 2 peaches - peeled, pitted, and thinly sliced, or more as needed
- 2 teaspoons hot water, or as needed

Direction

- Preheat oven to 400 degrees F (200 degrees C). Line 2 baking sheets with parchment paper.
- Cut each sheet of puff pastry into nine 3-inch squares. Dab a small amount of apricot preserves into the center of each square. Fan 3 slices of peach over the preserves, leaving a slim border of pastry exposed. Spoon a small amount of apricot preserves over the peach slices.
- Bake in the preheated oven, 1 baking sheet at a time, until puff pastry turns golden, about 10 minutes.
- Thin remaining apricot preserves with 2 teaspoons hot water in a small bowl to make a glaze.
- Spoon some of the glaze over each baked tartlet. Return to the oven and bake until tartlets are golden brown, about 2 minute more. Repeat with second baking sheet. Cool

tartlets on a wire rack before serving, about 10 minutes.

Nutrition Information

- Calories: 185 calories
- Total Fat: 10.4 g
- Cholesterol: 0 mg
- Sodium: 74 mg
- Total Carbohydrate: 21.5 g
- Protein: 2.1 g

250. Peach Tea

"This is a very light peach tea, great for a summer day."

Serving: 10 | Prep: 5 m | Cook: 15 m | Ready in: 20 m

Ingredients

- 3 cups water
- 3 family size tea bags
- 2 fresh peaches - peeled, pitted, and sliced
- 1 cup water
- 1 1/2 teaspoons stevia powder

Direction

- Bring 3 cups water to a boil in a saucepan over high heat. Add the tea bags, and steep for 15 minutes. Remove tea bags.
- Meanwhile, place peaches with 1 cup water into the jar of a blender, and blend until very smooth. Pour the peach mixture, tea, and stevia powder into a 1 gallon pitcher. Fill the pitcher to the top with water, and stir until blended.

Nutrition Information

- Calories: 5 calories
- Total Fat: 0 g
- Cholesterol: 0 mg
- Sodium: < 1 mg
- Total Carbohydrate: 1.6 g
- Protein: 0 g

251. Peach Upside Down Cake I

"This cake uses fresh peaches. Serve with whipped cream."

Serving: 9 | Prep: 20 m | Cook: 35 m | Ready in: 1 h

Ingredients

- 1/4 cup butter
- 1/2 cup packed light brown sugar
- 1/4 teaspoon ground nutmeg
- 5 fresh peaches - peeled, pitted and halved
- 1/2 cup butter, softened
- 1/2 cup white sugar
- 1 egg
- 1 1/4 cups all-purpose flour
- 2 teaspoons baking powder
- 1/2 teaspoon salt
- 1/2 cup milk

Direction

- Preheat oven to 375 degrees F (190 degrees C).
- Melt 1/4 cup butter or margarine in an 8-inch square pan. Sprinkle with brown sugar and nutmeg. Arrange peach halves, cut side down, in pan.
- In a large bowl, cream the butter and sugar until light and fluffy. Beat in egg. Stir together flour, baking powder and salt. Add flour mixture to creamed mixture alternately with milk, beating well after each addition. Spread batter over peaches.
- Bake in preheated oven until lightly browned on top, 35 to 40 minutes. Remove cake from oven, and let stand in pan for 5 minutes; invert onto serving platter.

Nutrition Information

- Calories: 318 calories
- Total Fat: 16.4 g
- Cholesterol: 62 mg
- Sodium: 366 mg
- Total Carbohydrate: 40.7 g
- Protein: 3.1 g

- Cholesterol: 31 mg
- Sodium: 234 mg
- Total Carbohydrate: 41.3 g
- Protein: 2.5 g

252. Peach Upside Down Cake II

"This citrus-flavored cake recipe features a layer of cherries and canned peaches for a delicious spin on the pineapple-flavored classic."

Serving: 10

Ingredients

- 1/4 cup butter, softened
- 1/2 cup packed brown sugar
- 1 1/2 cups sliced canned peaches, drained
- 6 cherries, pitted and halved
- 1/3 cup shortening
- 1/2 cup white sugar
- 1 egg
- 1 1/4 cups cake flour
- 1 1/2 teaspoons baking powder
- 1/2 teaspoon salt
- 1/2 teaspoon orange zest
- 1/2 cup orange juice

Direction

- Spread butter or margarine in bottom of 8 inch round baking dish. Sprinkle with brown sugar and arrange very well drained peaches and halved cherries on top.
- In a large bowl, cream shortening and sugar together thoroughly. Blend in unbeaten egg, and beat well.
- In a separate bowl, sift together flour, baking powder and salt. Add these dry ingredients to creamed mixture alternately with the juice. Stir in orange rind until evenly distributed.
- Bake at 350 degrees F (175 degrees C) for 45 to 50 minutes, or until cake is done. Allow cake to cool 5 to 10 minutes in the pan. Invert over serving plate to remove cake, and allow syrup to drain a minute.

Nutrition Information

- Calories: 279 calories
- Total Fat: 12.2 g

253. Peach UpsideDown Cake III

"Low-fat and delicious. Made with fresh peaches."

Serving: 12 | Prep: 30 m | Cook: 20 m | Ready in: 55 m

Ingredients

- 6 large fresh peaches
- 2/3 cup white sugar
- 2 tablespoons unsalted butter
- 1 cup all-purpose flour
- 1 teaspoon baking powder
- 1/2 teaspoon baking soda
- 1/2 teaspoon ground cinnamon
- 1/4 teaspoon salt
- 1 tablespoon canola oil
- 1 egg
- 1 teaspoon vanilla extract
- 1 teaspoon almond extract
- 1/2 cup low-fat buttermilk

Direction

- Preheat the oven to 375 degrees. Bring a large saucepan of water to a boil.
- Score the stem end of each peach and place the peaches in the boiling water. Boil for about 1 minute, or until the skins soften. Transfer to a bowl of cold water to cool, then peel, halve and pit the peaches.
- In a 9-inch cast-iron skillet, combine 1/3 cup of the sugar with 1 tablespoon of the butter. Cook over medium heat for 3 to 5 minutes, or until the sugar begins to melt. Add the peaches to the skillet, cut-side up, in one layer (the fruit should fit tightly). Remove the pan from the heat and set aside.
- In a medium bowl, combine the flour, baking powder, baking soda, cinnamon and salt; set aside.

- In a large bowl, with an electric mixer at medium speed, beat the remaining 1/3 cup sugar and 1 tablespoon butter with the oil until combined. Add the egg, beating until smooth, then beat in the vanilla and almond extract. With the mixer at low speed, add the buttermilk and the reserved flour mixture, beating until just incorporated.
- Spoon the batter evenly over the peaches in the skillet, place the skillet in the oven and bake, uncovered, at 375 degrees F (190 degrees C), for 20 to 25 minutes, or until a cake tester inserted into the center of the cake comes out clean.
- Transfer the skillet to a wire rack to cool for 3 to 4 minutes. Loosen the edges of the cake with a knife. Invert the cake onto a serving plate. If any of the peaches stick to the skillet, remove them with a knife and replace them on the cake.

Nutrition Information

- Calories: 137 calories
- Total Fat: 3.7 g
- Cholesterol: 21 mg
- Sodium: 161 mg
- Total Carbohydrate: 23.8 g
- Protein: 2 g

---

254. Peach Whirligigs

"My mother-in-law makes this yummy dish every summer when peaches are in season. When my husband and I got married I just had to have the recipe to carry on the tradition! In autumn, replace the peaches with apples and you have a delicious fall dessert as well!"

Serving: 6 | Prep: 20 m | Cook: 25 m | Ready in: 45 m

Ingredients

- 5 large fresh peaches - peeled, pitted, and sliced
- 2 cups water
- 1 1/2 cups white sugar
- 2 tablespoons cornstarch
- 1 1/3 cups buttermilk baking mix
- 2 tablespoons white sugar
- 2 tablespoons margarine, melted
- 1/3 cup milk
- 2 tablespoons margarine, softened
- 1/4 cup white sugar
- 1 teaspoon ground cinnamon

Direction

- Preheat oven to 425 degrees F (220 degrees C).
- In large saucepan over medium heat, combine peaches, water, 1 1/2 cups sugar and cornstarch. Cook, stirring constantly, until mixture boils. Boil for one minute, then reduce heat to low to keep warm.
- In a large bowl, stir together baking mix, 2 tablespoons sugar, melted margarine and milk to form a soft dough. Remove to floured surface and knead 8 to 10 times. Roll out into a 9 inch square.
- Spread softened margarine over dough. Combine 1/4 cup sugar with cinnamon, and sprinkle mixture over dough. Roll dough into a log shape and cut into 6 - 1 1/2 inch slices. Pour hot peach mixture into an 8x8 inch baking dish. Place roll slices, cut side up, on top of peach mixture.
- Bake in preheated oven 20 to 25 minutes, until puffed and golden. Serve warm.

Nutrition Information

- Calories: 459 calories
- Total Fat: 11.4 g
- Cholesterol: 1 mg
- Sodium: 428 mg
- Total Carbohydrate: 89 g
- Protein: 2.5 g

255. Peach Wrinkle

"Delicious with fresh peaches. This recipe has been made for several generations in our family. A favorite for summer. Can also be made with other fruits, but peaches have always been the best!"

Serving: 8 | Prep: 20 m | Cook: 40 m | Ready in: 1 h

Ingredients

- 6 fresh peaches - peeled, pitted, and sliced
- 1/2 cup white sugar
- 1/4 cup butter, softened
- 1 cup white sugar
- 2 eggs
- 1/2 cup milk
- 1 1/2 cups all-purpose flour
- 4 teaspoons baking powder
- 1/4 teaspoon salt

Direction

- Preheat oven to 325 degrees F (165 degrees C). Grease a baking dish.
- Mix peaches with 1/2 cup sugar in a bowl. Arrange in the bottom of the prepared baking dish.
- Beat butter and 1 cup sugar together in a bowl until creamy. Add eggs and milk; stir to combine. Mix flour, baking powder, and salt together in a separate bowl; add to butter mixture. Stir until fully incorporated. Pour batter evenly over peaches.
- Bake in the preheated oven until center is set and bounces back when lightly pressed, 40 to 45 minutes.

Nutrition Information

- Calories: 327 calories
- Total Fat: 7.5 g
- Cholesterol: 63 mg
- Sodium: 384 mg
- Total Carbohydrate: 61.3 g
- Protein: 4.6 g

256. PeachaBerry Pie

"This is a great way to use up fresh peaches that are ripening too fast. The berries add a hint of tart to the sweet peaches. Easy to make and looks great."

Serving: 8 | Prep: 25 m | Cook: 45 m | Ready in: 1 h 25 m

Ingredients

- 4 cups fresh peaches - peeled, pitted, and sliced
- 1 cup fresh raspberries
- 3/4 cup white sugar
- 3 tablespoons all-purpose flour
- 1 teaspoon ground cinnamon
- 2 (9 inch) pie crusts
- 2 tablespoons butter, softened and cut into pieces
- 1 tablespoon coarse granulated sugar

Direction

- Preheat oven to 400 degrees F (200 degrees C).
- Place peaches and berries in a colander for about 15 minutes to drain any excess fluid, then transfer to a large bowl. Gently toss with sugar, flour, and cinnamon. Transfer to a pie crust. Dot with butter, and top with remaining crust. Cut vents in top crust, and sprinkle with coarse sugar.
- Bake 45 minutes in the preheated oven, until crust is golden brown.

Nutrition Information

- Calories: 301 calories
- Total Fat: 13.4 g
- Cholesterol: 8 mg
- Sodium: 228 mg
- Total Carbohydrate: 44.1 g
- Protein: 1.9 g

257. PeachBasil White Sangria

"My inventive twist on a delicious white sangria - perfect for summer! Use any un-oaked white wine, such as Pinot Grigio."

Serving: 6 | Prep: 10 m | Ready in: 10 m

Ingredients

- 1 (750 milliliter) bottle Pinot Grigio
- 1 fresh peach, chopped
- 1/2 cup peach schnapps
- 1/2 cup chopped fresh basil
- 2 tablespoons agave nectar
- ice cubes
- 1 fresh peach, sliced

Direction

- Stir Pinot Grigio, 1 chopped peach, peach schnapps, basil, and agave nectar together in a pitcher; add ice. Pour into glasses and garnish with peach slices.

Nutrition Information

- Calories: 202 calories
- Total Fat: 0.1 g
- Cholesterol: 0 mg
- Sodium: 10 mg
- Total Carbohydrate: 19.5 g
- Protein: 0.2 g

258. Peaches and Cream Cookies

"Basic, fluffy sugar cookie with fresh peaches (made out of desperation because my family had so many peaches from our trees!)."

Serving: 24

Ingredients

- 1 cup shortening
- 1 1/2 cups white sugar
- 2 eggs
- 1 cup fresh peaches, pitted and chopped
- 3 cups all-purpose flour

- 1 teaspoon salt
- 1/2 tablespoon baking soda
- 3/4 cup chopped walnuts

Direction

- Preheat oven to 325 degrees F (165 degrees C). Grease a cookie sheet.
- Beat shortening and sugar together. Blend eggs and fruit into the shortening and sugar mixture. Stir flour, salt, baking soda and nuts into the egg mixture; mix well.
- Drop dough by teaspoonfuls onto the greased cookie sheet. The cookies will double in size while baking, so set the cookies far apart on the cookie sheet. Bake for 12 to 15 minutes.

Nutrition Information

- Calories: 212 calories
- Total Fat: 11.5 g
- Cholesterol: 16 mg
- Sodium: 177 mg
- Total Carbohydrate: 25.3 g
- Protein: 2.7 g

259. Peaches and Cream Pie I

"This pie has a delicious graham cracker crust, cream filling, and fruit on top."

Serving: 8

Ingredients

- 18 cinnamon graham crackers
- 1/8 cup white sugar
- 6 tablespoons butter
- 1/2 (8 ounce) package cream cheese, softened
- 1/2 cup confectioners' sugar
- 1/2 cup frozen whipped topping, thawed
- 1 (3 ounce) package peach flavored Jell-O® mix
- 1 (3 ounce) package non-instant vanilla pudding mix
- 1 1/4 cups water

- 1 (16 ounce) can sliced cling peaches, drained

Direction

- Place graham crackers in a plastic bag, and seal. Using a rolling pin or a hammer, crush into fine crumbs. Combine crumbs and sugar. Stir in melted butter or margarine. Press mixture over bottom and up sides of a 9 inch pie pan.
- Bake at 375 degrees F (190 degrees C) for 6 to 9 minutes, or until edges are brown.
- Beat together cream cheese and sugar in a medium-size bowl until well mixed. Stir in whipped topping. Spread mixture evenly into crust. Arrange fruit in an attractive pattern over the top of pie.
- Stir together gelatin, pudding mix, and water in a medium-size saucepan until smooth. Place over medium-low heat; stir constantly until mixture comes to boil. Let cool 5 minutes. Spoon gelatin mixture over fruit. Refrigerate 4 hours, or until set.

Nutrition Information

- Calories: 337 calories
- Total Fat: 15.4 g
- Cholesterol: 38 mg
- Sodium: 265 mg
- Total Carbohydrate: 48.1 g
- Protein: 3.2 g

260. Peaches and Cream Pie II

"Very good peach-like pie with really good whipped topping on the top. Everyone must try this! Garnish with nuts if desired."

Serving: 24 | Prep: 45 m | Ready in: 1 h 45 m

Ingredients

- 1 1/2 cups all-purpose flour
- 3/4 cup butter, softened
- 3/4 cup chopped pecans
- 1 tablespoon white sugar

- 1 (8 ounce) package cream cheese, softened
- 2 cups frozen whipped topping, thawed
- 1 cup confectioners' sugar
- 1 1/2 cups white sugar
- 4 tablespoons cornstarch
- 3 cups warm water
- 2 (3 ounce) packages peach flavored Jell-O® mix
- 5 fresh peaches - peeled, pitted, and sliced
- 1 (12 ounce) container frozen whipped topping, thawed

Direction

- Preheat oven to 350 degrees F (175 degrees C). Lightly grease a 9x13 inch baking pan.
- In a medium bowl, mix together flour, butter, pecans and 1 tablespoon sugar. Press mixture into bottom of baking pan.
- Bake in preheated oven for 15 minutes. Remove from oven and let cool.
- In a large bowl, beat together cream cheese and confectioners' sugar until smooth. Gently stir in the 2 cups whipped topping. Spread over cooled crust. In a small bowl, stir together the 1 1/2 cups sugar and cornstarch. Pour the sugar mixture into a saucepan and stir in the 3 cups water. Cook over medium heat, stirring frequently until clear and thick. Stir in gelatin and remove from heat.
- Combine the gelatin mixture with the peaches. Spread entire mixture over cream cheese layer. Top with 12 ounce container of whipped topping. Cover and refrigerate for an hour.

Nutrition Information

- Calories: 296 calories
- Total Fat: 14.8 g
- Cholesterol: 26 mg
- Sodium: 96 mg
- Total Carbohydrate: 37.7 g
- Protein: 2.5 g

261. Peaches and Cream Pudding

"Delicious, refreshing, and oh-so-peachy! This summer pudding is a great alternative to banana pudding."

Serving: 6 | Prep: 10 m | Cook: 20 m | Ready in: 2 h 30 m

Ingredients

- 2 peaches, thinly sliced
- 1 pinch ground cinnamon, or more to taste
- 4 cups milk
- 6 egg yolks, beaten
- 1 cup white sugar
- 2/3 cup all-purpose flour
- 1 tablespoon vanilla extract

Direction

- Arrange sliced peaches in the bottom of a serving bowl; sprinkle with cinnamon.
- Combine milk, egg yolks, sugar, and flour together in a saucepan; cook and stir over medium-low heat until pudding thickens and clings to the back of a spoon, about 20 minutes. Remove from heat and stir in vanilla. Pour pudding over prepared peaches. Refrigerate until chilled, about 2 hours.

Nutrition Information

- Calories: 328 calories
- Total Fat: 7.7 g
- Cholesterol: 218 mg
- Sodium: 76 mg
- Total Carbohydrate: 54.5 g
- Protein: 9.5 g

262. Peaches and Cream Wontons

"Fried wontons are filled with a cream cheese and peach filling."

Serving: 24 | Prep: 30 m | Cook: 15 m | Ready in: 55 m

Ingredients

- 1 (8 ounce) package cream cheese, softened
- 1 fresh peach - peeled, pitted, and diced
- 1/4 cup confectioners' sugar
- 1 1/2 teaspoons vanilla extract
- 1 cup vegetable oil for frying, or as needed
- 24 wonton wrappers
- 1/2 cup water

Direction

- Beat cream cheese with an electric mixer on low in a bowl until slightly fluffy. Add peach, confectioners' sugar, and vanilla extract; beat until mixed. Cover bowl with plastic wrap and refrigerate to chill slightly, about 10 minutes.
- Heat vegetable oil in a deep-fryer or large saucepan to 350 degrees F (175 degrees C).
- Place a wonton wrapper on a work surface; spoon about 1 tablespoon cream cheese mixture into the center. Pour water into a small bowl, dip your finger in the water, and swipe all 4 sides of the wrapper. Fold one corner of the wrapper over the filling, forming a triangle shape. Press the edges of the wrapper down to seal all the sides. Repeat with remaining wrappers and filling.
- Fry 4 to 5 wontons at a time in the hot oil until lightly browned, about 3 minutes per side. Remove with a slotted spoon; drain on a paper towel-lined plate. Repeat with remaining wontons.

Nutrition Information

- Calories: 71 calories
- Total Fat: 4.3 g
- Cholesterol: 11 mg
- Sodium: 74 mg
- Total Carbohydrate: 6.5 g
- Protein: 1.5 g

263. Peaches and Pistachios Yogurt Cup

"Sweet and salty come together in this peach and pistachio-flavored yogurt cup."

Serving: 1

Ingredients

- 1 (6 ounce) container Yoplait® Original Yogurt Harvest Peach
- 2 tablespoons diced fresh peaches, divided
- 3 teaspoons shelled roasted pistachio nuts, divided

Direction

- Remove 1 tablespoon yogurt from yogurt container. Stir in 1 tablespoon of the diced peaches and 2 teaspoons of the pistachio nuts. Top with the remaining peaches and pistachios. Enjoy!

Nutrition Information

- Calories: 145 calories
- Total Fat: 4.1 g
- Cholesterol: < 1 mg
- Sodium: 119 mg
- Total Carbohydrate: 19.4 g
- Protein: 6.9 g

264. Peaches and Tequila Sunrise Sauce

"This is a marinade I came up with that I use mostly on pork tenderloin, but is good on steaks, chicken and fish as well."

Serving: 12 | Prep: 10 m | Cook: 15 m | Ready in: 25 m

Ingredients

- 1/2 cup peach preserves
- 1/4 cup Worcestershire sauce
- 1/4 cup apple cider vinegar
- 1 cup orange juice
- 2 (1.5 fluid ounce) jiggers tequila
- 1/4 cup chopped onion
- 1 clove garlic, minced
- salt and pepper to taste

Direction

- In a medium bowl, stir together the peach preserves, Worcestershire sauce, vinegar, orange juice, tequila, onion, garlic, salt and pepper. Use half of the mixture to marinate your meat. Pour the remainder into a saucepan, and bring to a boil. Boil for about 10 minutes, or until thickened. Use as a sauce for your cooked meat.

Nutrition Information

- Calories: 68 calories
- Total Fat: 0 g
- Cholesterol: 0 mg
- Sodium: 56 mg
- Total Carbohydrate: 12.9 g
- Protein: 0.2 g

265. Peaches N Cream Banana Breakfast Smoothie

"This is a lightly tasting smoothie that will fill you up! Perfect breakfast smoothie! Made with instant oatmeal, yogurt and banana."

Serving: 2 | Prep: 5 m | Ready in: 5 m

Ingredients

- 1 1/4 cups milk
- 1/4 cup vanilla yogurt
- 1 banana, broken into chunks
- 1 packet peaches and cream flavor instant oatmeal
- 2 packets granular no-calorie sucralose sweetener (such as Splenda®) (optional)
- 5 ice cubes

Direction

- Place the milk, yogurt, banana, instant oatmeal, sweetener, and ice cubes into a blender. Cover, and puree until smooth. Pour into glasses to serve.

Nutrition Information

- Calories: 223 calories
- Total Fat: 4.8 g
- Cholesterol: 14 mg
- Sodium: 180 mg
- Total Carbohydrate: 39.2 g
- Protein: 8.7 g

266. Peaches n Cream Pie

"A wonderfully, easy pie to make that is good warm or cold, and makes its own crust!"

Serving: 8

Ingredients

- 3/4 cup all-purpose flour
- 1 (3 ounce) package non-instant vanilla pudding mix
- 3 tablespoons butter
- 1 egg
- 1/2 cup milk
- 2 1/2 cups canned sliced peaches, syrup reserved
- 1 (8 ounce) package cream cheese
- 1/2 cup white sugar
- 1 tablespoon white sugar
- 1 teaspoon ground cinnamon

Direction

- Preheat the oven to 350 degrees F (175 degrees C). Drain peaches and reserve the syrup; set aside.
- Combine flour, pudding mix, margarine, egg, and milk; beat well. Pour into a greased 8 or 9 inch pie pan. Arrange drained peaches on top of mixture, just to edges.

- Cream together softened cream cheese, sugar, and 3 tablespoons reserved peach syrup. Spoon mixture carefully on top of peaches, just to edges. Sprinkle sugar and cinnamon on top.
- Bake at 350 degrees F (175 degrees C) for 30 to 35 minutes. Do not over bake.

Nutrition Information

- Calories: 353 calories
- Total Fat: 15.2 g
- Cholesterol: 67 mg
- Sodium: 214 mg
- Total Carbohydrate: 49.6 g
- Protein: 5.3 g

267. Peaches n Creme Smores

"In peach season, we want to eat them constantly. Why not layer them with marshmallow crème and crispy graham crackers for a super summery s'more?"

Serving: 2 | Prep: 5 m | Cook: 3 m | Ready in: 10 m

Ingredients

- 2 HONEY MAID Honey Grahams, broken in half
- 4 tablespoons marshmallow creme
- 1 fresh peach, pitted and thinly sliced

Direction

- Top each of 2 cracker halves with 2 tablespoons marshmallow creme. Top with sliced peaches and remaining cracker. Gently press. Serve immediately.

Nutrition Information

- Calories: 101 calories
- Total Fat: 1.4 g
- Cholesterol: 0 mg
- Sodium: 81 mg
- Total Carbohydrate: 21.8 g
- Protein: 0.9 g

268. Peaches n Mint Juice

"Refreshing combination of juices and herbs. Great for energy levels and your skin!"

Serving: 1 | Prep: 5 m | Ready in: 5 m

Ingredients

- 3 large peaches or nectarines, cubed
- 1 large apple, quartered
- 1 lime
- 2 sprigs fresh mint

Direction

- Juice the peaches, apple, and lime with a juice extractor. Transfer the juice to a blender with the mint leaves. Blend quickly to combine the juice and mint thoroughly.

Nutrition Information

- Calories: 232 calories
- Total Fat: 0.5 g
- Cholesterol: 0 mg
- Sodium: 19 mg
- Total Carbohydrate: 60.8 g
- Protein: 1.3 g

269. Peaches with Burrata Basil and Raspberry Balsamic Syrup

"Juicy peaches snuggle into creamy Burrata cheese, with a sweet/tart balsamic reduction drizzled over the top. Bright fresh basil and flakes of crunchy sea salt finish off this easy, impressive summertime appetizer."

Serving: 4 | Prep: 10 m | Cook: 5 m | Ready in: 15 m

Ingredients

- 1 (4 ounce) ball Burrata cheese, at room temperature
- 1 peach, sliced
- 1 tablespoon thinly sliced fresh basil leaves
- 2 tablespoons extra-virgin olive oil
- 3 tablespoons raspberry balsamic vinegar
- flaked sea salt
- freshly ground black pepper (optional)

Direction

- Gently tear open the Burrata cheese to expose the soft, creamy core and place it in the middle of a plate. Arrange peach slices in and around the cheese. Sprinkle basil leaves over cheese and top with olive oil.
- Bring raspberry balsamic vinegar to a boil in a small saucepan; reduce heat to medium-low and simmer until vinegar reduces to a thick syrup, about 5 minutes. Spoon balsamic syrup over peaches and cheese; season with sea salt and black pepper.

Nutrition Information

- Calories: 159 calories
- Total Fat: 12.8 g
- Cholesterol: 20 mg
- Sodium: 176 mg
- Total Carbohydrate: 3.9 g
- Protein: 4.1 g

270. PeachMangoHabanero Wing Sauce

"Delicious peach-mango habanero sauce for your chicken wings. Sweet and spicy. These guys bite back!"

Serving: 16 | Prep: 10 m | Cook: 10 m | Ready in: 20 m

Ingredients

- 1 large mango, peeled and pitted
- 1 small fresh peach, halved and pitted
- 2 habanero peppers, stemmed
- 1/4 cup unsalted butter
- 4 cloves garlic, minced
- 1/2 cup brown sugar
- 2 teaspoons Worcestershire sauce
- 1 teaspoon minced fresh ginger root
- salt and ground black pepper to taste

Direction

- Blend mango, peach, and habanero peppers in a food processor or blender until smooth.
- Melt butter in a saucepan over medium heat; cook and stir garlic until fragrant, about 1 minute. Add mango mixture, brown sugar, Worcestershire sauce, ginger, salt, and pepper; reduce heat to low and simmer until sauce is smooth and slightly thickened, about 8 minutes.

Nutrition Information

- Calories: 57 calories
- Total Fat: 2.9 g
- Cholesterol: 8 mg
- Sodium: 9 mg
- Total Carbohydrate: 8.2 g
- Protein: 0.2 g

271. Peachy Baked Pancake

"A great alternative to the everyday pancake. This recipe calls for sliced peaches, but any fruit can be substituted. Try bananas and chocolate chips for a special treat."

Serving: 4 | Prep: 10 m | Cook: 30 m | Ready in: 40 m

Ingredients

- 3 tablespoons margarine
- 3 eggs
- 1 cup all-purpose flour
- 1 cup milk
- 1 peach, sliced
- 1/4 cup white sugar, or to taste

Direction

- Preheat oven to 350 degrees F (175 degrees C).
- Put margarine in a pie dish and melt in the preheating oven.
- Mix eggs, flour, and milk in a bowl; pour over melted butter. Arrange peach slices atop the egg mixture. Sprinkle sugar over the peach slices.

- Bake in preheated oven until the pancake is firm in the center, about 30 minutes.

Nutrition Information

- Calories: 317 calories
- Total Fat: 12.7 g
- Cholesterol: 128 mg
- Sodium: 166 mg
- Total Carbohydrate: 41 g
- Protein: 9.5 g

272. Peachy Bread Pudding with Caramel Sauce

"This rich and creamy bread pudding is a truly decadent and comforting dessert."

Serving: 10 | Prep: 15 m | Cook: 1 h 10 m | Ready in: 1 h 35 m

Ingredients

- 2 cups fresh peaches - peeled, pitted and halved
- 1 (14 ounce) can sweetened condensed milk
- 3 eggs, lightly beaten
- 1 1/4 cups hot water
- 1/4 cup butter, melted
- 1 teaspoon ground cinnamon
- 1 teaspoon vanilla extract
- 4 cups French bread, torn into small pieces
- CARAMEL SAUCE
- 1/2 cup brown sugar
- 1/2 cup butter
- 2 tablespoons light corn syrup
- 1 tablespoon rum

Direction

- Preheat an oven to 325 degrees F (165 degrees C). Grease a 9x13-inch baking dish.
- Chop the peaches and lightly mash them in a mixing bowl. Combine the sweetened condensed milk and the eggs; add them to the peaches and mix well. Stir in the hot water,

melted butter, cinnamon, and vanilla. Stir the French bread into to the custard mixture until the bread is completely moistened. Turn the pudding into the prepared baking dish.

- Bake until a knife inserted in the center of the pudding comes out clean, about 1 hour and 10 minutes.
- While the pudding is baking, combine the brown sugar, 1/2 cup butter, corn syrup, and rum in a saucepan. Bring to a boil over medium heat and simmer for 3 to 4 minutes or until just slightly thickened. Let cool slightly.
- Remove the pudding from the oven and let it cool for about ten minutes before serving. Serve warm with the caramel sauce. Cool and cover any leftover pudding and store it in the refrigerator.

Nutrition Information

- Calories: 456 calories
- Total Fat: 19.5 g
- Cholesterol: 106 mg
- Sodium: 449 mg
- Total Carbohydrate: 60.9 g
- Protein: 10.1 g

273. Peachy Broccoli Chicken

"This is a great recipe. It's delicious and a whole meal in one serving!"

Serving: 4 | Prep: 15 m | Cook: 40 m | Ready in: 55 m

Ingredients

- 1 cup uncooked long grain white rice
- 2 cups water
- 1 tablespoon vegetable oil
- 2 skinless, boneless chicken breast halves
- salt and pepper to taste
- 1 (15 ounce) can peaches in light syrup, diced, syrup reserved
- 1 (10 ounce) package frozen broccoli florets
- 2 tablespoons boiling water

Direction

- In a pot, bring the rice and water to a boil. Cover, reduce heat to low, and simmer 20 minutes.
- Heat the oil in a skillet over medium heat, and cook the chicken 8 minutes on each side, or until juices run clear. Season with salt and pepper. Remove from skillet, and cut into bite-size pieces.
- Place the peaches and syrup in the skillet, and cook 15 minutes, until syrup is reduced by about 1/2 and thickened.
- Place the broccoli and water in a microwave-safe dish, cover, and cook 5 minutes on High in the microwave, or until tender.
- Return the chicken to the skillet with the peaches. Mix in the broccoli, and continue cooking 5 minutes, until heated through and coated with the syrup. Serve over the cooked rice.

Nutrition Information

- Calories: 360 calories
- Total Fat: 5.9 g
- Cholesterol: 36 mg
- Sodium: 55 mg
- Total Carbohydrate: 58.2 g
- Protein: 19.4 g

274. Peachy Cake

"An extremely light and easy to make cake that is topped with fresh peach slices. The perfect ending to a summer meal!"

Serving: 10 | Prep: 20 m | Cook: 45 m | Ready in: 1 h 5 m

Ingredients

- 1 1/4 cups all-purpose flour
- 2 tablespoons cornmeal
- 2 teaspoons baking powder
- 1/8 teaspoon salt
- 2 eggs

- 1/3 cup light brown sugar
- 2/3 cup milk
- 1 tablespoon butter, melted
- 3 tablespoons light brown sugar
- 4 fresh peaches - peeled, pitted, and sliced

Direction

- Preheat oven to 350 degrees F (175 degrees C). Grease and flour a 10 inch springform pan. Combine the flour, cornmeal, baking powder and salt. Set aside.
- In a medium bowl, beat eggs and 1/3 cup brown sugar. Stir in the flour mixture, mixing just until combined. Gradually beat in the milk. Set aside.
- Pour batter into prepared pan. Arrange peach slices on top of batter. Drizzle with melted butter and sprinkle with 3 tablespoons brown sugar.
- Pour batter into prepared pan. Bake in the preheated oven for 45 minutes, or until a toothpick inserted into the center of the cake comes out clean. Allow to cool 5 minutes in the pan before removing.

Nutrition Information

- Calories: 149 calories
- Total Fat: 2.7 g
- Cholesterol: 42 mg
- Sodium: 135 mg
- Total Carbohydrate: 27.9 g
- Protein: 3.6 g

275. Peachy Chicken

"This quick and easy recipe was passed on to me by my Grandma when I moved away from home. It makes a nice meal for family or guests served alongside steamed rice and a tossed salad. Kids love the peachy, creamy sauce!"

Serving: 7

Ingredients

- 6 pounds skinless, boneless chicken breast halves
- 3/4 cup all-purpose flour
- 2 teaspoons salt
- 1/2 teaspoon ground black pepper
- 1 1/2 teaspoons paprika
- 2 tablespoons vegetable oil
- 1 cup blanched slivered almonds
- 1 1/4 cups water
- 1 (10.75 ounce) can beef consomme
- 2 tablespoons ketchup
- 1 cup reduced fat sour cream
- 1 (15 ounce) can sliced peaches
- 1/2 cup grated Parmesan cheese

Direction

- Combine the flour, salt, pepper, and paprika in a shallow dish. Dredge chicken pieces. Set flour mixture aside.
- In a skillet, heat oil over medium heat, and brown chicken pieces. Transfer browned chicken pieces to an oiled baking dish. Set aside.
- Add the almonds to the skillet, and stir over medium heat until golden. Stir in the remaining flour mixture, and add the water, beef consume and ketchup. Cook until thick and bubbly. Remove from heat, and stir in the sour cream. Pour sauce over chicken. Cover.
- Bake at 350 degrees F (175 degrees C) for 40 minutes. Remove from oven, and top with drained peach slices. Sprinkle with Parmesan cheese. Return to oven. Bake uncovered for 20 minutes more, until cheese is brown and chicken is done.

Nutrition Information

- Calories: 729 calories
- Total Fat: 22.8 g
- Cholesterol: 244 mg
- Sodium: 1094 mg
- Total Carbohydrate: 26 g
- Protein: 98.6 g

276. Peachy Chicken Picante

"This is a quick and easy recipe to prepare, made with what everyone has on hand in the kitchen, and is delicious! (Note: When I am in a real hurry, I julienne the chicken and add all of the ingredients all at once into the skillet until the chicken is cooked through; then serve over rice.)"

Serving: 4 | Prep: 15 m | Cook: 25 m | Ready in: 40 m

Ingredients

- 1 (15 ounce) can sliced peaches
- 4 skinless, boneless chicken breast halves
- 1 tablespoon olive oil
- 1/2 cup red bell pepper, diced
- 1/2 cup chunky salsa
- 1 tablespoon frozen orange juice concentrate, thawed
- salt and pepper to taste

Direction

- Drain peaches, reserving liquid, and set aside.
- Season chicken with salt and pepper to taste. In a large skillet, heat oil over medium heat. Add chicken and sauté for 9 to 10 minutes, turning once, until chicken is no longer pink in center. Remove chicken from skillet.
- Add bell pepper to skillet, reduce heat and sauté for 2 minutes, stirring, until pepper is crisp and tender. Add the reserved peach liquid, salsa and orange juice to the skillet and bring all to a boil, scraping up browned bits from the bottom of the skillet. Add the peaches and stir until hot. Add the chicken. Spoon sauce and peaches over chicken until it is coated/glazed, then serve.

Nutrition Information

- Calories: 266 calories
- Total Fat: 7.2 g
- Cholesterol: 72 mg
- Sodium: 274 mg
- Total Carbohydrate: 21.1 g
- Protein: 27.2 g

277. Peachy Ginger Soup

"A zippy peach soup that is perfect for a hot summer evening. For a spicier soup, use fresh ginger root."

Serving: 6 | Prep: 30 m | Ready in: 30 m

Ingredients

- 3 1/2 pounds fresh peaches - peeled, pitted and chopped
- 1 teaspoon ground ginger
- 1 1/3 cups heavy cream
- 2 tablespoons rum

Direction

- Puree the peaches and ginger together in a food processor or blender. Stir in heavy cream and rum. Chill. Serve cold.

Nutrition Information

- Calories: 245 calories
- Total Fat: 19.6 g
- Cholesterol: 72 mg
- Sodium: 28 mg
- Total Carbohydrate: 13.9 g
- Protein: 1.2 g

278. Peachy Keen Smoothie

"I invented this recipe when I started running out of smoothie components. I think it tastes like a cross between peaches and cream, and egg nog (there are no eggs in it though). The oats and/or wheat germ can be omitted for a smoother smoothie. If using frozen peaches, omit the ice cubes."

Serving: 2 | Prep: 10 m | Ready in: 10 m

Ingredients

- 1 cup sliced peaches
- 4 cubes ice (optional)
- 1/4 teaspoon ground nutmeg
- 1/2 teaspoon vanilla extract
- 1/2 teaspoon honey
- 2 teaspoons wheat germ

- 1 tablespoon rolled oats
- 1 cup vanilla soy milk

Direction

- Place the peaches, ice, nutmeg, vanilla extract, honey, wheat germ, oats, and soy milk into a blender. Cover, and puree until smooth. Pour into glasses to serve.

Nutrition Information

- Calories: 111 calories
- Total Fat: 2.7 g
- Cholesterol: 0 mg
- Sodium: 66 mg
- Total Carbohydrate: 16.4 g
- Protein: 4.9 g

279. Peachy Korean BBQ Salad

"This main course salad features grilled slices of pork loin, mixed greens, sugar snap peas, fresh peaches, cashews all tossed in an Asian sesame and ginger vinaigrette."

Serving: 6 | Prep: 15 m | Cook: 25 m | Ready in: 40 m

Ingredients

- 1 Smithfield® Mesquite Seasoned Loin Filet
- 2 fresh ripe peaches
- 1 (7 ounce) package mixed salad greens
- 1 1/2 cups sugar snap peas
- 1 cup cashews
- 1 red onion, thinly sliced
- 2 tablespoons Wish-Bone Light® Asian with Sesame Ginger vinaigrette

Direction

- Heat charcoal or gas grill to medium.
- Grill loin filet about 25 minutes, turning occasionally, until internal temperature reaches 150 degrees F. Cool slightly and thinly slice.
- Slice peaches and onion, set aside.

- To make salad, layer salad greens, peas, onion, peaches and sliced filet in large bowl. Garnish with cashews. Serve with Asian sesame vinaigrette.

Nutrition Information

- Calories: 403 calories
- Total Fat: 29.8 g
- Cholesterol: 63 mg
- Sodium: 264 mg
- Total Carbohydrate: 16.8 g
- Protein: 17.8 g

280. Peachy Mango Cucumber Tea Smoothie

"Peach and mango give this smoothie its delicate color, while cucumber lightens up the texture. A touch of yogurt and ginger gives it a palate-pleasing finish."

Serving: 2 | Prep: 10 m | Ready in: 10 m

Ingredients

- 1 cup brewed black tea (such as Gold Peak®), chilled
- 1 cup frozen peach slices
- 1 cup mango chunks
- 1 cup peeled and chopped cucumber
- 1/2 cup plain Greek yogurt
- 1 teaspoon grated fresh ginger
- 1 teaspoon honey (optional)

Direction

- Combine tea, peach, mango, cucumber, yogurt, ginger, and honey in a blender. Blend until smooth.

Nutrition Information

- Calories: 156 calories
- Total Fat: 5.3 g
- Cholesterol: 11 mg
- Sodium: 42 mg
- Total Carbohydrate: 25.2 g

- Protein: 3.8 g

281. Peachy Oatmeal

"Bring the taste of peach crisp to your morning bowl of cereal!"

Serving: 1 | Prep: 5 m | Cook: 3 m | Ready in: 8 m

Ingredients

- 1/2 (15 ounce) can sliced peaches, drained
- 1/2 cup water
- 1/2 cup milk
- 1/2 cup quick-cooking oats
- 2 tablespoons packed brown sugar
- 1/4 teaspoon ground cinnamon, or more to taste
- 1 pinch salt

Direction

- Stir peaches, water, milk, oats, brown sugar, cinnamon, and salt together in a microwave-safe bowl.
- Cook in microwave on High, stirring every 60 seconds, until the oats are softened, about 3 minutes. Stir one final time before serving.

Nutrition Information

- Calories: 411 calories
- Total Fat: 5.1 g
- Cholesterol: 10 mg
- Sodium: 72 mg
- Total Carbohydrate: 84.5 g
- Protein: 10.7 g

282. Peachy Pork Chops

"This recipe is good and easy, two things that definitely work for me! This is wonderful served with wild rice."

Serving: 4

Ingredients

- 4 (1 1/4 inch) thick pork chops
- salt and pepper to taste
- 1 tablespoon vegetable oil
- 1 (29 ounce) can sliced peaches, drained and syrup reserved
- 3 tablespoons brown sugar
- 1 teaspoon ground ginger

Direction

- Heat oil in a large skillet over medium heat. Trim all visible fat from chops and season with salt and pepper to taste. Brown chops in vegetable oil.
- Combine reserved peach syrup, brown sugar and ginger. Pour over chops and bring to a boil. Add peaches and cook, uncovered for 15 to 20 minutes or until liquid is reduced to half and thick. Turn chops occasionally to insure even cooking. Serve!

Nutrition Information

- Calories: 388 calories
- Total Fat: 9.4 g
- Cholesterol: 69 mg
- Sodium: 93 mg
- Total Carbohydrate: 48.4 g
- Protein: 26.4 g

283. Peachy Rye Julep

"Crushed ice, and plenty of it, is key to the julep and other smashes. It's what, in pre-freezer days, made this cocktail style seem so very indulgent."

Serving: 1 | Prep: 5 m | Ready in: 5 m

Ingredients

- 2 slices fresh peach, plus more for garnish
- 4 sprigs fresh mint, plus more for garnish
- 2 teaspoons turbinado sugar
- 1 1/2 fluid ounces rye whiskey
- 2 dashes bitters (such as Angostura®)
- 1 1/2 cups crushed ice

Direction

- In a silver julep cup or old-fashioned glass, muddle peach, mint, and sugar until peach is well smashed and sugar is dissolved. Add rye whiskey, bitters, and 1 cup crushed ice. Stir until well chilled. Mound glass with remaining 1/2 cup ice. Garnish with additional mint and a peach slice.

Nutrition Information

- Calories: 153 calories
- Total Fat: 0.1 g
- Cholesterol: 0 mg
- Sodium: 9 mg
- Total Carbohydrate: 11.3 g
- Protein: 0.4 g

284. Peachy Turkey Burger over Greens with Endive Bacon Avocado and Gorgonzola

"A delicious bun-less grilled turkey burger infused with summer peaches, jalapeno, and onions and served over mixed greens with endive, bacon, avocado, gorgonzola, and some more peaches. I created this recipe for my blog, Celiac and Allergy Friendly Epicurean by Jackie Ourman, however, it is a fantastic meal for all and does not need to be made gluten free. You can just use regular soy and teriyaki sauces. Toss salad with mustard vinaigrette if you like."

Serving: 4 | Prep: 30 m | Cook: 20 m | Ready in: 50 m

Ingredients

- 1 tablespoon canola oil
- 1/2 red onion, chopped
- 1/2 jalapeno pepper, seeded and minced
- 2 cloves garlic, minced
- 1 pound ground turkey
- 1 tablespoon gluten-free teriyaki sauce (such as Kikkoman®)
- 1 tablespoon tamari (gluten-free soy sauce)
- 1 peach, halved, divided
- salt and ground black pepper to taste
- 1 head endive, chopped
- 1 (5 ounce) bag spring mix lettuce
- 1 firm ripe avocado, cubed
- 1/4 cup crumbled Gorgonzola cheese
- 4 bacon strips, cooked and chopped

Direction

- Heat canola oil in a skillet over medium heat; add onion, jalapeno, and garlic. Cook until onions are translucent, 10 to 12 minutes. Cool to room temperature, about 15 minutes.
- Mix the onion mixture, ground turkey, teriyaki sauce, and soy sauce together in a bowl using a fork. Chop half the peach and mix gently into the bowl with the turkey mixture. Season with salt and pepper. Form into 4 patties.
- Preheat grill for medium heat and lightly oil the grate.
- Cook turkey burgers on the preheated grill until no longer pink in the center and the

juices run clear, about 4 minutes per side. An instant-read thermometer inserted into the center should read at least 165 degrees F (74 degrees C).

- Combine endive and spring mix in a bowl. Top with avocado, Gorgonzola cheese, and bacon. Serve alongside turkey burgers.

Nutrition Information

- Calories: 391 calories
- Total Fat: 24.8 g
- Cholesterol: 100 mg
- Sodium: 798 mg
- Total Carbohydrate: 14.1 g
- Protein: 30.8 g

285. Pennys Smoothie

"Banana, blueberries and peaches blended with yogurt and fruit syrup. Use any flavor of syrup to taste. My kids like to freeze this for ice pops."

Serving: 3 | Prep: 10 m | Ready in: 10 m

Ingredients

- 1 banana
- 1/4 cup frozen blueberries
- 3/4 cup frozen peach slices
- 1/4 cup yogurt
- 2 tablespoons all fruit blueberry syrup
- 1/8 cup rice milk

Direction

- In a blender, combine banana, frozen blueberries, frozen peach slices, yogurt and syrup. Blend until smooth. Add rice milk and blend to desired consistency. Pour into glasses and serve.

Nutrition Information

- Calories: 139 calories
- Total Fat: 0.7 g
- Cholesterol: 1 mg

- Sodium: 24 mg
- Total Carbohydrate: 33.1 g
- Protein: 2.1 g

286. Perfect Individual Peach Cobblers

"This yummy peach cobbler was developed by my mom and me one night after dinner. It hits the spot if you are having a sweet craving, but it isn't super high in calories. This recipe will work in a 9x11-inch glass baking dish as well. Add a bit of ice cream if desired and enjoy!"

Serving: 8 | Prep: 15 m | Cook: 10 m | Ready in: 45 m

Ingredients

- 8 cups diced fresh peaches
- 1/2 cup water
- 1/2 cup white sugar
- 1 pinch ground cinnamon
- 1 pinch ground nutmeg
- 2 tablespoons butter, cut into small pieces
- 1 (8 ounce) can refrigerated reduced-fat crescent roll dough
- 1 tablespoon water, or as needed
- 1 teaspoon brown sugar, or to taste

Direction

- Preheat oven to 375 degrees F (190 degrees C).
- Place 1 cup peaches into 8 individual ramekins. Mix 1/2 cup water and white sugar together in a bowl; stir until sugar is dissolved. Evenly divide sugar mixture over peaches. Sprinkle peaches with cinnamon and nutmeg. Dot about 3/4 teaspoon butter onto each serving of peaches.
- Unroll and separate crescent roll dough; completely cover peaches in each ramekin with 1 piece of dough. Cut small slits into each roll for ventilation during baking. Lightly brush each roll with water and sprinkle each with about 1/8 teaspoon brown sugar. Arrange ramekins onto a baking sheet.

- Bake in the preheated oven until cobblers are browned, 11 to 13 minutes. Allow cobblers to cool for 20 minutes before serving.

Nutrition Information

- Calories: 211 calories
- Total Fat: 7.5 g
- Cholesterol: 8 mg
- Sodium: 260 mg
- Total Carbohydrate: 33.2 g
- Protein: 2.1 g

287. Perfect Peach Smoothie

"This delightfully light smoothie makes for the perfect start to a summer day."

Serving: 1 | Prep: 5 m | Ready in: 5 m

Ingredients

- 1 large peach, sliced and frozen
- 1 banana, cut into pieces and frozen
- 1/2 cup orange juice
- 1/2 cup soy milk
- 1 tablespoon ground flax seed (optional)

Direction

- Blend peach, banana, orange juice, soy milk, and flax seed in a blender until smooth.

Nutrition Information

- Calories: 297 calories
- Total Fat: 5.7 g
- Cholesterol: 0 mg
- Sodium: 72 mg
- Total Carbohydrate: 57.5 g
- Protein: 7.4 g

288. Pickled Peaches

"These peaches are very different and very yummy. We had a bumper crop of peaches one year and I remember my grandmother making these. We ate them for months and I still love them."

Serving: 32

Ingredients

- 4 cups sugar
- 2 cups white vinegar
- 4 (3 inch) cinnamon sticks
- 15 whole cloves
- 4 pounds fresh peaches - peeled, pitted, and sliced

Direction

- Pour sugar and vinegar into a large saucepan, and stir to dissolve sugar. Add cinnamon sticks and cloves, and bring to a boil. Cover and boil for about 5 minutes. Strain out the cloves and cinnamon sticks, or you can leave them in for a stronger flavor.
- Pack peaches into hot sterile 1 pint jars to within 1 inch of the rim. Fill each jar with syrup to within 1/2 inch from the top. Wipe rims with a clean dry cloth, and seal with new lids and screwbands. Process in a hot water bath for 10 minutes.

Nutrition Information

- Calories: 110 calories
- Total Fat: 0 g
- Cholesterol: 0 mg
- Sodium: 3 mg
- Total Carbohydrate: 28.3 g
- Protein: 0.1 g

289. Pierced Fuzzy Navel

"Actually stumbled across this when making Fuzzy Navels. It was a suggested recipe. Thought it might be good to share...interesting. Great party drink. Scales well."

Serving: 1 | Prep: 5 m | Ready in: 5 m

Ingredients

- 1 fluid ounce peach schnapps
- 1 fluid ounce vodka
- 3 fluid ounces orange juice
- 1 dash grenadine (optional)
- ice cubes

Direction

- Pour the peach schnapps, vodka, orange juice into a shaker with ice. Shake, then strain into a glass. Top with a splash of grenadine if you like.

290. Plum Peach Chicken

"My son is in the stage where he is eating adult food, but only chicken and starches. I came up with this delicious recipe to help get some more fruit in him!"

Serving: 3 | Prep: 20 m | Cook: 50 m | Ready in: 1 h 10 m

Ingredients

- 3 plums, pitted and roughly chopped
- 1 peach, pitted and roughly chopped
- 1/4 cup mixed fruit and vegetable juice drink (such as Juicy Juice Harvest Surprise®)
- 1 pinch crushed red pepper flakes, or to taste
- 1 pinch ground paprika, or to taste
- 1 pinch ground cinnamon, or to taste
- 3 skinless, boneless chicken breast halves
- salt and ground black pepper to taste
- 1 plum, pitted and chopped
- 1 peach, pitted and chopped

Direction

- Preheat oven to 375 degrees F (190 degrees C). Spray a 9x9-inch baking dish with cooking spray.
- Place 3 plums and 1 peach into the work bowl of a food processor with the juice drink, red pepper flakes, paprika, and cinnamon; process until smooth. Sprinkle the chicken on both sides with salt and pepper; place into the prepared baking dish. Pour about 3/4 of the fruit sauce over the chicken. Set the remaining sauce aside.
- Bake the chicken in the preheated oven until the sauce has thickened and baked onto the meat, the chicken is no longer pink inside, and the juices run clear, about 50 minutes. An instant-read thermometer inserted into the center should read at least 165 degrees F (74 degrees C).
- Place each chicken breast on a plate and spoon the reserved fruit sauce over the chicken. Place 1 chopped plum and 1 chopped peach into a bowl, and mix the fruit together; garnish each chicken breast with 1/3 of the chopped fruit.

Nutrition Information

- Calories: 195 calories
- Total Fat: 3.1 g
- Cholesterol: 67 mg
- Sodium: 66 mg
- Total Carbohydrate: 16 g
- Protein: 25.2 g

291. Pluma Moos

"Pluma Moos is a traditional Mennonite festive fruit soup served warm as a side dish or dessert on Christmas eve and morning by many families in Canada. Traditionally dried fruit was used but our family recipe calls for canned fruit."

Serving: 12 | Prep: 10 m | Cook: 2 h | Ready in: 2 h 10 m

Ingredients

- 1 (29 ounce) can peaches in light syrup

- 1 (29 ounce) can pears in light syrup
- 1 (16.5 ounce) can pitted dark sweet cherries in heavy syrup
- 1/2 cup dried pitted prunes
- 1/2 cup raisins
- 2 mandarin orange peels
- 2 cinnamon sticks

Direction

- Pour peaches, pears, cherries, and all syrups from the canned fruit into a large pot. Stir in prunes, raisins, mandarin orange peels, and cinnamon sticks; bring to a boil. Reduce heat to low and simmer until slightly thick, about 2 hours.
- Serve warm. Remove orange peels and cinnamon sticks before serving.

Nutrition Information

- Calories: 153 calories
- Total Fat: 0.1 g
- Cholesterol: 0 mg
- Sodium: 11 mg
- Total Carbohydrate: 40 g
- Protein: 1.1 g

292. Polynesian Peach Chicken

"This is a delicious, fairly quick, attractive main dish. Serve over rice."

Serving: 6 | Prep: 20 m | Cook: 1 h 5 m | Ready in: 1 h 25 m

Ingredients

- 1/2 cup all-purpose flour
- 1/2 teaspoon salt
- 1/4 teaspoon ground black pepper
- 3 pounds bone-in chicken pieces
- 1/4 cup corn oil
- 1 1/2 cups water
- 1 onion, chopped
- 1 green bell pepper, cut into strips
- 1 (15 ounce) can peach halves, liquid reserved
- 1 tablespoon soy sauce

- 3 tablespoons distilled white vinegar
- 1 tablespoon cornstarch
- 4 tomatoes, chopped (optional)
- salt and black pepper to taste

Direction

- Combine the flour in a plastic bag with 1/2 teaspoon salt and 1/4 teaspoon black pepper. Add the chicken pieces, and toss to coat evenly with flour. Heat the corn oil in a Dutch oven over medium heat. Shake the excess flour from the chicken pieces, and place into the hot oil. Cook until browned on all sides turning occasionally, about 15 minutes. Pour in the water, cover, and reduce the heat to medium-low. Cook 30 minutes.
- After 30 minutes, stir in the onion and green bell pepper. Cook and stir until the chicken is no longer pink at the bone, and the onion is tender, about 10 minutes. Pour 2 tablespoons of the reserved peach juice into a small bowl, and set aside. Pour the remaining peach juice into the pot along with the soy sauce and vinegar; bring to a boil over medium-high heat. Dissolve the cornstarch in the reserved peach juice, and stir into the boiling sauce. Cook and stir until the sauce thickens and is no longer cloudy, about 1 minute. Stir in the peach halves and chopped tomatoes. Cook and stir until the peaches are hot and the tomatoes are beginning to fall apart, about 5 minutes. Season to taste with salt and pepper before serving.

Nutrition Information

- Calories: 478 calories
- Total Fat: 26.7 g
- Cholesterol: 97 mg
- Sodium: 449 mg
- Total Carbohydrate: 25.8 g
- Protein: 33.8 g

293. Pork Chops with a Riesling Peach Sauce

"Boneless pork chops are covered with peaches cooked in white wine."

Serving: 4 | Prep: 10 m | Cook: 30 m | Ready in: 40 m

Ingredients

- 1 tablespoon olive oil
- salt and black pepper to taste
- 4 boneless pork chops
- 1 cup Riesling wine
- 3 under ripe peaches, pitted, and cut into 12 wedges each
- 1 teaspoon ground cinnamon
- 1/4 teaspoon ground nutmeg
- 1 tablespoon brown sugar

Direction

- Preheat an oven to 350 degrees F (175 degrees C). Cover a baking sheet with aluminum foil.
- Heat the olive oil in a large skillet over medium-high heat. Season the pork chops with salt and pepper. Brown the pork chops in the hot oil until golden brown on both sides, about 3 minutes per side. Place the pork chops on the prepared baking sheet and bake in the preheated oven until the pork is no longer pink in the center, about 20 minutes. An instant-read thermometer inserted into the center should read 145 degrees F (63 degrees C).
- While the pork chops are baking, pour the Riesling wine into the skillet, and bring to a simmer, using a wooden spoon to scrape up all of the browned bits of pork. Simmer until the wine has reduced to half its original volume then add the peaches and sprinkle in the cinnamon, nutmeg, and brown sugar. Reduce the heat to medium, and cook until the peaches are tender but not mushy, about 15 minutes. Spoon the peach sauce over the pork chops to serve.

Nutrition Information

- Calories: 214 calories

- Total Fat: 7.7 g
- Cholesterol: 36 mg
- Sodium: 28 mg
- Total Carbohydrate: 10 g
- Protein: 14.4 g

294. Pork with Peaches StirFry

"A yummy stir-fry that's quick and easy to make, this one's sure to impress! Pork, vegetables, and peaches are stir-fried over high heat to produce a dish that can be served with either noodles or steamed rice. You can replace the broccoli with snow peas or baby corn. Be sure to get peaches packed in juice."

Serving: 4 | Prep: 30 m | Cook: 20 m | Ready in: 4 h 50 m

Ingredients

- 1/4 cup lemon juice
- 1/4 cup soy sauce
- 1/2 teaspoon ground ginger
- 1/2 teaspoon garlic powder
- 1 pound cubed pork meat
- 2 teaspoons peanut oil, or sesame oil
- 1 large onion, diced
- 1 large carrot, sliced
- 1 cup broccoli florets
- 1 (15 ounce) can sliced peaches, with juice
- 1 tablespoon all-purpose flour

Direction

- In a glass bowl or casserole dish, combine the lemon juice, soy sauce, ground ginger, and garlic powder. Place the pork into the dish, cover and refrigerate for several hours or overnight.
- Heat the oil in a wok over medium-high heat. Add the pork, marinade and onion, and cook stirring constantly until the meat is cooked through. Throw in the carrot and broccoli, and cook for a few minutes, then add the peaches with the juice, and bring the mixture to a boil. Sprinkle the flour over the mixture, and stir in.

Cook, stirring, until the sauce thickens. Serve over rice or noodles.

Nutrition Information

- Calories: 307 calories
- Total Fat: 12.1 g
- Cholesterol: 73 mg
- Sodium: 981 mg
- Total Carbohydrate: 23.3 g
- Protein: 27.4 g

295. Pudding Fruit Salad

"This is kinda like a homemade fruit cocktail. A perfect side dish with any meal."

Serving: 8 | Prep: 10 m | Cook: 5 m | Ready in: 35 m

Ingredients

- 1 (29 ounce) can pear slices, drained and cut into bite-size pieces
- 1 (28 ounce) can sliced peaches, drained and cut into bite-size pieces with 1 cup liquid reserved
- 1 (20 ounce) can pineapple tidbits, drained
- 1 (4.6 ounce) package non-instant vanilla pudding mix

Direction

- Mix pears, peaches, and pineapple in a serving bowl.
- Stir pudding mix into reserved liquid from the peaches in a small saucepan over medium-low heat; cook and stir until the pudding dissolves completely and the mixture is bubbling, about 5 minutes. Pour the pudding mixture over the fruit mixture and stir to coat.
- Refrigerate salad until chilled completely, at least 20 minutes.

Nutrition Information

- Calories: 199 calories
- Total Fat: 0.2 g

- Cholesterol: 0 mg
- Sodium: 130 mg
- Total Carbohydrate: 51 g
- Protein: 1.3 g

296. Quick and Easy Peach Cobbler

"Soooo easy."

Serving: 18

Ingredients

- 1 cup self-rising flour
- 1 cup white sugar
- 1 cup milk
- 2 (16 ounce) cans sliced peaches in heavy syrup
- 1/2 cup butter

Direction

- Melt butter or margarine in 9 x 13 inch pan.
- Mix together the flour, sugar, and milk. Pour mixture into the pan. Spread peaches, including syrup, evenly around the pan.
- Bake at 350 degrees F (175 degrees C) for 30 to 40 minutes, until the crust turns golden brown. Let cool for about 10 minutes before serving.

Nutrition Information

- Calories: 158 calories
- Total Fat: 5.4 g
- Cholesterol: 15 mg
- Sodium: 134 mg
- Total Carbohydrate: 26.2 g
- Protein: 1.6 g

297. Quick and Easy Peach Pie Egg Rolls with Raspberry Sauce

"I had to make a dessert really quickly because we had some friends over for dinner. Unfortunately I lent out my car and was unable to make it to the grocery store. All I had was a can of peach pie filling, some raspberry jam, cream cheese, egg roll wrappers, and some vanilla ice cream in the freezer."

Serving: 6 | Prep: 25 m | Cook: 20 m | Ready in: 45 m

Ingredients

- 1 (21 ounce) can peach pie filling
- 1/2 teaspoon ground cinnamon
- 1/4 teaspoon ground allspice
- 1/4 teaspoon ground cloves
- 1/4 teaspoon ground ginger
- 1/4 teaspoon ground nutmeg
- 1/4 teaspoon pumpkin pie spice
- 1 pinch salt
- 12 egg roll wrappers
- 1 (8 ounce) package cream cheese, softened
- 1/2 cup water
- 1 quart canola oil for frying
- 1/2 cup raspberry jam
- 1 tablespoon honey
- 1 quart vanilla ice cream
- 1/4 cup confectioners' sugar

Direction

- In a large bowl, mix the peach pie filling, cinnamon, allspice, cloves, ginger, nutmeg, pumpkin pie spice, and salt.
- Spread one side of each egg roll wrapper with about 1 tablespoon cream cheese. Top cream cheese with 1 tablespoon of the pie filling mixture. Fold the wrappers over the mixture. Moisten the ends with a small amount of water, and seal.
- Heat the oil in a large skillet over medium-high heat. Drop the egg rolls a few at a time into the hot oil. Fry until golden brown. Drain on paper towels.
- In a bowl, mix the raspberry jam, honey, and remaining water. Add more water as

necessary to obtain a syrup like texture. Serve the warm egg rolls over ice cream, top with the raspberry jam mixture, and sprinkle with confectioners' sugar.

Nutrition Information

- Calories: 675 calories
- Total Fat: 37.7 g
- Cholesterol: 81 mg
- Sodium: 290 mg
- Total Carbohydrate: 78.8 g
- Protein: 8.6 g

298. Quick Peach Cobbler

"This is a quick dessert that is pretty good. It has been around for a while, but I added a new twist. Serve warm with ice cream."

Serving: 6 | Prep: 15 m | Cook: 45 m | Ready in: 1 h

Ingredients

- 1/2 cup butter, melted
- 1 cup self-rising flour
- 1 cup white sugar
- 1 cup milk
- 1 (28 ounce) can sliced peaches
- 1 teaspoon almond extract
- 2 teaspoons ground cinnamon

Direction

- Preheat oven to 350 degrees F (175 degrees C). Place butter in a 9x9-inch baking pan; melt in the preheating oven.
- Mix flour, sugar, and milk together in bowl until smooth. Open peaches and add almond extract to the peaches and juice.
- Pour peaches over melted butter in the 9x9-inch pan; spoon batter atop peaches without mixing. Sprinkle with cinnamon.
- Bake in the preheated oven until bubbling and top is lightly browned, about 45 to 60 minutes.

Nutrition Information

- Calories: 421 calories
- Total Fat: 16.4 g
- Cholesterol: 44 mg
- Sodium: 396 mg
- Total Carbohydrate: 66.6 g
- Protein: 4.4 g

299. Quick Peach Melba

"Turn on the appliances: For Quick Peach Melba, microwave fresh peaches in a little peach schnapps. Raspberry sauce will zip together fast in a food processor or a blender."

Serving: 8 | Prep: 10 m | Cook: 11 m | Ready in: 2 h 21 m

Ingredients

- 1/4 cup peach schnapps or peach juice
- 4 large peaches, halved, pitted
- 1 (12 ounce) jar seedless raspberry jam
- 1 (12 ounce) package frozen raspberries, thawed
- 1/2 cup slivered almonds, toasted in a 300-degree oven for 6 to 8 minutes
- 1 quart premium vanilla ice cream

Direction

- Pour schnapps in a microwave-safe pan or pie plate large enough to hold peach halves in a single layer. Place peaches, cut side down in pan. Microwave on high Pour schnapps in a microwave-safe pie plate large enough to hold all peach halves in a single layer. Place peaches cut side down in pan. Microwave on high for 3 minutes. Turn peaches over and microwave about 2 minutes longer, until the fruit is tender when poked with a sharp knife. Let peaches cool, then peel. Refrigerate. for 3 minutes.
- Transfer jam to a microwave-safe measuring cup; microwave on high 1 to 2 minutes until partially melted. In a food processor, puree

jam and raspberries. Set a fine-mesh strainer over a bowl; strain sauce to remove seeds, pressing with a rubber spatula. Discard seeds. Refrigerate.
- Put 1/2 cup ice cream in each of eight shallow bowls, then a peach half, 2 Tbs. sauce and 1 Tb. almonds. Serve.

Nutrition Information

- Calories: 365 calories
- Total Fat: 10.8 g
- Cholesterol: 29 mg
- Sodium: 57 mg
- Total Carbohydrate: 62.5 g
- Protein: 4 g

300. Quick Savory Grilled Peaches

"Grilled peaches are given a slightly savory treatment to make them an excellent summertime side dish."

Serving: 12 | Prep: 10 m | Cook: 5 m | Ready in: 20 m

Ingredients

- 2 tablespoons olive oil
- 1/2 teaspoon chopped fresh basil
- 1/4 teaspoon chopped fresh thyme
- salt and ground black pepper to taste
- 6 fresh peaches, halved and pitted

Direction

- Preheat grill for medium heat and lightly oil the grate.
- Whisk olive oil, basil, thyme, salt, and pepper together in a bowl. Allow flavors to combine for 5 minutes. Brush oil mixture on inside flesh of peach halves.
- Grill peaches, flesh sides down until softened and grill marks appear, about 4 minutes.

Nutrition Information

- Calories: 32 calories
- Total Fat: 2.3 g
- Cholesterol: 0 mg
- Sodium: 2 mg

- Total Carbohydrate: 3 g
- Protein: 0 g

301. Raspberry Peach Crumble

"This is a showstopper, perfect for summer. Serve with vanilla ice cream to make it a perfect dessert. Use frozen fruit, if the fresh is not in season."

Serving: 6 | Prep: 15 m | Cook: 35 m | Ready in: 50 m

Ingredients

- 1 pint fresh raspberries
- 3 fresh peaches, pitted and chopped
- 2 tablespoons lemon juice
- 1/3 cup white sugar
- 1 pinch cinnamon
- 1 cup rolled oats
- 1/2 cup unsalted butter
- 1/4 cup brown sugar
- 1/4 cup white sugar
- 1 teaspoon vanilla extract
- 1 teaspoon salt
- 1 pinch cinnamon

Direction

- Preheat oven to 350 degrees F (175 degrees C). Lightly grease 6 small ramekins.
- In a bowl, mix the raspberries, peaches, lemon juice, 1/3 cup white sugar, and 1 pinch cinnamon.
- In a separate bowl, mix the oats, butter, brown sugar, 1/4 cup white sugar, vanilla, salt, and 1 pinch cinnamon.
- Fill the prepared ramekins with equal amounts of the raspberry and peach mixture, and top with equal amounts of the oats mixture. Arrange the ramekins on a baking sheet.
- Bake 35 minutes in the preheated oven, until crisp and golden brown. Cool 10 minutes before serving.

Nutrition Information

- Calories: 327 calories
- Total Fat: 16.5 g
- Cholesterol: 41 mg
- Sodium: 394 mg
- Total Carbohydrate: 44.3 g
- Protein: 2.5 g

302. RaspberryPeach Pie

"Simple, quick, delicious recipe that can be made all year round. Serve alone or with fresh-made whipped cream. Yummy!"

Serving: 8 | Prep: 15 m | Cook: 45 m | Ready in: 1 h

Ingredients

- 1 (10 ounce) package frozen unsweetened raspberries, thawed
- 1 (10 ounce) package frozen unsweetened sliced peaches
- 1 1/3 cups white sugar, divided
- 6 tablespoons all-purpose flour
- 1 prepared double pie crust

Direction

- Preheat an oven to 450 degrees F (230 degrees C).
- Mix raspberries, peaches, 1 cup sugar, and flour in a large bowl.
- Press one pie crust into a pie dish; pour fruit mixture into pie crust. Sprinkle remaining 1/3 cup sugar over fruit.
- Cut designs in the second pie crust using a cookie cutter and arrange pie crust over fruit. Pinch the edges of the bottom and top crusts together to seal.
- Bake in the preheated oven for 10 minutes. Reduce oven temperature to 375 degrees F (190 degrees C) and continue baking until crust is golden brown and fruit filling is bubbly, about 35 minutes more.

Nutrition Information

- Calories: 406 calories
- Total Fat: 15 g
- Cholesterol: 0 mg
- Sodium: 234 mg
- Total Carbohydrate: 65.3 g
- Protein: 4.1 g

303. Really Quick Peach Cobbler

"This recipe is for the super busy family. It has been used in our family for years."

Serving: 10 | Prep: 15 m | Cook: 30 m | Ready in: 45 m

Ingredients

- 3/4 cup white sugar
- 2 tablespoons all-purpose flour
- 1/4 teaspoon ground nutmeg
- 1/4 teaspoon ground cinnamon
- 1 (22 ounce) can cling peaches in heavy syrup
- 1/4 cup butter, cut into chunks, divided
- 1 (15 ounce) package pastry for a double crust 9-inch pie, cut into 1-inch strips

Direction

- Preheat oven to 350 degrees F (175 degrees C).
- Mix sugar, flour, nutmeg, and cinnamon together in a bowl.
- Pour peaches into the bottom of a glass 9x13-inch baking dish. Sprinkle sugar mixture over peaches and mix well. Scatter 1/2 of the butter chunks over the peach mixture. Arrange pastry strips over peach mixture in a crisscross or striped pattern. Scatter remaining butter chunks over pie pastry.
- Bake in the preheated oven until crust is golden brown and crisp, 30 to 40 minutes.

Nutrition Information

- Calories: 348 calories
- Total Fat: 17.6 g
- Cholesterol: 12 mg

- Sodium: 239 mg
- Total Carbohydrate: 46.3 g
- Protein: 2.9 g

304. Really Simple Bellinis

"Just 2 ingredients and a blender is all that is needed for a nice cold peach beverage! You can adjust the ratio to your liking. Add a dash of grenadine for a more colorful drink! Enjoy!"

Serving: 8 | Prep: 5 m | Ready in: 35 m

Ingredients

- 1 (15 ounce) can sliced peaches, chilled
- 1 (750 milliliter) bottle champagne, chilled

Direction

- Blend chilled peaches and their juice in a blender until smooth. Pour into a chilled glass until 1/2 full. Top with champagne; gently stir.

Nutrition Information

- Calories: 101 calories
- Total Fat: 0 g
- Cholesterol: 0 mg
- Sodium: 7 mg
- Total Carbohydrate: 8.6 g
- Protein: 0.4 g

305. ReBar ReVive Shake

"Lived in Israel for a few years and lived on Re:Bar's shakes, now that I'm back in America I can't get them. This tastes almost exactly the same as their Re:Vive shake does. It's my favorite one! For a thicker shake freeze your yogurt before blending."

Serving: 1 | Prep: 5 m | Ready in: 5 m

Ingredients

- 1 (6 ounce) tub vanilla-flavored yogurt (such as Yoplait®)
- 6 frozen peach slices
- 3 fluid ounces orange juice
- 6 tablespoons slivered almonds
- 6 tablespoons granola

Direction

- Blend yogurt, peach slices, orange juice, almonds, and granola in a blender until smooth.

Nutrition Information

- Calories: 667 calories
- Total Fat: 33.9 g
- Cholesterol: 8 mg
- Sodium: 131 mg
- Total Carbohydrate: 68.1 g
- Protein: 24.3 g

306. Red Currant and Peach Applesauce

"Your basic applesauce with a savory twist. Serve warm or refrigerate in an air-tight container."

Serving: 8 | Prep: 15 m | Cook: 30 m | Ready in: 55 m

Ingredients

- 12 small apples - peeled, cored, and sliced
- 5 small fresh peaches - peeled, pitted, and sliced
- 1/2 cup brewed hibiscus herbal tea
- 1 tablespoon dried marjoram
- 1/2 teaspoon ground ginger
- 1/2 teaspoon ground allspice
- 4 cups fresh red currants

Direction

- Bring the apples, peaches, and tea to a light boil in a large wok-style pan. Reduce heat to medium-high heat; cook and stir until fruit is soft, about 30 minutes. Drain any excess liquid from the pan. Let fruit mixture cool slightly.
- Stir marjoram, ground ginger, ground allspice into the fruit mixture. Fold currants into the mixture.

Nutrition Information

- Calories: 117 calories
- Total Fat: 0.4 g
- Cholesterol: 0 mg
- Sodium: 3 mg
- Total Carbohydrate: 30.3 g
- Protein: 1.2 g

307. Ritas Roasted Peach Salsa

"This recipe is a little different, in a good way! I was experimenting in my kitchen and thought it was good enough to share! It's super easy to make and is just as easy to modify.

I purposely omitted the broiler temperature, as broiling is done to taste."

Serving: 4 | Prep: 20 m | Cook: 10 m | Ready in: 1 h 30 m

Ingredients

- 2 tomatoes, halved
- 1 small peach, halved and pitted
- 1/2 white onion, halved
- 1/2 red bell pepper, halved
- 1/2 yellow bell pepper, halved
- 1 clove garlic, minced
- 1 tablespoon lemon juice
- 1 teaspoon white sugar, or to taste
- 1/2 teaspoon salt

- 1/2 teaspoon chopped fresh parsley, or to taste

Direction

- Set oven rack about 6 inches from the heat source and preheat the oven's broiler.
- Arrange tomatoes, peach, onion, red bell pepper, yellow bell pepper, and garlic on a baking sheet.
- Broil in the preheated oven until vegetables and peach are browned and tender and tomato skins can be peeled off, 10 to 15 minutes.
- Dice the roasted vegetable and peach and transfer to a bowl. Add lemon juice, sugar, salt, and parsley; toss to coat. Refrigerate at least 1 hour for flavors to blend.

Nutrition Information

- Calories: 38 calories
- Total Fat: 0.2 g
- Cholesterol: 0 mg
- Sodium: 296 mg
- Total Carbohydrate: 8.6 g
- Protein: 1.2 g

308. Roasted Beet Peach and Goat Cheese Salad

"This salad is a bit of work, but it's so delicious and always impresses guests. Mache can be hard to find, so you may omit it and just use arugula, but it adds a great nutty flavor if you can find it."

Serving: 2 | Prep: 20 m | Cook: 1 h 20 m | Ready in: 2 h 40 m

Ingredients

- 2 beets, scrubbed
- 1 bunch mache (lamb's lettuce), rinsed and dried
- 1 bunch arugula, rinsed and dried
- 2 fresh peaches - peeled, pitted, and sliced
- 2 shallots, chopped
- 1/4 cup pistachio nuts, chopped

- 1 (4 ounce) package goat cheese, crumbled
- 1/4 cup walnut oil
- 2 tablespoons balsamic vinegar
- salt and pepper to taste

Direction

- Preheat oven to 375 degrees F (190 degrees C). Wrap each beet in two layers of aluminum foil, and place onto a baking sheet. Bake in the preheated oven until the beets are tender, about 1 hour and 20 minutes. Allow the beets to cool slightly, then remove the skins. Let the beets cool to room temperature, or refrigerate until cold. Once cooled, thinly slice the beets.
- Place the mache and arugula into a large mixing bowl. Add the sliced beets and peaches; sprinkle with the shallots, pistachios, and goat cheese. In a separate bowl, whisk together the walnut oil, balsamic vinegar, salt, and pepper until emulsified, and pour over the salad mixture. Toss well, and serve.

Nutrition Information

- Calories: 667 calories
- Total Fat: 52.8 g
- Cholesterol: 45 mg
- Sodium: 474 mg
- Total Carbohydrate: 31.7 g
- Protein: 23.2 g

309. Roasted Fruit Compote

"Peach, plum, and apricot halves are topped with a sweet and spicy sugar mixture and baked until tender."

Serving: 8 | Prep: 20 m | Cook: 20 m | Ready in: 40 m

Ingredients

- 1 tablespoon soft butter
- 4 ripe firm peaches, peeled, halved, pitted
- 4 ripe firm plums peeled, halved, pitted
- 4 ripe firm apricots peeled, halved, pitted
- 1/2 cup Sugar In The Raw®
- 1/2 teaspoon ground cardamom or cinnamon

- 1/4 teaspoon ground ginger
- 1/4 teaspoon ground nutmeg
- 1 teaspoon grated lemon peel
- 3 tablespoons fresh lemon juice
- Mascarpone cheese

Direction

- Heat oven to 400 degrees F. Butter 13x9-inch (3-quart) baking dish with 1 tablespoon butter. Place fruit in single layer, cut sides of fruit facing up, in dish. In small bowl, mix Sugar In The Raw, cardamom, ginger, nutmeg and lemon peel. Sprinkle sugar mixture generously over fruit. Drizzle lemon juice over fruit. Bake 20 minutes or until fruit is tender and juices are bubbly. Spoon fruit into 8 dessert dishes and drizzle with some of the roasting juices. Top with spoonfuls of mascarpone.

Nutrition Information

- Calories: 168 calories
- Total Fat: 8.1 g
- Cholesterol: 21 mg
- Sodium: 20 mg
- Total Carbohydrate: 23.6 g
- Protein: 1.6 g

310. Rosy Ginger Peach Smoothie

"With yogurt, honey, and ginger, this is a refreshing twist on your everyday smoothie."

Serving: 2 | Prep: 10 m | Ready in: 10 m

Ingredients

- 1 fresh peach, sliced
- 1 (6 ounce) container strawberry-flavored yogurt
- 1/2 cup milk
- 1/2 cup strawberries
- 1 tablespoon honey
- 1/8 teaspoon ground ginger

Direction

- Place peach slices, yogurt, milk, strawberries, honey, and ground ginger in a blender; cover and blend until smooth.

Nutrition Information

- Calories: 132 calories
- Total Fat: 1.3 g
- Cholesterol: 7 mg
- Sodium: 88 mg
- Total Carbohydrate: 25.6 g
- Protein: 5.3 g

311. Sex on the Beach I

"It will make your hot day into a cool day! You should try it on a hot day."

Serving: 1 | Prep: 2 m | Ready in: 2 m

Ingredients

- 1 fluid ounce peach schnapps
- 1/4 fluid ounce light rum
- 1/4 fluid ounce banana liqueur
- 1/2 fluid ounce sweetened coconut cream
- 1 fluid ounce orange juice
- 5 fluid ounces crushed ice

Direction

- In a blender, combine peach schnapps, rum, banana liqueur, coconut cream, orange juice and crushed ice. Blend until smooth. Pour into a glass and serve.

312. Sheilas Peach Cobbler with Pecans

"Homemade peach cobbler with fresh-picked peaches baked in a cast iron skillet. Serve with your favorite ice cream, (my husband loves pecan pralines and cream). I made this recipe up because I was ready to be finished with the peaches! LOL! You can use any baking type dish you like. It was old fashioned and baked nicely in the cast iron skillet."

Serving: 6 | Prep: 15 m | Cook: 30 m | Ready in: 45 m

Ingredients

- 3 cups sliced fresh peaches
- 2 teaspoons lemon juice
- 1 1/2 cups white sugar
- 1 cup chopped pecans (optional)
- 1 teaspoon ground cinnamon
- 1 1/2 cups self-rising flour, or as needed
- 1/2 cup white sugar
- 1/2 cup brown sugar
- 1 teaspoon ground cinnamon
- 1/4 cup butter, melted
- 2 tablespoons butter, cut into small pieces
- 1 tablespoon raw sugar, or as desired

Direction

- Preheat oven to 400 degrees F (200 degrees C).
- Stir peaches with lemon juice in a bowl to prevent fruit from browning. Transfer to a cast iron skillet and stir in 1 1/2 cup white sugar, pecans, and 1 teaspoon cinnamon. Bring to a soft boil, stirring often.
- Whisk self-rising flour, 1/2 cup white sugar, brown sugar, and 1 teaspoon cinnamon in a bowl. Stir melted butter into the mixture (batter should resemble cooked oatmeal). Spoon batter over hot peach filling in the skillet; dot topping with 2 tablespoons of butter pieces and sprinkle with raw sugar.
- Bake cobbler in the preheated oven until topping is golden brown, about 30 minutes.

Nutrition Information

- Calories: 668 calories
- Total Fat: 24.9 g
- Cholesterol: 31 mg
- Sodium: 485 mg
- Total Carbohydrate: 110.9 g
- Protein: 4.9 g

313. Simply Southern Bento Box

"Tasty bites of Southern favorites!"

Serving: 2 | Prep: 25 m | Cook: 5 m | Ready in: 45 m

Ingredients

- Southern Pimento Cheese:
- 1/3 cup shredded extra-sharp Cheddar cheese
- 2 tablespoons cream cheese, softened
- 1 1/2 tablespoons mayonnaise
- 1 1/2 tablespoons pimento peppers, drained and chopped
- 1 teaspoon chopped jalapeno pepper (optional)
- 1/8 teaspoon garlic powder
- 1/8 teaspoon ground cayenne pepper (optional)
- 1/8 teaspoon onion powder
- salt and ground black pepper to taste
- Deviled Eggs:
- 2 eggs
- 2 teaspoons mayonnaise
- 1/8 teaspoon paprika
- 1/8 teaspoon mustard powder
- Creamy Cucumber Salad:
- 1/2 cup sour cream
- 2 tablespoons apple cider vinegar
- 1 clove garlic, minced
- 1 teaspoon dill weed
- 2 cucumbers, sliced
- salt and ground black pepper to taste
- 6 crackers, or as desired
- 1 peach, sliced

Direction

- Combine Cheddar cheese, cream cheese, 1 1/2 tablespoons mayonnaise, pimento peppers, jalapeno pepper, garlic powder, cayenne pepper, onion powder, salt, and black pepper in the bowl of a stand mixer fitted with a paddle attachment. Beat at medium speed until thoroughly combined. Transfer to the refrigerator.

- Place eggs in a saucepan and cover with water. Bring to a boil, remove from heat, and let eggs stand in hot water for 15 minutes. Remove eggs from hot water, cool under cold running water, and peel. Cut in half lengthwise.
- Mash yolks, 2 teaspoons mayonnaise, paprika, and mustard powder together in a bowl. Spoon filling into egg whites. Transfer to the refrigerator.
- Mix sour cream, apple cider vinegar, garlic, and dill together in a bowl. Add cucumbers; stir to combine. Season with salt and pepper. Transfer to the refrigerator.
- Place pimento cheese in a small container; surround with crackers. Add 2 deviled egg halves, cucumber salad, and sliced peaches to divided sections of the bento box.

Nutrition Information

- Calories: 549 calories
- Total Fat: 43.6 g
- Cholesterol: 253 mg
- Sodium: 608 mg
- Total Carbohydrate: 25.2 g
- Protein: 16.9 g

314. Single Crust Peach Pie

"My mother made this pie several times a month in the fall with fresh peaches from the Western Slope of Colorado, the BEST peaches in the world! It is still one of our family's favorites!"

Serving: 8 | Prep: 30 m | Ready in: 1 h 20 m

Ingredients

- 3/4 cup white sugar
- 2 tablespoons butter, softened

- 1/3 cup all-purpose flour
- 1/4 teaspoon ground nutmeg
- 6 fresh peaches - pitted, skinned, and sliced
- 1 recipe pastry for a 9 inch single crust pie

Direction

- Cream sugar and butter or margarine together. Add flour and nutmeg; mix until mealy. Spread 1/2 of mixture in pie crust. Arrange peaches on top of crumb mixture. Sprinkle remaining crumb mixture on top of peaches.
- Bake at 450 degrees F (230 degrees C) for ten minutes. Reduce heat to 350 degrees F (175 degrees C). Continue baking for 40 minutes, or until brown.

Nutrition Information

- Calories: 250 calories
- Total Fat: 10.4 g
- Cholesterol: 8 mg
- Sodium: 140 mg
- Total Carbohydrate: 37.5 g
- Protein: 2 g

315. Skillet Peach Pie

"Peach cobbler made in a skillet. In place of pie crust, try using biscuits."

Serving: 6 | Prep: 15 m | Cook: 30 m | Ready in: 45 m

Ingredients

- 1 (10 ounce) package pie crust mix
- 6 fresh peaches - pitted, skinned, and sliced
- 1/2 cup white sugar
- 1/2 teaspoon salt
- 1/4 teaspoon ground cinnamon
- 1 1/2 tablespoons butter

Direction

- Preheat oven to 425 degrees F (220 degrees C).
- Make crust mix according to package directions. Roll dough out so that it fits an 8

inch skillet or frying pan; make sure there is overhang.

- Place peaches into pastry lined pan. Sprinkle with sugar, salt and cinnamon. Dot with butter. Fold the dough edges over towards center; leave a small space in center uncovered. Bake in preheated oven for 25 to 30 minutes until fruit is bubbly and crust is browned.

Nutrition Information

- Calories: 360 calories
- Total Fat: 17.7 g
- Cholesterol: 8 mg
- Sodium: 575 mg
- Total Carbohydrate: 47.4 g
- Protein: 3.3 g

---

316. Slow Cooked Apple Peach Sauce

"This is a yummy fresh summer fruit sauce and because you make it in a slow cooker it doesn't heat up your kitchen!"

Serving: 12 | Prep: 10 m | Cook: 5 h | Ready in: 5 h 10 m

Ingredients

- 10 Macintosh apples, cored and chopped
- 4 fresh peaches, pitted and chopped
- 1 tablespoon ground cinnamon

Direction

- Put fruit into a slow-cooker; sprinkle with cinnamon. Turn slow-cooker to high. Cover, and cook for 3 hours on high, then switch to low for 2 hours. Stir before serving.

Nutrition Information

- Calories: 69 calories
- Total Fat: 0.2 g
- Cholesterol: 0 mg
- Sodium: 3 mg

- Total Carbohydrate: 18.3 g
- Protein: 0.3 g

---

317. Slow Cooker Fruit Cobbler

"This easy dessert is always a hit in my house. It is especially good for entertaining; your guests think you slaved away baking when all you did was throw a few simple ingredients into the slow cooker! My favorite fruit mixture is peach/berry but any fruit your family loves will work. Serve hot with a scoop of vanilla ice cream."

Serving: 8 | Prep: 10 m | Cook: 3 h | Ready in: 3 h 10 m

Ingredients

- cooking spray
- 2 cups frozen peach slices
- 2 cups mixed frozen berries
- 2 tablespoons cornstarch
- 1 teaspoon vanilla extract
- 1/2 cup brown sugar
- 1/2 teaspoon ground cinnamon
- 1/2 teaspoon nutmeg
- 1 (18.25 ounce) package white cake mix
- 1/2 cup melted butter

Direction

- Lightly spray the slow cooker with cooking spray. Mix peaches and berries together in the slow cooker; sprinkle with cornstarch and toss to coat.
- Stir vanilla into berry mixture; add brown sugar, cinnamon, and nutmeg. Pour cake mix over berry mixture and drizzle with melted butter.
- Cook in the slow cooker set to High until bubbling, 3 to 3 1/2 hours.

Nutrition Information

- Calories: 511 calories
- Total Fat: 18.8 g
- Cholesterol: 31 mg
- Sodium: 514 mg
- Total Carbohydrate: 84.7 g

- Protein: 3.7 g

318. Slow Cooker Moroccan Chicken

"Tasty, easy, and impressive! Serve with couscous or rice."

Serving: 6 | Prep: 15 m | Cook: 5 h 15 m | Ready in: 5 h 30 m

Ingredients

- 1 pound skinless, boneless chicken breast halves - cut into 2 inch pieces
- 4 cloves garlic, chopped
- 1 large onion, chopped
- 1 (28 ounce) can diced tomatoes
- 3 fresh peaches - peeled, pitted, and sliced
- 1 (15 ounce) can garbanzo beans, drained
- 1 cup chopped dried apricots
- 2 teaspoons ground cumin
- 1 teaspoon ground ginger
- 1 teaspoon cinnamon
- 1/2 teaspoon ground coriander
- 1/2 teaspoon cayenne pepper
- 2 cups chicken broth
- 1 tablespoon cornstarch
- 1 tablespoon water
- 3 tablespoons chopped fresh cilantro
- 1/3 cup slivered almonds, toasted

Direction

- Place chicken in the bottom of a slow cooker. Add the garlic, onion, tomatoes, peaches, garbanzo beans, dried apricots, cumin, ginger, cinnamon, coriander, and cayenne pepper. Pour in the chicken broth. Cook on Low for 5 hours.
- Remove the chicken and keep warm. Mix the cornstarch and water in a small bowl. Stir the cornstarch mixture into the slow cooker. Cook on High until the sauce has thickened, about 15 minutes. Return the chicken to the slow cooker and heat through. Top with fresh cilantro and almonds before serving.

Nutrition Information

- Calories: 284 calories
- Total Fat: 5.5 g
- Cholesterol: 39 mg
- Sodium: 385 mg
- Total Carbohydrate: 37.9 g
- Protein: 20.7 g

319. Slow Cooker Peach Cobbler

"Easy way to enjoy this delicious Southern dessert. Serve warm topped with vanilla ice cream."

Serving: 6 | Prep: 15 m | Cook: 4 h | Ready in: 4 h 15 m

Ingredients

- 3/4 cup old-fashioned oats
- 3/4 cup white sugar
- 2/3 cup brown sugar
- 1/2 cup all-purpose baking mix (such as Bisquick®)
- 3/4 teaspoon ground cinnamon
- 5 fresh peaches - peeled, pitted, and sliced

Direction

- Grease the inside of a 3- to 4-quart slow cooker crock.
- Mix oats, white sugar, brown sugar, baking mix, and cinnamon together in a bowl; stir in peaches and spoon mixture into prepared slow cooker.
- Cook on Low for 4 hours.

Nutrition Information

- Calories: 258 calories
- Total Fat: 2.2 g
- Cholesterol: 0 mg
- Sodium: 134 mg
- Total Carbohydrate: 59 g
- Protein: 2.1 g

320. Slow Cooker Peach Upside Down Cake

"Peaches caramelize with brown sugar in the bottom of your slow cooker for a warm, gooey upside-down cake."

Serving: 8 | Prep: 30 m | Cook: 2 h | Ready in: 3 h

Ingredients

- 3 (15 ounce) cans sliced peaches in heavy syrup, drained well
- 5 tablespoons butter, melted
- 2/3 cup packed light brown sugar
- 1 teaspoon cinnamon
- 1/2 teaspoon nutmeg
- 1 1/2 sticks butter, softened
- 1 cup white sugar
- 2 large eggs
- 1/2 teaspoon pure almond extract
- 2 cups flour
- 2 teaspoons baking powder
- 1/2 teaspoon salt
- 1 cup whole milk

Direction

- Spread peach slices between several layers of paper towels and let dry, gently pressing occasionally and replacing any soaked towels, 20 minutes.
- Meanwhile, pour melted butter over bottom of a 6-quart oval slow cooker. Stir together brown sugar, cinnamon, and nutmeg in a bowl and sprinkle over butter.
- Arrange peaches in a tight layer over brown sugar. (You may need to make a partial second layer to fit them all in.)
- Beat softened butter with white sugar in a large bowl with an electric mixer until light and fluffy, about 3 minutes. Beat in eggs, 1 at a time, beating well after each addition. Beat in almond extract.
- Whisk together flour, baking powder, and salt in a separate bowl. Working in batches, stir flour mixture into egg mixture alternately with milk, beginning and ending with flour mixture. Mix batter until well combined. Spoon over peaches and spread evenly.
- Drape paper towels over top of slow cooker (to absorb any condensation during baking), then cover with lid. Cook on High until a wooden skewer inserted into center of cake comes out clean, 2 to 2 1/2 hours.
- Remove lid and paper towels. Using oven mitts, remove ceramic liner from slow cooker and let cool 10 minutes. Run a knife around edge of cake and carefully turn out onto a serving platter.

Nutrition Information

- Calories: 654 calories
- Total Fat: 27.2 g
- Cholesterol: 114 mg
- Sodium: 486 mg
- Total Carbohydrate: 100.8 g
- Protein: 6.8 g

321. Smoothie for a Boss

"A tasty, sweet, nutritious smoothie that you'll crave every day!"

Serving: 2 | Prep: 10 m | Ready in: 10 m

Ingredients

- 2 cups milk
- 15 slices frozen peach, or more to taste
- 1 banana
- 3 1/2 ounces fruit yogurt
- 2 tablespoons chocolate sauce (optional)

Direction

- Pour milk into a blender; add peaches, banana, and yogurt. Blend mixture until smooth; add chocolate sauce and blend until smooth.

Nutrition Information

- Calories: 294 calories
- Total Fat: 5.7 g

- Cholesterol: 21 mg
- Sodium: 145 mg
- Total Carbohydrate: 50.6 g
- Protein: 11.2 g

- Cholesterol: 9 mg
- Sodium: 133 mg
- Total Carbohydrate: 39 g
- Protein: 2.7 g

322. Sour Cream Peach Pie

"This recipe combines the delicious flavors of peaches with sour cream and a hint of almond extract."

Serving: 8 | Prep: 10 m | Cook: 55 m | Ready in: 1 h 5 m

Ingredients

- 3/4 cup sour cream
- 1/2 cup white sugar
- 1/3 cup all-purpose flour
- 1/4 teaspoon almond extract
- 1 tablespoon all-purpose flour
- 1 (9 inch) unbaked pie crust
- 4 cups sliced fresh or frozen peaches
- 1/4 cup brown sugar

Direction

- Preheat the oven to 425 degrees F (220 degrees C).
- In a medium bowl, stir together the sour cream, white sugar, 1/3 cup flour and almond extract until smooth. Sprinkle 1 tablespoon of flour over the pie crust to prevent it from getting soggy. Alternate layers of peaches and the sour cream mixture, beginning with a layer of peaches and ending with a layer of sour cream.
- Bake for 20 minutes in the preheated oven. Reduce the heat to 350 degrees F (175 degrees C). Continue baking for an additional 35 minutes. Remove the pie from the oven and sprinkle brown sugar over the top. Set the oven to Broil, and broil for 2 to 3 minutes, until caramelized.

Nutrition Information

- Calories: 273 calories
- Total Fat: 12.1 g

323. Spiced Blackberry and Peach Compote

"A nutritious fruit compote that feels like fall. Serve over frozen yogurt or waffles or grain-free Dutch babies!"

Serving: 6 | Prep: 5 m | Cook: 25 m | Ready in: 30 m

Ingredients

- 3 tablespoons butter
- 2 tablespoons maple sugar
- 2 teaspoons grated fresh ginger
- 1 teaspoon ground cinnamon
- 1/2 teaspoon freshly grated nutmeg
- 3 cups frozen peach slices
- 1 cup frozen blackberries

Direction

- Melt butter in a saucepan over medium heat. Stir maple sugar, ginger, cinnamon, and nutmeg into the melted butter. Add peaches and stir to coat. Cook the peaches at a simmer until soft and the juices begin to thicken, about 20 minutes.
- Gently fold blackberries into the peach mixture; cook until the berries soften, about 5 minutes more.

Nutrition Information

- Calories: 100 calories
- Total Fat: 6 g
- Cholesterol: 15 mg
- Sodium: 44 mg
- Total Carbohydrate: 12.1 g
- Protein: 0.4 g

324. Spiced Peach Oatmeal Muffins

"These sweet and tender muffins are the perfect choice for a summer brunch."

Serving: 12 | Prep: 15 m | Cook: 20 m | Ready in: 35 m

Ingredients

- 1 cup quick cooking oats
- 1 cup buttermilk
- 1/3 cup brown sugar
- 1/3 cup applesauce
- 1/4 cup molasses
- 2 eggs
- 1 1/3 cups all-purpose flour
- 1 teaspoon baking soda
- 1 teaspoon baking powder
- 1 1/2 cups pitted and diced fresh peaches
- 2 tablespoons white sugar
- 1/2 teaspoon ground cinnamon

Direction

- Preheat oven to 400 degrees F (200 degrees C). Grease muffin cups or line with paper muffin liners.
- In a large bowl, mix together oats, buttermilk, brown sugar, applesauce, molasses and eggs. In a separate bowl, stir together flour, baking soda and baking powder. Stir flour mixture into eggs mixture, just until moistened. Fold in peaches. Spoon batter into prepared muffin cups.
- Bake in preheated oven for 15 minutes. While muffins are baking, combine 2 tablespoons sugar and 1/2 teaspoon cinnamon. After 15 minutes of baking, remove muffins from oven and sprinkle with cinnamon sugar. Return to oven and continue baking for 3 minutes, until a toothpick inserted into center of a muffin comes out clean.

Nutrition Information

- Calories: 147 calories
- Total Fat: 1.6 g
- Cholesterol: 32 mg
- Sodium: 173 mg
- Total Carbohydrate: 29.2 g
- Protein: 4.1 g

325. Spicy Mango Salsa

"This is the best mango salsa I have ever tasted! It's a refreshing, cool and spicy salsa that adds excitement to fish, poultry, pork or tortilla chips! You'll love it! If you're feeling adventurous, use fresh cilantro instead of basil-- wonderful!"

Serving: 10 | Prep: 10 m | Ready in: 2 h 10 m

Ingredients

- 2 cups diced fresh mango
- 2 cups fresh peaches, pitted and chopped
- 2 cloves garlic, minced
- 2 tablespoons chopped fresh ginger root
- 1/4 cup chopped fresh basil
- 2 serrano chile peppers, diced
- 1/4 cup fresh lime juice

Direction

- In a large bowl, mix together the mangoes, peaches or nectarines, garlic, ginger and basil or cilantro.
- Add the chilies and lime juice to taste; mix well. Allow to chill 2 hours before serving.

Nutrition Information

- Calories: 35 calories
- Total Fat: 0.1 g
- Cholesterol: 0 mg
- Sodium: 3 mg
- Total Carbohydrate: 8.7 g
- Protein: 0.4 g

326. Spicy Peach Chicken

"You can alter the 'spicy' part of this dish by how much hot sauce you use. Great broiled or grilled!"

Serving: 6 | Prep: 15 m | Cook: 25 m | Ready in: 40 m

Ingredients

- 1/3 cup peach preserves
- 1/4 cup honey
- 1 tablespoon spicy brown mustard
- hot pepper sauce to taste
- 1 (2 pound) whole chicken, cut into pieces, skin removed
- 2 tablespoons Creole seasoning

Direction

- Preheat the oven broiler.
- In a small bowl, mix peach preserves, honey, spicy brown mustard, and hot pepper sauce.
- Arrange chicken pieces on a medium baking sheet. Season with Creole seasoning. Brush with the peach preserves mixture, reserving some of the mixture for basting.
- Turning occasionally and basting often with reserved peach reserves mixture, broil 25 minutes in the preheated oven, until chicken is no longer pink and juices run clear.

Nutrition Information

- Calories: 261 calories
- Total Fat: 6.6 g
- Cholesterol: 76 mg
- Sodium: 585 mg
- Total Carbohydrate: 25.2 g
- Protein: 25 g

327. Spicy Peach Chutney

"This chutney closely resembles imported Indian chutneys and is good with all curry dishes. It is also great with cream cheese and crackers."

Serving: 96 | Prep: 8 h | Cook: 2 h | Ready in: 10 h

Ingredients

- 4 pounds sliced peeled peaches
- 1 cup raisins
- 2 cloves garlic, minced
- 1/2 cup chopped onion
- 5 ounces chopped preserved ginger
- 1 1/2 tablespoons chili powder
- 1 tablespoon mustard seed
- 1 teaspoon curry powder
- 4 cups packed brown sugar
- 4 cups apple cider vinegar
- 1/4 cup pickling spice

Direction

- In a large heavy pot, stir together the peaches, raisins, garlic, onion, preserved ginger, chili powder, mustard seed, curry powder, brown sugar and cider vinegar. Wrap the pickling spice in a cheesecloth bag, and place in the pot.
- Bring to a boil, and cook over medium heat uncovered until the mixture reaches your desired consistency. It will take about 1 1/2 hours to get a good thick sauce. Stir frequently to prevent scorching on the bottom.
- Remove the spice bag, and ladle into hot sterilized jars. Wipe the rims with a clean moist cloth. Seal with lids and rings, and process in a barely simmering water bath for 10 minutes, or the time recommended by your local extension for your area. The water should cover the jars completely.

Nutrition Information

- Calories: 51 calories
- Total Fat: 0.1 g
- Cholesterol: 0 mg
- Sodium: 5 mg
- Total Carbohydrate: 12.6 g
- Protein: 0.1 g

328. Spicy Peach Coleslaw

"Peaches are so sweet, juicy, and delicious, and they make a fantastic coleslaw."

Serving: 6 | Prep: 15 m | Ready in: 45 m

Ingredients

- Dressing:
- 1/4 cup mayonnaise
- 1 1/2 teaspoons Dijon mustard
- 1 tablespoon Asian chile pepper sauce (such as sambal oelek)
- 1/2 lemon, juiced
- 2 tablespoons rice vinegar
- 1 tablespoon vegetable oil
- 1/2 teaspoon white sugar
- salt to taste
- 1 pinch cayenne pepper, or to taste
- Coleslaw:
- 1/2 (2 pound) cabbage - quartered and thinly sliced
- 2 fresh peaches, pitted and chopped
- 1 tablespoon thinly sliced fresh chives
- 1 teaspoon thinly sliced fresh chives for garnish (optional)

Direction

- Whisk mayonnaise, Dijon mustard, Asian chile sauce, lemon juice, rice vinegar, vegetable oil, and sugar in a bowl until dressing is smooth. Season with salt and cayenne pepper.
- Place cabbage into a large bowl; add peaches and 1 tablespoon chives. Lightly toss until combined. Pour dressing over coleslaw and stir until coated.
- Cover coleslaw with plastic wrap and chill until flavors have developed and cabbage is slightly softened, about 30 minutes. Adjust seasoning, mix again, and sprinkle with 1 teaspoon chives before serving.

Nutrition Information

- Calories: 108 calories
- Total Fat: 9.6 g
- Cholesterol: 3 mg
- Sodium: 118 mg
- Total Carbohydrate: 5.6 g
- Protein: 0.6 g

329. Spicy PeachGlazed Pork Chops

"Sweet and spicy boneless pork chops made with a special sauce that includes peach preserves and white wine. Serve with sweet potato latkes."

Serving: 4 | Prep: 10 m | Cook: 20 m | Ready in: 30 m

Ingredients

- 1 cup peach preserves
- 1 1/2 tablespoons Worcestershire sauce
- 1/2 teaspoon chile paste
- 4 boneless pork chops
- 1 teaspoon ground ginger
- 1 pinch ground cinnamon
- salt and pepper to taste
- 2 tablespoons vegetable oil
- 1/2 cup white wine

Direction

- In a small bowl, mix together the peach preserves, Worcestershire sauce, and chile paste. Rinse pork chops, and pat dry. Sprinkle the chops with ginger, cinnamon, salt, and pepper.
- Heat oil in a large skillet over medium-high heat. Sear the chops for about 2 minutes on each side. Remove from the pan, and set aside.
- Pour white wine into the pan, and stir to scrape the bottom of the pan. Stir in the peach preserves mixture. Return the chops to the pan, and flip to coat with the sauce. Reduce heat to medium low, and cook the pork chops

for about 8 minutes on each side, or until done.

Nutrition Information

- Calories: 404 calories
- Total Fat: 11.5 g
- Cholesterol: 36 mg
- Sodium: 91 mg
- Total Carbohydrate: 58.2 g
- Protein: 13.2 g

330. Spiked Peach Jam with Ginger

"This is a great jam for peaches that are not picture-perfect but nice and ripe. The riper they are, the more juice they will release when marinating. Combined with ginger and amaretto liqueur, the peach jam tastes divine."

Serving: 40 | Prep: 30 m | Cook: 25 m | Ready in: 1 d 8 h 55 m

Ingredients

- 4 1/2 cups finely chopped, peeled peaches
- 4 tablespoons lemon juice
- 3 cups white sugar
- 1 teaspoon ground ginger
- 1 (1.75 ounce) package light pectin (such as Sure-Jell®)
- 1/3 cup amaretto liqueur, or more to taste

Direction

- Place peaches in a glass or plastic container with a lid and immediately mix with lemon juice to prevent browning. Stir in sugar and ginger. Cover and marinate in a cool place, 8 hours to overnight.
- Inspect 5 half-pint jars for cracks and rings for rust, discarding any defective ones. Immerse in simmering water until jam is ready. Wash new, unused lids and rings in warm soapy water.
- Transfer peaches and all accumulated liquid to a large pot. Stir in pectin and slowly bring mixture to a full rolling boil that does not stop

bubbling when stirred. Cook for 1 minute, stirring constantly.
- Remove from heat and stir in amaretto liqueur, adding more to taste.
- Ladle peach jam into the prepared jars, filling to within 1/4 inch of the top. Run a clean knife or thin spatula around the insides of the jars to remove any air bubbles. Wipe rims with a moist paper towel to remove any spills. Top with lids and tightly screw on rings.
- Place a rack in the bottom of a large stockpot and fill halfway with water. Bring to a boil and lower jars 2 inches apart into the boiling water using a holder. Pour in more boiling water to cover jars by at least 1 inch. Bring to a rolling boil, cover, and process for 10 minutes.
- Remove the jars from the stockpot and place onto a cloth-covered or wood surface, several inches apart. Let rest for 24 hours without moving. Gently press the center of each lid with a finger to ensure the lid does not move up or down. Remove the rings for storage and store in a cool, dark area.

Nutrition Information

- Calories: 70 calories
- Total Fat: 0 g
- Cholesterol: 0 mg
- Sodium: 13 mg
- Total Carbohydrate: 17 g
- Protein: 0 g

331. Spinach Salad with Peaches and Pecans

"A perfect summer salad with ripe peaches, baby spinach, and roasted pecans"

Serving: 4 | Prep: 10 m | Cook: 10 m | Ready in: 20 m

Ingredients

- 3/4 cup pecans
- 2 ripe peaches
- 4 cups baby spinach, rinsed and dried
- 1/4 cup poppyseed salad dressing

Direction

- Preheat oven to 350 degrees F (175 degrees C). Arrange pecans on a single layer on a baking sheet and roast in preheated oven for 7-10 minutes, until they just begin to darken. Remove from oven and set aside.
- Peel peaches (if desired) and slice into bite-sized segments. Combine peaches, spinach and pecans in a large bowl. Toss with dressing until evenly coated, adding a little additional dressing, if necessary.

Nutrition Information

- Calories: 253 calories
- Total Fat: 22.6 g
- Cholesterol: 5 mg
- Sodium: 132 mg
- Total Carbohydrate: 11.4 g
- Protein: 2.9 g

332. Strawberry Banana Blend

"A sweet refreshing blend of strawberries, bananas, and fresh fruit. Use any fresh fruit you choose. A healthy touch to a hot summer day."

Serving: 4 | Prep: 25 m | Ready in: 30 m

Ingredients

- 2 bananas, sliced
- 15 strawberries, hulled
- 1/2 cup fresh peaches, pitted and chopped
- 1 3/4 cups strawberry sorbet
- 1/3 cup orange juice

Direction

- In a blender combine the bananas and strawberries. Blend on medium speed until smooth. Blend in the peaches and orange juice. Scoop in the sorbet. Blend until smooth.

Nutrition Information

- Calories: 194 calories

- Total Fat: 0.4 g
- Cholesterol: 0 mg
- Sodium: 2 mg
- Total Carbohydrate: 48.1 g
- Protein: 1.1 g

333. Strawberry Peach Parfait

"Super tasty for a breakfast, a quick snack, or even dessert. Great for those days were you can't seem to stop thinking about the ice cream in your freezer."

Serving: 2 | Prep: 10 m | Ready in: 10 m

Ingredients

- 1 cup chopped fresh peach
- 1 cup chopped old fashioned donuts
- 1 (6 ounce) container strawberry yogurt

Direction

- Divide about 1/4 cup chopped peach into two small cups or bowls, followed by a layer of about 1/4 cup donuts. Spread about 1/2 of the yogurt over donuts, then repeat layers once more.

Nutrition Information

- Calories: 308 calories
- Total Fat: 14.9 g
- Cholesterol: 8 mg
- Sodium: 309 mg
- Total Carbohydrate: 37.4 g
- Protein: 5.5 g

334. Strawberry Peach Smoothie

"Quick, delicious and refreshing on a hot day. If you don't have fresh strawberries or peaches, you can substitute with frozen ones."

Serving: 1 | Prep: 10 m | Ready in: 10 m

Ingredients

- 3/4 cup vanilla-flavored soy milk
- 1 (1/2 cup) scoop vanilla ice cream
- 1/4 cup frozen sliced strawberries
- 4 sliced fresh strawberries
- 1 small fresh peach, sliced

Direction

- Pour soy milk into a blender and add vanilla ice cream, frozen strawberries, fresh strawberries, and peach slices. Blend until smooth and pour into a large glass.

Nutrition Information

- Calories: 225 calories
- Total Fat: 8.9 g
- Cholesterol: 29 mg
- Sodium: 142 mg
- Total Carbohydrate: 31.4 g
- Protein: 7.3 g

335. Strawberry Peach Smoothie from Yoplait

"A creamy, peach and orange smoothie is layered on top of a strawberry smoothie--pretty as a picture and oh so delicious."

Serving: 2 | Prep: 10 m | Ready in: 10 m

Ingredients

- 1 cup frozen strawberries
- 1 large banana, peeled and halved
- 1 (5.3 ounce) container Yoplait® Greek 100 Vanilla Yogurt, divided
- 1/4 cup milk
- 1 tablespoon honey (optional)
- 1 cup sliced frozen peaches
- 1/4 cup orange juice

Direction

- Combine the strawberries, half the banana, 1/2 container of yogurt, milk and honey (if using) in a blender and blend until smooth. Pour into 2 glasses and rinse out the blender.
- Combine the remaining half the banana, remaining yogurt, peaches and orange juice in the blender and blend until smooth. Pour over the strawberry smoothie layer and serve.

Nutrition Information

- Calories: 235 calories
- Total Fat: 1 g
- Cholesterol: 2 mg
- Sodium: 44 mg
- Total Carbohydrate: 45.9 g
- Protein: 9.5 g

336. Stuffed Baked Peaches

"Quick and light peaches with a twist, served warm or at room temp."

Serving: 4 | Prep: 15 m | Cook: 25 m | Ready in: 40 m

Ingredients

- 1/4 cup almonds
- 1/4 cup brown sugar
- 1/4 cup butter, cut into cubes
- 4 fresh peaches, peeled and halved
- 1/4 cup brandy-based orange liqueur (such as Grand Marnier®)
- 1/4 cup water

Direction

- Preheat oven to 350 degrees F (175 degrees C).
- Heat a small skillet over medium heat. Toast almonds in hot skillet until fragrant and lightly browned, about 3 minutes.

- Put almonds and brown sugar into a food processor bowl and process until almonds are chopped; add butter and pulse the mixture until completely blended.
- Arrange peaches with the cut sides facing up into the baking dish. Spoon 1 tablespoon almond mixture into the center of each peach. Pour liqueur and water into the baking dish; cover with aluminum foil.
- Bake in preheated oven until the peaches are tender, 20 to 30 minutes.

Nutrition Information

- Calories: 279 calories
- Total Fat: 16 g
- Cholesterol: 31 mg
- Sodium: 91 mg
- Total Carbohydrate: 27.4 g
- Protein: 2.1 g

337. Succulent Grilled Peaches with Honey Chevre

"The sweetness of the warmed peach goes so well with the creaminess of the goat cheese with a hint of honey. It's like getting cheesecake in a peach crust. "

Serving: 8 | Prep: 15 m | Cook: 5 m | Ready in: 20 m

Ingredients

- 6 ounces chevre (soft goat cheese)
- 2 tablespoons skim milk
- 1 tablespoon honey
- 4 fresh peaches, halved and pitted
- 8 mint leaves

Direction

- Preheat an outdoor grill for medium heat, and lightly oil the grate.
- Combine chevre cheese, milk, and honey in a small bowl.
- Grill the peaches cut sides down until peaches begin to caramelize and show grill marks, 5 to

7 minutes. Fill each peach half with 1 tablespoon of the cheese mixture. Garnish with a mint leaf, and serve warm.

Nutrition Information

- Calories: 99 calories
- Total Fat: 6.3 g
- Cholesterol: 17 mg
- Sodium: 113 mg
- Total Carbohydrate: 5.9 g
- Protein: 4.7 g

338. Sugar Free Peach and Banana Cobbler

"My own creation! This recipe is good for diabetics, but can easily be made as a non-diabetic dessert by using real sugar instead of a sugar substitute. This dessert is not super sweet, allowing the natural sweetness of the fruit to come through. If you like sweeter desserts, double the amount of the sugar substitute or sugar. You can use whatever sugar substitute is your preference."

Serving: 8 | Prep: 20 m | Cook: 30 m | Ready in: 1 h 10 m

Ingredients

- 8 white peaches, pitted and sliced
- 2 bananas, sliced
- 2 tablespoons all-purpose flour
- 1 teaspoon sugar substitute
- 1 cup all-purpose flour
- 2 teaspoons baking powder
- 1/2 teaspoon salt
- 1/2 teaspoon ground cinnamon
- 1/2 cup skim milk
- 1 egg
- 1 tablespoon corn oil
- 2 teaspoons sugar substitute
- 1/2 teaspoon vanilla extract

Direction

- Preheat oven to 350 degrees F (175 degrees C). Grease an 8x8-inch baking dish.

- Mix white peaches, bananas, 2 tablespoons flour, and 1 teaspoon sugar substitute in a bowl until the fruit is coated; spread into the bottom of the prepared baking dish.
- Whisk 1 cup flour, baking powder, salt, and cinnamon in the same bowl used to mix fruit; stir in skim milk, egg, corn oil, 2 teaspoons sugar substitute, and vanilla extract to make a batter. Pour batter in an even layer over the fruit.
- Bake in the preheated oven until cake is golden brown and a toothpick inserted into the middle of the cake layer comes out clean, about 30 minutes. Cool in pan on rack at least 20 minutes before serving.

Nutrition Information

- Calories: 160 calories
- Total Fat: 2.9 g
- Cholesterol: 24 mg
- Sodium: 283 mg
- Total Carbohydrate: 30.8 g
- Protein: 4.3 g

339. Summer Citrus and Peach Chicken Salad

"Spicy and sweet, creamy and crunchy, this summer salad is perfect for year-round enjoyment if you can get your hands on the produce!"

Serving: 8 | Prep: 40 m | Cook: 12 m | Ready in: 52 m

Ingredients

- 6 boneless, skinless chicken breast halves rinsed and patted dry
- 2 tablespoons olive oil
- sea salt and cracked black pepper to taste
- Dressing:
- 1 cup fresh squeezed orange juice
- 1/2 cup olive oil
- 2 tomatillos, husked and quartered
- 1 shallot, quartered
- 1 jalapeno pepper, stemmed and seeded, or more to taste
- 1 tablespoon cider vinegar
- 2 tablespoons chopped cilantro
- 1/2 teaspoon sea salt
- 1/4 teaspoon cracked black pepper, or to taste
- Salad:
- 8 cups mixed salad greens
- 4 fresh peaches - peeled, pitted, and sliced
- 2 avocados - peeled, pitted, and sliced
- 2 tablespoons chopped fresh mint
- dried orange slices (such as Simple Crisp™), or more to taste (optional)

Direction

- Preheat an outdoor grill for medium-high heat and lightly oil the grate.
- Drizzle chicken with 2 tablespoons olive oil; season with salt and pepper. Grill chicken until no longer pink in the center and the juices run clear, 6 to 8 minutes per side. An instant-read thermometer inserted into the center should read at least 165 degrees F (74 degrees C). Place chicken on a flat work surface and slice crosswise into strips.
- Place orange juice, 1/2 cup olive oil, tomatillos, shallot, jalapeno, vinegar, cilantro, 1/2 teaspoon salt, and 1/4 pepper in a blender. Puree until dressing is smooth.
- Place salad greens in a bowl. Drizzle dressing on top. Add chicken, peaches, avocados, and mint. Crumble dried oranges and sprinkle over the salad.

Nutrition Information

- Calories: 371 calories
- Total Fat: 26.6 g
- Cholesterol: 50 mg
- Sodium: 285 mg
- Total Carbohydrate: 13.9 g
- Protein: 20.7 g

340. Summer Fruit Galettes

"Here's a quick and easy way to create a beautiful summer fruit dessert. I love to use fresh peaches, strawberries and blueberries, but frozen fruits should also work. You can also use fresh nectarines or apricots in place of the peaches. It will look like you spent hours making this fancy 30 minute dessert! Pairs great with a scoop of vanilla ice cream."

Serving: 10 | Prep: 15 m | Cook: 14 m | Ready in: 29 m

Ingredients

- 2 (9 inch) refrigerated pie crusts
- 3 fresh peaches - peeled, pitted, and sliced
- 1 pint fresh strawberries, sliced
- 1/2 pint fresh blueberries
- 4 tablespoons white sugar, divided
- 4 tablespoons all-purpose flour, divided
- 6 tablespoons turbinado sugar, divided

Direction

- Preheat oven to 450 degrees F (230 degrees C).
- Lay out one pie crust on a baking sheet lined with parchment or on a baking stone, leaving room for the second pie crust next to it.
- Mix together the sliced peaches with half the blueberries, 2 tablespoons of the flour and 2 tablespoons of the sugar in a bowl. Pour over one pie crust leaving a 1-inch border. Fold up the uncovered border over the edge of the fruit and pinch into pleats. Sprinkle the crust and fruit filling with 3 tablespoons of turbinado (or raw) sugar.
- Lay out the second pie crust on the baking sheet. Mix together the sliced strawberries, the rest of the blueberries, 2 tablespoons of flour and 2 tablespoons of sugar in the bowl. Pour over the second pie crust and form the galette the same as the first. Sprinkle with 3 tablespoons of turbinado sugar.
- Bake in preheated oven until crust is lightly browned, 12 to 14 minutes. Sprinkle with more sugar if desired. Serve warm or at room temperature.

Nutrition Information

- Calories: 269 calories
- Total Fat: 12.1 g
- Cholesterol: 0 mg
- Sodium: 192 mg
- Total Carbohydrate: 37.9 g
- Protein: 2.9 g

341. Summer Fruit Salad

"YUMMY YUMMY!!!"

Serving: 10 | Prep: 40 m | Ready in: 1 h 40 m

Ingredients

- 1 fresh pineapple - peeled, cored, and chopped
- 1/2 cantaloupe - peeled, seeded, and chopped
- 2 fresh peaches, pitted and chopped
- 3 plums, pitted and chopped
- 2 bananas, chopped
- 2 oranges, peeled and cut into bite size pieces
- 2 kiwi fruit, peeled and chopped
- 2 fresh apricots, pitted and chopped
- 10 cherries, pitted and halved
- 15 seedless grapes
- 7 strawberries, chopped

Direction

- In a large salad bowl, lightly stir together the pineapple, cantaloupe, peaches, plums, bananas, oranges, kiwi fruit, apricots, cherries, grapes, and strawberries; chill for 1 hour before serving.

Nutrition Information

- Calories: 155 calories
- Total Fat: 0.6 g
- Cholesterol: 0 mg
- Sodium: 8 mg
- Total Carbohydrate: 39.3 g
- Protein: 2.2 g

342. Summer is Here Triple Berry Peach Pie

"The best part of summer is the fresh, juicy fruit available in grocery stores or farmers' markets. This pie is my own creation after visiting the market and seeing beautiful berries and peaches for sale. After experimenting with different fruits and sugar levels, I have put together a fresh berry and peach pie that just screams 'summer is here!'"

Serving: 8 | Prep: 30 m | Cook: 45 m | Ready in: 1 h 45 m

Ingredients

- For the Pie:
- 1 pastry for a 9 inch double crust pie
- 1 egg white, lightly beaten
- 3 fresh peaches - peeled, pitted, and sliced
- 1 pint fresh strawberries, hulled and large berries cut in half
- 1 pint fresh blueberries
- 2 (6 ounce) containers fresh raspberries
- 1/3 cup all-purpose flour
- 3 tablespoons cornstarch
- 1/2 cup brown sugar
- 1/2 cup white sugar
- 2 teaspoons ground cinnamon
- 1/4 teaspoon ground nutmeg
- 2 tablespoons butter, cut into small pieces
- For the Topping:
- 1 teaspoon ground cinnamon
- 1 tablespoon white sugar

Direction

- Preheat an oven to 350 degrees F (175 degrees C). Line a 9 inch pie plate with half of the dough and brush with half of the beaten egg white.
- Combine the sliced peaches, strawberries, blueberries, and raspberries in a large bowl; set aside. Mix the flour, cornstarch, brown sugar, 1/2 cup white sugar, 2 teaspoons cinnamon, and nutmeg together. Gently fold the flour mixture into the fruit, taking care not to crush the berries. Transfer the fruit mixture into the pastry-lined pie plate. The filling will be piled high but will cook down. Dot with butter.
- Top the filled pie with a lattice crust or a full top crust (cut decorative slits in the crust to allow steam to escape). Brush the top crust or lattice with the remaining egg white. Combine 1 teaspoon cinnamon and 1 tablespoon sugar and sprinkle the mixture on the crust. Place the pie on a baking sheet to catch drips.
- Bake the pie until the crust is golden brown and the filling is bubbly, 45 to 60 minutes. Turn off the oven and let the pie set for 30 minutes; transfer to a cooling rack. The filling will be loose if served warm, but will tighten up when the pie is completely cooled.

Nutrition Information

- Calories: 463 calories
- Total Fat: 18.4 g
- Cholesterol: 8 mg
- Sodium: 268 mg
- Total Carbohydrate: 72.1 g
- Protein: 4.9 g

343. Summer Peach Basil Cheddar Muffins

"Nothing says summer like a ripe, juicy peach and fresh fragrant basil. I love pairing fruits with cheese, and these were inspired by apple cheddar muffins my mom used to make. These savory sidekicks have just a hint of sweetness and make the perfect addition to your summer brunch table!"

Serving: 12 | Prep: 20 m | Cook: 25 m | Ready in: 45 m

Ingredients

- 4 fresh peaches, cut into 1/2-inch pieces
- 4 teaspoons finely minced fresh basil
- 1 tablespoon brown sugar
- 1 1/2 cups all-purpose flour
- 1 1/2 teaspoons baking powder
- 1/2 teaspoon baking soda
- 1/2 teaspoon salt

- 1 cup shredded extra-sharp Cheddar cheese (such as Sargento® Off the Block)
- 1/2 cup butter, room temperature
- 7 tablespoons brown sugar
- 2 eggs, room temperature
- 1/4 cup shredded extra-sharp Cheddar cheese (such as Sargento® Off the Block)

Direction

- Preheat oven to 350 degrees F (175 degrees C). Grease 12 muffin cups or line with paper liners.
- Mix peaches, basil, and 1 tablespoon brown sugar in a bowl; let sit until sugar dissolves, about 15 minutes.
- Sift flour, baking powder, baking soda, and salt together in a large bowl. Mix 1 cup Cheddar cheese into flour mixture.
- Beat butter and 7 tablespoons brown sugar in a bowl with an electric mixer until smooth and creamy. Add eggs, one at a time, until just combined; gently fold in peaches. Mix flour mixture, a little at time, into peach mixture until batter is just combined.
- Spoon batter into the prepared muffin cups. Sprinkle 1/4 cup Cheddar cheese over batter.
- Bake in the preheated oven until a toothpick inserted in the middle of a muffin comes out clean, about 25 minutes.

Nutrition Information

- Calories: 225 calories
- Total Fat: 12.4 g
- Cholesterol: 64 mg
- Sodium: 355 mg
- Total Carbohydrate: 23.4 g
- Protein: 5.7 g

344. Sweet and Easy Peach Dessert

"This is a simple dish with lots of flavor. Perfect way to use those summer peaches. It's also versatile, so feel free to experiment with other fruits."

Serving: 6 | Prep: 15 m | Cook: 1 h 5 m | Ready in: 1 h 20 m

Ingredients

- 1 1/2 teaspoons butter
- 4 fresh peaches - peeled, pitted, and diced
- 1/4 cup maple syrup
- 1 cup all-purpose flour
- 2 tablespoons all-purpose flour
- 1/2 teaspoon salt
- 1/2 cup unsalted butter
- 2 tablespoons sour cream
- 3 egg yolks, beaten
- 1 cup white sugar
- 3 1/3 tablespoons sour cream
- 2 tablespoons all-purpose flour
- 1 pinch salt

Direction

- Melt 1/2 tablespoon butter in a saucepan over medium heat. Stir peaches, maple syrup, and a pinch of salt together in the melted butter; cook, stirring occasionally, until the mixture is syrupy, about 10 minutes. Remove from heat and set aside to cool.
- Preheat oven to 425 degrees F (220 degrees C). Grease a 10x6-inch baking dish.
- Mix 1 cup plus 2 tablespoons flour and 1/2 teaspoon salt together in a bowl. Mash unsalted butter into the flour mixture until lumps are the size of small peas. Blend 2 tablespoons sour cream into the mixture; mix until you have a dough-like mixture. Pat the dough into the bottom and up the sides of the prepared baking dish.
- Bake in preheated oven until browned and crust-like, about 10 minutes.
- Spread peach mixture over the crust into an even layer.

- Beat egg yolks, sugar, 3 1/3 tablespoons sour cream, and 2 tablespoons flour together in a small bowl; pour evenly over the layer of peaches. Cover the dish with aluminum foil.
- Bake in the preheated oven for about 35 minutes. Remove aluminum foil and continue baking until a toothpick inserted into the center comes out clean, about 10 minutes. Let cool slightly before serving warm.

Nutrition Information

- Calories: 473 calories
- Total Fat: 21.5 g
- Cholesterol: 151 mg
- Sodium: 218 mg
- Total Carbohydrate: 66.8 g
- Protein: 4.6 g

345. Sweet Grilled Peaches

"Peaches are spruced up with a little honey and a dash of cinnamon before being packaged into foil and cooked on the grill. As my husband says, these taste like a peach cobbler without the crust!"

Serving: 4 | Prep: 5 m | Cook: 10 m | Ready in: 15 m

Ingredients

- 1 (16 ounce) package frozen peach slices
- 1/2 cup honey
- 2 tablespoons cinnamon

Direction

- Preheat a grill for medium heat.
- Place peaches onto a large piece of aluminum foil. Use two if necessary to hold in all of the peaches without spillage. Drizzle the honey over the peaches, and sprinkle with cinnamon. Close up the foil, sealing tightly.
- Place the foil packet onto the preheated grill, and cook for 10 minutes, turning once halfway through. Carefully open the packet, and serve.

Nutrition Information

- Calories: 244 calories
- Total Fat: 0.2 g
- Cholesterol: 0 mg
- Sodium: 9 mg
- Total Carbohydrate: 64.9 g
- Protein: 1 g

346. Sweet Potato Peach Bake

"Peaches and sweet potatoes complement each other so well in this Sweet Potato Peach Bake. This sweet and delicious casserole is perfect for the holidays, and can be dressed up with marshmallows or peach preserves."

Serving: 6 | Prep: 10 m | Cook: 40 m | Ready in: 50 m

Ingredients

- 1 (40 ounce) can Bruce's® Yams Cut Sweet Potatoes in Syrup, drained
- 1 (16 ounce) can sliced peaches (no sugar added), drained, juice reserved
- 1/2 teaspoon ground ginger
- 1/2 teaspoon salt
- 1/2 teaspoon pepper
- 1/4 cup brown sugar
- 1/3 cup chopped pecans

Direction

- Heat oven to 350 degrees F.
- Place Bruce's(R) Yams Cut Sweet Potatoes in a bowl and cut into slightly smaller pieces.
- Drain the peaches (reserving 4-5 slices for the top of the casserole) and add to the yams along with 1/2 cup peach juice, ground ginger, salt and pepper; stir to mix.
- Transfer to a 2 quart baking dish; set aside.
- In a separate bowl, stir together the brown sugar and pecans.
- Sprinkle over top of casserole and place reserved peach slices in a line down the center.
- Bake for 35-40 minutes until hot and bubbly.

Nutrition Information

- Calories: 354 calories
- Total Fat: 4.8 g
- Cholesterol: 0 mg
- Sodium: 269 mg
- Total Carbohydrate: 75.6 g
- Protein: 1.2 g

347. The Really Good Salad Recipe with Pieces of Fruit

"Garden salad with fruit, cooked sugared almonds, and an oil and vinegar dressing."

Serving: 8 | Prep: 15 m | Cook: 5 m | Ready in: 20 m

Ingredients

- 1 cup slivered almonds
- 1/2 cup white sugar
- 1/2 cup olive oil
- 1/4 cup distilled white vinegar
- 2 tablespoons white sugar
- salt and pepper to taste
- 1/2 head iceberg lettuce - rinsed, dried, and chopped
- 1/2 head leaf lettuce - rinsed, dried, and chopped
- 1 cup chopped celery
- 1/4 cup chopped fresh chives
- 1/2 cup dried, sweetened cranberries
- 1/2 cup mandarin orange segments, drained
- 1/2 cup sliced fresh peaches
- 1/2 cup diced mango
- 1/2 cup chopped fresh strawberries

Direction

- In a skillet over medium heat, cook and stir the almonds and 1/2 cup sugar 5 minutes, or until almonds are well-coated and lightly browned.
- In a bowl, mix the olive oil, vinegar, 2 tablespoons sugar, salt, and pepper. Set aside.
- In a large bowl, gently mix the almonds, iceberg lettuce, leaf lettuce, celery, chives, cranberries, mandarin orange, peaches, mango, and strawberries. Serve with desired amount of the oil and vinegar dressing.

Nutrition Information

- Calories: 317 calories
- Total Fat: 20.6 g
- Cholesterol: 0 mg
- Sodium: 24 mg
- Total Carbohydrate: 31.7 g
- Protein: 3.8 g

348. The Toxic Avenger

"This drink was invented with Ms. Sarah Johnson over games of Phantasmagoria 2 and bowls of Cajun popcorn. To fully enjoy this drink, make sure you drink it at least once while viewing the Troma movie of the same name."

Serving: 1 | Prep: 2 m | Cook: 1 m | Ready in: 3 m

Ingredients

- 3 fluid ounces white rum
- 6 fluid ounces peach daiquiri mix
- 1 dash Blue Curacao

Direction

- In a blender combine rum, daiquiri mix, and a good dash of Blue Curacao, add as much ice as desired and process until all ice is chopped. Drinks should be thick and a putrid, toxic-waste green but very fruity and delicious. Serve generously in tall glasses and enjoy!

349. Three CheeseStuffed French Toast

"This recipe is for those who enjoy baking and spending some time in the kitchen creating wonderful palate pleasing delights for those whose company we enjoy! So go on and give it a try, make someone's day by giving them brunch in bed!"

Serving: 8 | Prep: 30 m | Cook: 30 m | Ready in: 14 h 20 m

Ingredients

- 3/4 cup shredded mozzarella cheese
- 4 ounces cream cheese, softened
- 1 tablespoon ricotta cheese
- 3 tablespoons apricot jam
- 8 (2 inch thick) slices French bread
- 2 eggs, lightly beaten
- 1/2 cup milk
- 1 cup cornflakes cereal crumbs
- 2 tablespoons butter
- 2 cups apricot nectar
- 1/4 cup butter
- 2 tablespoons white sugar
- 2 teaspoons ground ginger
- 2 cups sliced fresh peaches
- 1/4 cup confectioners' sugar for dusting

Direction

- The night before: Split each bread slice four fifths of the way through. Spread the two sides apart so that they look like butterfly wings. Use a fork hollow out a shallow pocket on the inside of each slice. Discard the crumbs; set bread aside
- In a medium bowl, mix together the mozzarella, cream cheese and ricotta cheese. Stir in the apricot jam. Spoon 2 tablespoons of cheese mixture into each bread slice. Place slices in a 9x13 inch baking dish. Cover and chill 8 hours or overnight.
- The next morning: Preheat oven to 400 degrees F (200 degrees C). Pour apricot nectar into a small saucepan and simmer over medium heat. Stir in sugar and cornstarch; cook until thickened.
- Beat together eggs and milk. Dip bread slices into egg mixture and dredge in cornflakes crumbs. Melt 2 tablespoons butter in a large skillet over medium heat; cook bread 2 minutes on each side or until golden. Place in a lightly greased 9x13 inch baking dish. Bake at 400 degrees for 15 minutes.
- In a medium frying pan or skillet, heat 1/4 cup butter, 2 tablespoons sugar and ginger over medium heat. Add peaches and cook for 3 minutes.
- Arrange French toast slices on individual plates. Top each serving evenly with peach slices, sprinkle with powdered sugar. Serve with apricot syrup.

Nutrition Information

- Calories: 456 calories
- Total Fat: 18.2 g
- Cholesterol: 94 mg
- Sodium: 617 mg
- Total Carbohydrate: 61.5 g
- Protein: 13.6 g

350. Tinas Peach Cobbler

"This peach cobbler is absolutely the best I have ever tasted anywhere. It's well worth the time to make it. I have never met a person who didn't love this cobbler. You can put an egg wash on the crust if you wish."

Serving: 8 | Prep: 45 m | Cook: 50 m | Ready in: 1 h 35 m

Ingredients

- 8 cups fresh peaches - peeled, pitted, and sliced
- 2 cups white sugar
- 1/2 teaspoon ground nutmeg
- 1/3 cup unsalted butter
- 1 teaspoon vanilla extract
- 2 cups all-purpose flour, sifted
- 1 teaspoon salt
- 3/8 cup lard

- 3/8 cup shortening
- 1 egg
- 1/8 cup cold water

Direction

- Preheat oven to 350 degrees F (175 degrees C).
- In a large saucepan, combine peaches, sugar and nutmeg. Cook over medium heat, stirring occasionally, until mixture thickens and begins to bubble and peaches are tender, 10 minutes. Remove from heat and stir in butter and vanilla until butter is melted. Pour into a 9x13 inch baking dish.
- In a medium bowl, combine flour and salt. Blend in lard and shortening with pastry blender until mixture resembles pea-sized crumbs. Combine egg and cold water in a separate bowl and sprinkle mixture over pastry, a little at a time, stirring just until dough comes together. Roll out on a floured surface into a 9x13 inch rectangle. Lay crust over peach mixture.
- Bake in preheated oven 50 to 60 minutes, until crust is golden.

Nutrition Information

- Calories: 590 calories
- Total Fat: 27.9 g
- Cholesterol: 53 mg
- Sodium: 306 mg
- Total Carbohydrate: 81.9 g
- Protein: 4.1 g

351. Tipsy Peaches

"Sweet fried peaches with a hint of whiskey...good as a side dish or on top of vanilla ice cream for a tasty dessert. Use a good quality whiskey for the best flavor."

Serving: 4 | Prep: 15 m | Cook: 30 m | Ready in: 45 m

Ingredients

- 1 tablespoon butter
- 4 cups sliced fresh peaches

- 2 tablespoons brown sugar
- 1 teaspoon vanilla extract
- 1 (1.5 fluid ounce) jigger whiskey

Direction

- Melt butter in a skillet over medium heat. Add the peaches, and cook for about 10 minutes, stirring occasionally. Mix in the brown sugar, vanilla, and whiskey; simmer over medium heat for about 20 minutes, until peaches are soft and the sauce has darkened. Serve as a side dish or over ice cream.

Nutrition Information

- Calories: 113 calories
- Total Fat: 2.9 g
- Cholesterol: 8 mg
- Sodium: 28 mg
- Total Carbohydrate: 14.6 g
- Protein: 0.1 g

352. Too Easy Peach Cobbler

"This cobbler is made with slices of white bread instead of the traditional biscuit dough."

Serving: 6 | Prep: 20 m | Cook: 35 m | Ready in: 55 m

Ingredients

- 6 fresh peaches - pitted, skinned, and sliced
- 1 1/2 cups white sugar
- 2 tablespoons all-purpose flour
- 1 egg
- 1/2 cup butter, melted
- 5 slices white bread

Direction

- Preheat oven to 350 degrees F (175 degrees C). Butter an 8-inch square baking dish.
- Cut crust from bread slices, and cut each into 4 or 5 strips. Spread fruit into prepared pan, and cover with a layer of bread strips.

- Beat together butter, sugar, and flour; mix in egg. Pour mixture over the fruit and bread.
- Bake in preheated oven for 35 to 45 minutes, or until golden brown.

Nutrition Information

- Calories: 431 calories
- Total Fat: 16.9 g
- Cholesterol: 72 mg
- Sodium: 266 mg
- Total Carbohydrate: 68.6 g
- Protein: 3.1 g

353. Tuna Fish Tacos

"Picked and packed at its peak ripeness, canned peaches deliver nutrition, freshness and the flavors of summer to these wholesome tacos anytime of year!"

Serving: 4 | Prep: 15 m | Ready in: 30 m

Ingredients

- Salsa:
- 1 (15.25 ounce) can lite peach slices, drained and chopped
- 1 (4.25 ounce) can chopped green chilies, drained
- 1/4 cup finely chopped red onion
- 1 tablespoon fresh chopped parsley
- 1 tablespoon fresh squeezed lime juice
- 1/4 teaspoon hot pepper sauce (such as Tabasco®)
- Tacos:
- 1 (5 ounce) can albacore tuna packed in water, drained and flaked
- 8 (6 inch) corn, flour, or whole wheat tortillas, slightly warmed
- Finely shredded green cabbage (optional)
- Shredded Monterey Jack cheese (optional)
- Lime wedges (optional)

Direction

- Prepare Salsa: In medium bowl combine chopped peaches, green chiles, red onion, parsley, lime juice and Tabasco sauce. Cover and refrigerate until ready to serve.
- Prepare Tacos: Fill tortillas with flaked tuna; top with peach salsa. Serve with shredded cabbage and cheese if desired. Garnish with lime wedges if desired.

Nutrition Information

- Calories: 228 calories
- Total Fat: 2.4 g
- Cholesterol: 11 mg
- Sodium: 407 mg
- Total Carbohydrate: 42.3 g
- Protein: 12.4 g

354. Ultimate Fruit Smoothie

"This is a easy but healthy smoothie that anyone can make. A little tang and a dash of sweet combine to make an excellent smoothie!"

Serving: 1 | Prep: 10 m | Ready in: 10 m

Ingredients

- 1/2 cup 2% milk
- 1/2 cup orange juice
- 1/2 mango - peeled, seeded, and cut into chunks
- 1/2 fresh peach - peeled, pitted, and sliced
- 1/4 cup fresh pineapple chunks
- 2 strawberries

Direction

- Blend milk, orange juice, mango, peach, pineapple, and strawberries together in a blender until smooth.

Nutrition Information

- Calories: 225 calories
- Total Fat: 3.1 g
- Cholesterol: 10 mg
- Sodium: 56 mg
- Total Carbohydrate: 46.4 g

- Protein: 5.8 g

355. UnTofu Tofu Smoothie

"A great way to eat tofu -- without even knowing it! Very refreshing, especially for breakfast or as a snack. Tinker with it until you find the perfect combo for you."

Serving: 4 | Prep: 5 m | Ready in: 5 m

Ingredients

- 1/3 (10.75 ounce) package dessert tofu
- 3 frozen strawberries
- 5 frozen peach slices
- 1 (8 ounce) container strawberry yogurt
- 1 cup orange juice

Direction

- In a blender, combine tofu, strawberries, peach slices, yogurt and orange juice. Blend until smooth.

Nutrition Information

- Calories: 96 calories
- Total Fat: 0.6 g
- Cholesterol: 1 mg
- Sodium: 42 mg
- Total Carbohydrate: 19.9 g
- Protein: 3.3 g

356. UpsideDown Coffee Cake

"This is a gorgeous moist and gooey coffee cake! Use any type of fresh or frozen fruit, or combination of 2 fruits. Peach, cherry, blackberry and/or red raspberry are some of the best. The deep baking pan is required due to the bubbling caramel sauce and the height of the cake. Every time I serve it I get rave reviews!"

Serving: 16 | Prep: 45 m | Cook: 1 h 30 m | Ready in: 2 h 15 m

Ingredients

- 1/2 cup butter
- 2 cups light brown sugar
- 3 cups fresh peaches, pitted and sliced
- 2/3 cup margarine
- 1 1/3 cups white sugar
- 4 eggs
- 2 teaspoons vanilla extract
- 1 1/3 cups milk
- 3 1/3 cups all-purpose flour
- 4 teaspoons baking powder
- 1/2 teaspoon salt
- 1 teaspoon ground cinnamon

Direction

- Preheat oven to 350 degrees F (175 degrees C). Use a deep sided 10 inch pan, or wrap the outside of a 10 inch springform pan with aluminum foil to prevent leaking. Sift together the flour, baking powder, salt and cinnamon. Set aside.
- In a saucepan over medium heat, combine brown sugar and 1/2 cup butter. Bring to a boil, then pour into bottom of springform pan. Sprinkle with sliced peaches.
- In a large bowl, cream together 2/3 cup margarine and the white sugar until light and fluffy. Beat in the eggs one at a time, then stir in the vanilla. Beat in the flour mixture alternately with the milk. Pour batter over caramel and fruit in pan.
- Bake in the preheated oven for 90 minutes, or until a toothpick inserted into the center of the cake comes out clean. Cool in pan for 10 minutes, then invert onto serving platter and

carefully remove pan. Be extremely careful of hot caramel and fruit juices! Serve warm.

Nutrition Information

- Calories: 418 calories
- Total Fat: 15.1 g
- Cholesterol: 63 mg
- Sodium: 326 mg
- Total Carbohydrate: 66.5 g
- Protein: 5.1 g

---

357. Vegan and GlutenFree Naked Cake with Peaches and Coconut Cream

"A stunning vegan naked cake with fruity peaches and coconut cream. Decorate with fresh flowers for a truly spectacular result."

Serving: 12 | Prep: 40 m | Cook: 45 m | Ready in: 2 h 45 m

Ingredients

- Cakes:
- 2 3/4 cups gluten-free all-purpose baking flour
- 1 1/4 cups white sugar
- 1 teaspoon baking soda
- 1 teaspoon gluten-free baking powder
- 1 cup cold water
- 1/3 cup vegetable oil
- 1 teaspoon vanilla extract
- Filling:
- 1 (14 ounce) can cream of coconut
- 2 teaspoons vanilla extract
- 2 tablespoons white sugar
- 1 (15 ounce) can canned peaches in syrup, drained and cubed
- 2 tablespoons confectioners' sugar, or to taste

Direction

- Preheat oven to 375 degrees F (190 degrees C). Grease 3 8-inch cake pans and line with parchment paper.
- Combine flour, sugar, baking powder, and baking soda in a large bowl. Whisk together water, oil, and vanilla extract in a second bowl. Make a well in the center of the flour mixture and pour in water-mixture. Mix well with a wooden spoon until batter is well combined, 3 to 5 minutes.
- Divide cake batter evenly into prepared cake pans. Rest for 15 minutes.
- Bake in the preheated oven until a toothpick inserted in the middle comes out clean, about 45 minutes. Carefully remove from oven. Cool for 5 minutes in pans and turn out onto wire racks. Cool completely before filling and decorating.
- Pour coconut cream in a mixing bowl and chill in freezer for 5 minutes. Remove from freezer and whisk in vanilla extract. Whisk in sugar gradually until stiff peaks form. Spoon coconut cream into a piping bag with a large tip.
- Place one of the cakes on a serving plate. Pipe about half of the cream in concentric circles to cover the top of the cake. Arrange half of the peaches on this first layer. Add the second cake layer and repeat, using up the rest of the cream and the peaches. Lightly dust the top of the cake with confectioners' sugar and serve.

Nutrition Information

- Calories: 386 calories
- Total Fat: 12.4 g
- Cholesterol: 0 mg
- Sodium: 159 mg
- Total Carbohydrate: 68.7 g
- Protein: 3.7 g

358. Warm Peaches and Nuts Salad

"Warm peaches and sauteed vegetables and nuts on top of a bed of greens make for a delicious summer dish."

Serving: 2 | Prep: 25 m | Cook: 15 m | Ready in: 40 m

Ingredients

- 2 tablespoons extra-virgin olive oil
- 1 cup shredded red cabbage
- 1 small carrot, shredded
- 1/2 yellow squash, thinly sliced
- 1/2 red bell pepper, diced
- 1/2 small onion, sliced
- 1/2 cup red wine
- 1/4 cup sliced almonds
- 1/4 cup chopped walnuts
- 2 fresh peaches - pitted, skinned, and sliced
- 4 cups mixed baby greens
- 1/4 cup raspberry vinaigrette

Direction

- Heat the olive oil in a skillet over medium heat. Cook the cabbage, carrot, squash, bell pepper, and onion in the oil until the onion is translucent, 5 to 7 minutes. Stir the red wine, almonds, and walnuts into the vegetable mixture, reduce heat to low, and simmer 5 minutes.
- While the vegetable mixture simmers, heat a small skillet over medium heat; cook the peach slices in the skillet until completely warmed, about 5 minutes.
- Place 2 cups of the baby greens on each of 2 plates. Top each portion of the greens with about half of the vegetable mixture and the warmed peaches. Drizzle each salad with about half of the raspberry vinaigrette. Serve promptly.

Nutrition Information

- Calories: 468 calories
- Total Fat: 29.7 g
- Cholesterol: 0 mg
- Sodium: 489 mg
- Total Carbohydrate: 35.2 g
- Protein: 8.1 g

359. White Peach Sangria

"A refreshing white wine sangria that is always a hit at parties."

Serving: 6 | Prep: 10 m | Ready in: 2 h 10 m

Ingredients

- 1 (750 milliliter) bottle dry white wine
- 3/4 cup peach flavored vodka
- 6 tablespoons frozen lemonade concentrate, thawed
- 1/4 cup white sugar
- 1 pound white peaches, pitted and sliced
- 3/4 cup seedless red grapes, halved
- 3/4 cup seedless green grapes, halved

Direction

- In a large pitcher, combine dry white wine, peach vodka, lemonade concentrate and sugar. Stir until sugar is dissolved. Add sliced peaches, red and green grapes.
- Refrigerate sangria until well chilled, at least 2 hours, or overnight to blend flavors. Serve over ice, and use a slotted spoon to include sliced peaches and grapes with each serving.

360. White Peach Sorbet

"This tastes exactly like a white peach!"

Serving: 6 | Prep: 30 m | Ready in: 1 h 30 m

Ingredients

- 5 ripe white peaches
- 2 teaspoons lemon juice
- 2 teaspoons white sugar, or to taste

Direction

- Peel white peaches, leaving a little bit of peach skin to add texture and color. Cut chunks from peaches into a bowl and discard pits. Add lemon juice.

- Puree peaches and lemon juice with an immersion blender until smooth. Stir in sugar to taste. Blend again. Chill peach mixture in refrigerator for 1 hour.
- Pour peach mixture into an ice cream freezer and freeze according to manufacturer's instructions.

Nutrition Information

- Calories: 38 calories
- Total Fat: 0.2 g
- Cholesterol: 0 mg
- Sodium: < 1 mg
- Total Carbohydrate: 9.3 g
- Protein: 0.7 g

361. White Peach Spring Sangria with Elderflower Liqueur

"A delicious and refreshing white peach sangria recipe using Wente® chardonnay and St. Germaine® liqueur!"

Serving: 6 | Prep: 10 m | Ready in: 2 h 10 m

Ingredients

- 1 (750 milliliter) bottle chardonnay wine (such as Wente®)
- 1 cup elderflower liqueur (such as St. Germain®)
- 2 fresh peaches, sliced
- 1 pint fresh strawberries, sliced
- 1/2 cup fresh raspberries, or more to taste
- 1/2 cup fresh blueberries, or more to taste
- 1/2 cup fresh blackberries, or more to taste
- ice cubes

Direction

- Pour chardonnay and elderflower liqueur into a pitcher; add peaches, strawberries, raspberries, blueberries, and blackberries. Stir and let fruit soak for at least 2 hours.

- Fill wine glasses with ice and pour in sangria.

Nutrition Information

- Calories: 278 calories
- Total Fat: 0.3 g
- Cholesterol: 0 mg
- Sodium: 12 mg
- Total Carbohydrate: 28.3 g
- Protein: 0.5 g

362. White PeachLavender Compote

"White peaches and lavender are a lovely combination as long as you use the lavender sparingly to avoid an overwhelming lavender flavor. You can use yellow peaches if you can't find white ones."

Serving: 4 | Prep: 5 m | Cook: 5 m | Ready in: 1 h 10 m

Ingredients

- 1 1/2 pounds white peaches, pitted and shopped
- 1/2 tablespoon lavender honey
- 5 sprigs lavender flowers

Direction

- Combine peaches, honey, and lavender flowers in a microwave-safe bowl and cook for 5 minutes on high power. Discard lavender flowers.
- Transfer peach mixture to a blender; blend until smooth. Cover with plastic wrap and refrigerate for 1 hour. Serve chilled.

Nutrition Information

- Calories: 76 calories
- Total Fat: 0.5 g
- Cholesterol: 0 mg
- Sodium: 1 mg
- Total Carbohydrate: 18.7 g
- Protein: 1.7 g

363. White Peachy Sangria

"This sweet and yummy recipe is good for even those that do not like wine. Great on a hot day or paired with a dessert, ESPECIALLY a cheesecake or something fruity!"

Serving: 20 | Prep: 30 m | Ready in: 8 h 30 m

Ingredients

- 4 (750 milliliter) bottles moscato wine
- 4 (12 fluid ounce) cans or bottles lemon-lime soda (such as Sprite®)
- 1 cup brandy
- 1 cup peach schnapps
- 2 fresh peaches, pitted and sliced
- 1 (16 ounce) package fresh strawberries, sliced
- 2 mangos - peeled, seeded, and sliced
- 1/2 fresh pineapple - peeled, cored, and cut into chunks
- 1 (6 ounce) container fresh raspberries

Direction

- Stir moscato wine, lemon-lime soda, brandy, peach schnapps, peaches, strawberries, mangos, pineapple chunks, and raspberries together in a large container and chill 8 hours or overnight.

Nutrition Information

- Calories: 376 calories
- Total Fat: 0.2 g
- Cholesterol: 0 mg
- Sodium: 24 mg
- Total Carbohydrate: 40.9 g
- Protein: 0.7 g

364. White Sangria

"WONDERFUL!!! A wonderful punch made with white wine, mango and orange slices. Peach schnapps, cognac and ginger ale round out this summer party drink."

Serving: 32 | Prep: 30 m | Ready in: 1 h 30 m

Ingredients

- 1/2 cup peach schnapps
- 1/2 cup cognac
- 1/4 cup white sugar
- 4 oranges, sliced into rounds
- 2 mangos, peeled and sliced
- 4 (750 milliliter) bottles dry white wine, chilled
- 1 liter ginger ale, chilled

Direction

- In a pitcher, combine peach schnapps, cognac, sugar, sliced oranges and sliced mangos. Chill for at least an hour.
- Pour fruit mixture into a large punch bowl. Stir in white wine and ginger ale.

365. Whole Grain Carrot Peach Muffins

"A soft healthy whole grain muffin bursting with sweet peaches and topped with an oat streusel. Plus a hidden veggie surprise."

Serving: 12 | Prep: 25 m | Cook: 15 m | Ready in: 45 m

Ingredients

- Topping:
- 2 tablespoons butter, slightly softened
- 1/4 cup rolled oats
- 1 tablespoon dark brown sugar
- 1 tablespoon all-purpose flour
- 1/4 teaspoon ground cinnamon
- Muffins:
- 1/2 cup all-purpose flour
- 1/2 cup white whole-wheat flour
- 1/2 cup oat flour
- 1 1/2 teaspoons baking powder

- 1 teaspoon ground cinnamon
- 1/2 teaspoon baking soda
- 1/2 cup canola oil
- 1/2 cup white sugar
- 2 large eggs
- 1 teaspoon vanilla extract
- 1 1/2 cups diced peaches
- 1 cup grated carrots

Direction

- Preheat oven to 350 degrees F (175 degrees C). Line a muffin pan with paper liners.
- Combine butter, rolled oats, dark brown sugar, 1 tablespoon all-purpose flour, and 1/4 teaspoon cinnamon in a bowl. Mix with a fork or fingers until crumbly.
- Whisk 1/2 cup all-purpose flour, white whole-wheat flour, oat flour, baking powder, 1 teaspoon cinnamon, and baking soda together in a large bowl.
- Whisk oil, sugar, eggs, and vanilla extract together in a separate bowl. Pour into flour mixture; fold until batter is just combined. Fold peaches and carrots in gently.
- Spoon batter into prepared muffin pan, about 2/3 full. Sprinkle with oat topping.
- Bake in the preheated oven until an inserted toothpick comes out clean, about 15 minutes. Cool in the pan for 5 to 10 minutes; transfer muffins to a wire rack to cool completely.

Nutrition Information

- Calories: 214 calories
- Total Fat: 12.7 g
- Cholesterol: 36 mg
- Sodium: 140 mg
- Total Carbohydrate: 22.8 g
- Protein: 3.1 g

Index

A

Ale, *74, 192*

Allspice, 31, 58, 68, 78, 80, 85, 107, 117, 135, 159, 163

Almond, 14, 16, 19, 27, 34, 43, 50, 53, 61, 75, 83, 92–94, 99–103, 112, 117, 130–131,

137–138, 148, 159–160, 163, 169–171, 177–178, 184, 190

Almond extract, 14, 16, 43, 50, 53, 83, 92, 101–103, 117, 130, 137, 159, 170–171

Almond milk, *61, 112*

Apple, 28, 39, 41, 45–46, 49, 51, 59, 62, 64, 66, 83, 91, 105–106, 135, 138, 143, 145, 163,

166–168, 173, 181

Apricot, 13, 61, 68, 79, 93, 135, 164, 169, 180, 185

Apricot jam, *68, 185*

Avocado, *75, 91, 105, 152–153, 179*

B

Bacon, *59, 126–127, 152–153*

Baking, 10–12, 15–19, 23–25, 27–28, 30, 36–40, 42, 44–48, 50–55, 57–59, 62, 65–71, 79,

81–86, 91–92, 94–101, 103, 107–118, 120–123, 125–129, 134–141, 146–148, 153, 155, 157,

159, 161–162, 164–173, 176, 178–183, 185–186, 188–189, 192–193

Baking powder, 12, 15–16, 23–25, 36, 39, 46, 48, 51–53, 57–58, 62, 65–67, 69, 79, 81–82,

84–86, 99–100, 108–110, 112–116, 121–122, 125, 134–137, 139, 147–148, 170, 172,

178–179, 181–182, 188–189, 192–193

Balsamic vinegar, *21, 27, 34, 49, 72, 75–77, 145, 164*

Banana, 15–16, 19–20, 24, 39, 60–63, 91–93, 106, 142–144, 146, 153–154, 165, 170, 176–180

Banana bread, *19*

Barbecue sauce, *106*

Basil, 21, 29, 67, 73–74, 77, 104, 126–127, 140, 145, 160, 172, 181–182

Beans, *61–62, 169*

Beef, *22, 38, 62, 148*

Berry, 11, 20, 23, 34, 46, 51, 96, 108, 116, 139, 168, 171, 181

Biscuits, *24, 51, 58, 130, 167*

Black pepper, 21, 26–27, 32–33, 44, 59, 72–73, 75, 77–78, 91, 93, 97, 102, 104–106, 126–127,

131, 145, 148, 152, 155–157, 160, 166–167, 179

Blackberry, *25–26, 33, 69, 96, 171, 188, 191*

Blueberry, 15, 23–26, 34–35, 37, 48–49, 51, 60, 62–63, 81, 87, 100, 108, 113, 132, 153,

180–181, 191

Boar, *26*

Brandy, *27, 133, 177, 192*

Bread, 19, 22, 26–28, 58, 70, 77, 84, 89–90, 94–95, 103–104, 109, 120, 125–126, 146–147,

185–187

Broccoli, *147, 157*

Broth, *97, 169*

196

Y

Yam, *183*

Z

Zest, 33, 42, 53, 56–57, 66–67, 81, 87, 89–90, 122, 132, 137

Conclusion

Thank you again for downloading this book!

I hope you enjoyed reading about my book!

If you enjoyed this book, please take the time to share your thoughts and post a review on Amazon. It'd be greatly appreciated!

Write me an honest review about the book – I truly value your opinion and thoughts and I will incorporate them into my next book, which is already underway.

Thank you!

If you have any questions, **feel free to contact at:** *chefemilychan@gmail.com*

Emily Chan

www.TheCookingMAP.com/Emily-Chan

Made in the USA
Middletown, DE
09 July 2023

34761541R00117